Families -- Beyond the Nuclear Ideal

Science, Ethics and Society

GENERAL EDITORS: Professors **John Sulston** and **John Harris**
(respectively Chair and Director of the Institute for Science, Ethics and Innovation (iSEI) at the University of Manchester)

In conjunction with the Institute for Science, Ethics and Innovation, this series examines the major issues surrounding the impact of science and technology and the ethical issues generated by new discoveries.

Books in the series highlight the interplay between science and society; new technological and scientific discoveries; how they impact on our understanding of ourselves and our place in society; and the responsibility of science to the wider world.

Themes covered in the series include:

- Global justice
- The scope, limits and future of humanity
- Public health
- Technological governance
- Intellectual property
- Chronic poverty
- Climate change
- Environment

The series will appeal to policy-makers, academic readers and students in diverse disciplines including sociology, international relations, law, bioethics, physical and life sciences, and medicine.

Books already published in the series:

International Governance of Biotechnology:
Needs, Problems and Potential
Catherine Rhodes
ISBN 9781849660655 (Hardback)
ISBN 9781849660778 (Ebook)

Scientific Freedom
Edited by Simona Giordano, John Coggon and
Marco Cappato
ISBN 9781849668996 (Hardback)
ISBN 9781849669016 (Ebook)

Families – Beyond the Nuclear Ideal
Edited by Daniela Cutas and Sarah Chan
9781780930107 (Hardback)
9781780930121 (Ebook)

Forthcoming:

Bioscience and the Good Life
Iain Brassington
ISBN 9781849663380 (Hardback)
ISBN 9781849663397 (Ebook)

Humans and Other Animals: Challenging the
Boundaries of Humanity
Sarah Chan
ISBN 9781780932187 (Hardback)
ISBN 9781780932545 (Ebook)

Global Health and International Community
Edited by John Coggon and Swati Gola
ISBN 9781780933979 (Hardback)

Families – Beyond the Nuclear Ideal

Edited by Daniela Cutas and Sarah Chan

B L O O M S B U R Y

LONDON · NEW DELHI · NEW YORK · SYDNEY

Bloomsbury Academic
An imprint of Bloomsbury Publishing Plc

50 Bedford Square
London
WC1B 3DP
UK

1385 Broadway
New York
NY 10018
USA

www.bloomsbury.com

Bloomsbury is a registered trade mark of Bloomsbury Publishing Plc

First published 2012
Paperback edition first published 2014

British Library Cataloguing-in-Publication Data
A catalogue record for this book is available from the British Library.

ISBN: HB: 978-1-7809-3010-7
PB: 978-1-4725-7160-1
EPDF: 978-1-7809-3012-1
EPUB: 978-1-7809-3013-8

Contents

Notes on Contributors

Adrienne Asch is the Edward and Robin Milstein Professor of Bioethics and Director of the Center for Ethics at Yeshiva University. Trained in philosophy, social work, and social psychology, she has been in the field of bioethics since the mid-1980s. Her co-edited volumes include *Prenatal Testing and Disability Rights* (Georgetown University Press, 2000), and *The Double-Edged Helix: Social Implications of Genetics in a Diverse Society* (Johns Hopkins University Press, 2002). She is at work on a book about collaborative reproduction.

Sarah Chan was educated at the University of Melbourne where she received degrees in law and biological science. She spent a number of years as a research scientist in a molecular biology laboratory before taking up an opportunity to work in the area of science policy and stem cell ethics. In 2005 she moved to Manchester where she took up a research post at the Centre for Social Ethics and Policy, University of Manchester, and studied for a Master's degree in Health Care Ethics and Law. Since 2008 she has been a Research Fellow in Bioethics and Law at the University's new Institute for Science, Ethics and Innovation, and in 2009 was appointed Deputy Director of the Institute. Her research interests and publications cover areas including the ethics of gene therapy and genetic information, enhancement, research ethics, stem cells, animal ethics, transhumanism, and the ethics of science and innovation.

Daniela Cutas is Research Fellow at the Department for Health, Ethics and Society, Maastricht University, as well as at the Department of Philosophy, Linguistics and Theory of Science, University of Gothenburg, and Lecturer at the Department of Historical, Philosophical and Religious Studies, Umeå University. Her background is in philosophy, health care ethics and law, and political science. Her research interests include the ethics and policy of close personal relationships and family formation, ethics of reproductive technologies, and research ethics. She has published in journals such as *Bioethics, Human Fertility, Health Care Analysis, Reproductive BioMedicine Online, Journal of Medical Ethics*.

Dossie Easton has been a licensed Marriage and Family Therapist in private practice in San Francisco for the past twenty years. She is also a certified supervisor for MFT interns, and a certified continuing education provider for professionals. Along with her private practice, she teaches many classes and workshops in the United States, Canada and Europe. She is co-author with Janet Hardy of *The Ethical Slut: A Practical Guide to Polyamory, Open Relationships and Other Adventures; The New Bottoming Book; The New Topping Book; When Someone You Love Is Kinky* and *Radical Ecstasy: S/M Journeys to Transcendence*.

Susanna Graham is a Wellcome Trust funded PhD student at the Centre for Family Research, University of Cambridge. Her research explores the decision-making and experiences of single women embarking upon motherhood through the use of donor sperm. By taking an empirical approach to bioethics she aims to explore how these women morally conceive of their choice. With A. Braverman, she is the author of the forthcoming 'Solo and Selective: Men and Women Choosing to become Single Mothers by Choice', in M.P.M. Richards, J. Appleby and G. Pennings (eds), *Reproductive Donation: Policy, Practice and Bioethics*, Cambridge: Cambridge University Press.

David Gurnham is Reader in Law at the University of Southampton. His research interests are medical law and ethics, criminal law and law-and-literature. Recent publications include 'Bioethics as Science-Fiction: Making Sense of Habermas's *The Future of Human Nature*', *Cambridge Quarterly of Healthcare Ethics* 2012, 21: 235; 'Reproduction, Right, and the Welfare Interests of Children: the times they aren't a-changin'', *King's Law Journal* 2012, 23: 29 (with José Miola); 'Risky Sex and Manly Diversions: Historical and Social Contours of Consent in HIV-Transmission and Rough Horseplay Cases', in A. Alghrani, R. Bennett and S. Ost (eds), *The Criminal Law & Bioethical Conflict: Walking the Tightrope*, Cambridge: Cambridge University Press, 2012, forthcoming; 'Legal Authority and Savagery in Judicial Rhetoric: sexual violence and the criminal courts', International Journal of Law in Context 2011, 7: 117–137; and the monograph: Memory, Imagination, Justice: Intersections of Law and Literature, Farnham: Ashgate 2009. David is Assistant Editor at Contemporary Issues in Law, on the International Editorial Board of the *International Journal of Law in Context*, and guest editor on a number of forthcoming special issues.

Thomas Hartvigsson is a PhD student in practical philosophy at the University of Gothenburg. His main areas of interest are sexual and family ethics. His bachelor thesis discusses the issue of incest between consenting adults, and his master thesis examines the issue of parental discretion in respect to circumcision of young children. He is currently working on a paper examining the ethical aspects of Islamic banking practices.

Paul D. Hastings is a Professor of Psychology at the University of California Davis. He studies the contributions of physiological regulation and parental socialization to children's adaptive and maladaptive social-emotional development, at the Center for Mind & Brain. Recent major publications include: Hastings, P.D., Ruttle, P., Serbin, L.A., Mills, R.S.L., Stack, D.M. and Schwartzman, A.E. (2011), 'Adrenocortical stress reactivity and regulation in preschoolers: Relations with parenting, temperament, and psychopathology', *Developmental Psychobiology*, doi: 10.1002/dev.20545; Hastings, P.D., Shirtcliff, E.A., Klimes-Dougan, B., Allison, A.L., DeRose, L., Kendziora, K.T., Usher, B.A. and Zahn-Waxler, C. (2011), 'Allostasis and the development of internalizing and externalizing problems: Changing relations with physiological systems across adolescence', *Development & Psychopathology*, doi: 10.1017/ S095457941000538.

Sujatha Jesudason is the Director of the CoreAlign initiative at the University of California, San Francisco, a "think and do tank" working to develop and implement a 30-year strategy for winning reproductive rights in the United States. Before this, she was the founder and Executive Director of *Generations Ahead*, a non-profit organization that shapes and informs public policies on genetic technology, advocating for its equitable and wise use. From examining the fault lines in efforts to curtail sex selection to exposing attempts to pit reproductive rights against disability rights, Sujatha works to forge unlikely collaborations and look past forced simplifications. With over twenty years as an advocate for women's rights, Sujatha has worked at Asian Communities for Reproductive Justice, 9 to 5 National Association of Working Women and the Center for Genetics and Society. A leading voice on the ethics of genetic innovations, women's rights and racial justice, Sujatha holds a doctorate in sociology from the University of California, Berkeley.

Mianna Lotz is a Lecturer in the Department of Philosophy at Macquarie University, Sydney, Australia. She teaches primarily in ethics, bioethics and applied ethics, and her main research specializations are in the areas of reproductive ethics, parenthood, research ethics, and children's rights and welfare. She has published in journals such as *Bioethics, Journal of Applied Philosophy, Journal of Social Philosophy* and *Lancet*, and is currently a chief investigator on an ARC-funded Linkage project on ethical, legal and regulatory issues in surgical innovation. She has served on the Macquarie University Research Ethics Committee (Human Subjects) since 2006, and is currently Chair of the Macquarie Arts Faculty Research Ethics Committee.

Kerry Lynn Macintosh is a Professor at Santa Clara University School of Law, California, USA. She is an expert in the law of assisted reproductive technologies and human cloning. Her work identifies the social and legal costs of banning technologies that are misunderstood or controversial for political reasons. In her recent article, 'Brave New Eugenics: Regulating Assisted Reproductive Technologies in the Name of Better Babies', Macintosh explains how safety regulation of *in vitro fertilisation* is a new form of eugenics practiced against a vulnerable population of infertile men and women. In her first cloning book, *Illegal Beings: Human Clones and the Law* (Cambridge University Press, 2005), she makes the case that cloning bans violate the United States Constitution. In her forthcoming book, *Human Cloning: Four Fallacies and Their Legal Consequences* (Cambridge University Press, 2013), she reveals the role that essentialist intuitions about cloning and clones have played in bringing about a misguided drive to ban human cloning, whether for reproduction or stem cell research.

Simon Căbulea May is Assistant Professor of Philosophy at Florida State University and was a 2010–11 Visiting Fellow at the Center for Ethics and Public Affairs at Tulane University. His research primarily concerns conflicts of moral conviction in public life. He has published articles on moral compromise and on political legitimacy in *Philosophy and Public Affairs*.

Julie McCandless is a Lecturer in Law at the London School of Economics and Political Science. She teaches in the fields of medical and family law. Her research focuses on the legal regulation of gender and the family. Her PhD was an examination of law, gender and parenthood in the context of assisted reproduction and was awarded by Keele University in 2010. She has published recently in the *Modern Law Review* and *Feminist Legal Studies* on the amendments pertaining to parenthood in the Human Fertilisation and Embryology Act 2008.

Christian Munthe is Professor of Practical Philosophy at the University of Gothenburg. His research focuses on ethics, value and policy issues in the intersection of health, science, technology, the environment and society. His latest publications include *The Price of Precaution and the Ethics of Risk* (Springer, 2011) and *The Ethics of Screening in Health Care and Medicine* (Springer, 2011). Christian Munthe's work on this chapter has been undertaken within the project Alcopop-TV Culture, funded by the Daphne III Program of the European Commission, contract no: JUST/2009/DAP3/AG/1251 - 30-CE-0390165/00-49.

Melinda Roberts is a Professor of Philosophy at the College of New Jersey. She received her PhD in philosophy from the Five-College PhD Program (Amherst, Massachusetts) and J.D. from the University of Texas School of Law. She is especially interested in the formulation and analysis of alternative ('person-affecting') forms of maximizing consequentialism. Related interests include the nonidentity problem, the mere addition paradox, the repugnant conclusion and other problems in population ethics; also, reproductive ethics, abortion and wrongful life. Books include *Abortion and the Moral Significance of Merely Possible Persons* (2010), *Harming Future Persons: Ethics, Genetic and the Nonidentity Problem*, co-edited with David Wasserman (2009) and *Child Versus Childmaker: Future Persons and Present Duties in Ethics and the Law* (1998).

Joanna E. Scheib is jointly appointed as Associate Adjunct Professor of Psychology at the University of California Davis and as Research Director at The Sperm Bank of California, the first organization in the USA to offer open-identity sperm donation. She conducts research and develops policy on family-building through donor conception. Recent publications include: Ravitsky, V. and Scheib, J.E. (2010), 'Donor-conceived individuals' right to know', *Hastings Center Bioethics Forum*, 40(4), Scheib, J.E. and Ruby, A. (2009); 'Beyond consanguinity risk: Developing donor birth limits that consider psychosocial risk factors', *Fertility & Sterility*, 91: e12; Scheib J.E. and Cushing RA. (2007), 'Open-identity donor insemination in the USA: Is it on the rise?', *Fertility & Sterility*, 88: 231–232.

Mary Lyndon (Molly) Shanley is Professor of Political Science on the Margaret Stiles Halleck Chair at Vassar College. Her current academic work engages social justice issues in family formation. She sings in a community chorus and directs a women's writing group at the county jail. She is author of *Feminism, Marriage and the Law in Victorian England* (Princeton, 1989), *Making Babies, Making Families: What Matters Most in an Age of Reproductive Technologies, Surrogacy, Adoption, and Same-Sex and Unwed Parents* (Beacon, 2001), and editor, with Carole Pateman, of *Feminist Interpretations and Political Theory* (Penn State, 1990), among other works.

Maura Irene Strassberg is Professor of Law at Drake Law School, USA. Her main areas of interest are legal ethics, same-sex marriage, and polygamy. She is the author of, among others, 'Foreword to Same-Sex Marriage Symposium', *Drake Law Review*, 58: 879–887 (2010); 'The Crime of Polygamy', *Temple Political and Civil Rights Law Review*, 12: 353 (2007); 'The Challenge of Post-Modern Polygamy: Considering Polygamy', Capital Law Review, 31: 439 (2003); and 'Distinctions of Form or Substance: Monogamy, Polygamy, and Same-sex Marriage', *North Carolina Law Review*, 75: 1501–1624 (1997).

Preface and Acknowledgments

Recent decades have seen various challenges to the entrenched ideal of the nuclear family. Alterations in traditional family structures as a product of socio-cultural change, such as increased divorce rates and single parenthood, or the socio-political acceptance of partnerships beside traditional marriages; greater availability of reproductive choice as a result of assisted reproductive technologies; and increased uptake of alternative lifestyles as their practitioners become more willing to speak out and knowledge (though not always acceptance) of such lifestyles increases – all of these lead to questions about what sorts of personal relationships and families we should form, or be allowed to form. While there has been a proliferation of self-help literature that aims to inform, explain and provide practical guidance as to how to manage these 'alternative' relationships, and considerable work has been done in the fields of sociology, social anthropology and psychology in this area, much less exists in the academic literature by way of philosophical and ethical analysis.

Our book offers a modest overview and analysis of some of these close personal relationship and family types from an ethical perspective, drawing on cognate disciplines such as law and sociology to present what we hope is a broad and balanced coverage of relevant issues.

We wish to thank our authors, who have devoted their time, energy and thought to this project, both in the preparation of their individual contributions, and in reading each other's chapters and providing constructive feedback to help develop the collection as a unified whole. Work on the volume has been an enriching experience for us because of them.

We also thank Richard Ashcroft and Mihaela Miroiu for their expert reviewing of some of the chapters, and John Harris for his support and encouragement.

Daniela Cutas and Sarah Chan

Abbreviations

ACOG	American College of Obstetricians and Gynecologists
ART	Assisted Reproductive Technology
ASRM	American Society for Reproductive Medicine
CBCL	Child Behavior Check List
CRC	UN Convention on the Rights of the Child
DCN	Donor Conception Network
DI	Donor insemination
HFEA	Human Fertilisation and Embryology Authority
ICSI	Intracytoplasmic sperm injection
IVF	In vitro fertilisation
RCU	Reproductive Caring Unit
SMC	Single Mothers by Choice
UPA	Uniform Parentage Act

1

Introduction

Perspectives on private and family life

Daniela Cutas and Sarah Chan

That children should be conceived *naturally*, born to and raised by their two young, heterosexual, married to each other, genetic parents; that this relationship between parents is also the ideal relationship between romantic or sexual partners; and that romance and sexual intimacy ought to be at the core of our closest personal relationships – all these elements converge towards the ideal of the *nuclear family*.

In this book, then, the expression *nuclear family* will be used to denote families composed of a mother and a father romantically involved with each other, and their genetically related children that they have conceived *naturally*. We believe it quite uncontroversial to say that these are the core characteristics of the nuclear family standard. Calling units consisting of two parents and their adopted children, or same-sex couples and the children that they raise, *nuclear families*, corresponds to more generous interpretations of the concept or departures from the ideal, with varying degrees of acceptability.

We will not in this volume investigate how and why this formula came about. The nuclear family may have been the norm for some decades in the Western world, but it has not always been so, historically speaking (see for example Nicholson 1997), and is not so in some other contemporary cultures (see for example Stacey 2011). Whatever the age and coverage of the concept, the way *family* is defined in legislation as well as in the wider society has a prescriptive component (Archard 2010: 2): it determines whose private life is more, or less, scrutinized; who can be a parent and what sorts of organization of private and family life are encouraged, tolerated or even allowed at all; which associations will be supported, both socially and materially; and so on.

In contrast to the nuclear family ideal, real-life scenarios and choices in the realm of close personal relationships and family formation strategies display a variety of forms: electively or circumstantially single parents, unmarried couples, homosexual partnerships and parenting by homosexual couples, life-long close friendships preferred over sexually intimate alternatives, polyamory, poly-parental families, electively or circumstantially childless families[1], families created with medical or social assistance and so forth. These *alternative* relationship and family structures challenge the privileged status of the nuclear family as the preferable mode of family life for all, and the one to be endorsed and encouraged by society. Efforts to make the concept of *family* more elastic, however, or even to gain recognition for other forms of organizing one's private and family life as equally legitimate to the nuclear family, are faced with a variety of forms of resistance. These range from at the mildest tolerant acceptance, to outright rejection, often citing concerns of the threat to family values or the destruction of 'the family' that their acceptance represents.

In this book, we explore some of the possibilities offered by various relationship and family structures and examine the arguments to recommend or disqualify them as legitimate family units in our societies. Our aim is to re-examine and critically evaluate the norms and normativities surrounding personal relationships and families in Western societies, and to challenge the widespread assumption that nuclear families are the best, or even the only acceptable units at the core of personal relationships. We address in particular modes of reproduction and parenthood and the consequences for children of being raised in families that do not conform to the nuclear family model, one reason for focusing on this particular aspect being that the issue of parenting raises heightened sensitivity and resistance to *alternative* lifestyles. We also consider alternative modes of interpersonal relationships, such as romantic or sexual intimate relationships that deviate from widely and explicitly accepted heterosexual, monogamous and marital norms.

The nuclear family: A sexual family

A constitutive part of the nuclear family ideal is the presumption of sexual interaction between the parents. Often, this translates as a presumption of heterosexual interaction. Indeed, in most legislatures *parental dimorphism* (McCandless and Sheldon 2011; McCandless in this volume) is a required ingredient of bi-parenting: thus the parents of any child have to be of opposite sex (namely, one *mother* and one *father*). Even where digressions from this rule are permitted, the parents must not be in kin relationships to each other (for example siblings, parent-child) that would not allow them to form a socially or legally acceptable *couple* (*Ibid.*). And, as the conjugal couple is valorized as the ideal (or perhaps even the only legitimate) parental combination for the formation of families, the couple at the heart of the nuclear family remains the ideal (or perhaps even the only legitimate) scenario in which sex should take place.

The concept of the nuclear family as the 'sexual family' has been explicated at length by Fineman (1995). Her critique targets the privilege-conferring preference, entrenched in law and policy as well as social, cultural, political and popular discourse, for the 'appropriate intimacy' of the sexual family (Fineman 1995: 1), in the form of a husband and wife who are 'sexually affiliated' to each other. Intimacy and family connections, Fineman points out, are much more varied than the sexual family, and may include dependent parents, adult children living with their parents, plural sexual groupings and nonsexual intimate connections. There is no reason, she argues, why the sexual family should be privileged economically and legally: the sexual family is an overly simplified paradigm that fails to deliver as an appropriate basis of family theory (Fineman 1995: 160).

In line with this critique, varied experiences in the area of personal relationships suggest that *one size does not fit all* (Stacey 2011) and that the nuclear family ideal, in fact, does not fit most. Divorce rates have increased in the last decades (on average, 1 in 2.3 marriages in Europe end in divorce; Eurostat 2011), as have the numbers of adults not marrying or not cohabiting with romantic partners. Over 35 per cent of households in a number of countries (for example Norway, Sweden, Finland, Germany) are made of one person. In several European countries (such as Bulgaria, France, Iceland), the number of out-of-wedlock children has topped 50 per cent (Eurostat 2011). These children and adults are outside of the socially and legally protected unit of the nuclear family, at least some of them (the children) as a result of processes and conditions over which they have no control.

This raises difficulties particularly regarding the care of these children, as to how their interests can or should be safeguarded, and the role of the state in ensuring this care. Considering the interests of children over whose parenting several adults compete, decisions have to be made that can realistically be implemented: who should be awarded parenting privileges when several adults have a claim to be awarded them? Who has a right to have access to a child parented by someone else? How far do parental claims to privacy extend? Who should make these decisions? Who should be considered to be a parent, who should be allowed to be a parent, and what influence does the nuclear family ideal have on our thinking in this regard?

Mater semper certa est

The Latin formula embodies a particular, biological, understanding of establishing parentage: we know who the mother is, because she gives birth to the child, but we never really know who the father is. Until relatively recently, it was always the case that the genetic mother (who provided the egg) and the birth mother were one and the same; thus saying that it is always clear who the mother is (i.e. the birth mother) corresponds to equating 'genetic mother' with 'mother' and, analogously, saying that it is never clear who the father is, equates 'genetic father' with 'father'. Yet social and technological changes make identifying who *should* be regarded as a child's parents even less certain: as it seems, *mater incerta est, pater incertus est.*

Perhaps most commonly, the people deemed to be a child's parents (with associated rights and responsibilities) have been, *by default*, those who conceived her or, in the case of married couples, the birth mother and her husband (in spite of the genetic uncertainty). Here again the pervasiveness of the nuclear family ideal can be seen: when the predominant condition of this structure obtains, in the form of the married couple, legal and social presumptions follow suit in deeming any children born to the wife to be a product of that union. Such presumptions have also operated in reverse to dictate that the nuclear family is the proper, the best or the only context in which children *ought* to be produced. A historical expression of this is found in the social stigma once attached to children born out of wedlock. More recently, law and policy in the area of assisted reproduction have, either through explicit provisions or through their application in practice, reinforced the primacy of the nuclear family as the ideal or most legitimate reproductive environment. In so doing, they have tended to cleave to the nuclear ideal in determining what sorts of environments are appropriate for the creation and raising of children and therefore which sorts of 'families' are eligible for reproductive assistance. Yet this model fails to account for many of the contexts in which children are actually born and the ways in which families are formed.

Social practices as well as the use of reproductive technologies have compounded the difficulties associated with any straightforward decision-making criteria for parenting. Who a child's parents are, or should be, has never been a straightforward determination. Children were conceived by and born to unmarried women, or conceived by married women with men to whom they were not married. People could adopt children. The children's main attachment figures may have been people other than their legal parents (grandparents, for example). Today, birth mothers need not be either the genetic mothers, or the intending mothers. These separations of reproductive and caretaking contributions, together with their more and more widespread occurrence (and increasing social acknowledgment), force the re-evaluation of assumptions as to who should have priority in parenting claims. Further, they contribute to the increasing separation between reproduction and parenting, as well as, implicitly, to increasing competition over parenting.

When genetic parents, surrogate mothers, commissioning parents, financial, and social parents, all compete for recognition as the legal parents of the same children, whose claims should prevail and on what grounds? There are two main perspectives that have been taken in the process of decision-making in such cases: (a) that of the competitors and their claims to particular children, and (b) that of the children themselves. Some of the research presented in this volume (Scheib and Hastings; Graham; Asch) indicates that, as far as children's interests are concerned, the most important aspects of parenting seem to consist in the quality of the relationships within the family, rather than in the form that the family takes (whether there are one or two parents in the home; whether or not they are in a romantic relationship with each other; their sex or sexual orientation). From the perspective of children's interests, then, it may be that the ideal of the nuclear family is misguided or at least not best placed to serve these interests (see Munthe and Hartvigsson, and Lotz, in this volume). From the perspective of those adults who cannot or choose not to conform to the nuclear family model, it is likewise important to be able to find their own ways of leading their private lives within a supportive social environment.

Those who have contributed to a child's existence or wellbeing may feel they each have relevant claims to being recognized as legal parents or, at the very least, to being allowed to have a relationship with the children. The current *status quo* in many states is such that once they have been accepted as a child's legal parents, or custodial parents, people are allowed to prevent others from having access to the child. This is sometimes defended by claims to familial privacy, or by the need to protect the child's wellbeing. The first claim depends on careful distinctions in the area of the balance between parental discretion and the responsibilities that they have as parents. The strength and justification of both claims depend on what concepts of parental rights and responsibilities we adopt, as well as on outcomes for children of the different possible choices. What they should not depend blindly upon, however, is an assumption that the nuclear family is either most (or solely) deserving of protective privacy, or the best structure to ensure the wellbeing of children.

Policing private life

While the influence of the sexual, nuclear family ideal may be most prominent in the sphere of reproduction and parenting, not least because it is here most strongly and publicly promoted under the banner of children's interests and rights, it also has powerful and pervasive effects on the lives of people outside their role as parents, or who are not parents. As Fineman describes it, '[t]he characterization of some family groupings as deviant legitimates state intervention and the regulation of relationships well beyond what would be socially tolerated if directed at more traditional family forms' (Fineman 2009: 46).

This 'regulation of relationships' may occur indirectly, through legal and social privileges accorded to relationships that meet the ideal, and through analogous privileges extended to relationships that satisfy some aspects of the ideal, usually in proportion to how closely they conform to it. One example of this is the recognition accorded in many jurisdictions to what is often called *de facto* or common-law marriage – the requirements of which, to be validly established, include virtually all the tropes of the nuclear family couple save for actual *de jure* matrimony.

In certain cases, however, direct state intervention dictates what forms of relationship are allowed and what types of activities are permitted within personal relationships. Laws that not only do not permit polygamy but criminalize it proscribe certain relationship forms, as they prescribe others. Historical laws prohibiting homosexual activity (particularly between males) have been repealed in some jurisdictions but remain active in many. Even within England, where homosexual behaviour *per se* is no longer a crime, the attitude of the courts to particular practices seems to depend on the sexual orientation of the parties to the act: the 'Spanner case', *R v Brown*, involved acts of homosexual sadomasochism that were considered by the House of Lords to constitute assault occasioning actual bodily harm, thus rendering these activities criminal. While the judicial reasoning in *Brown* did not explicitly condemn homosexuality, its characterization of homosexual sadomasochism as violent, transgressive and dangerous to public health, morality and civilization, together with the contrasting attitude taken by English courts to cases of heterosexual sadomasochism, have been interpreted by some analysts (White 2006; Houlihan 2011) as discriminating between homosexual and heterosexual practices and enforcing 'a moralistic jurisprudential model of socio-sexuality which is heteronormative and procreative' (Houlihan 2011: 32).

Towards the post-nuclear family?

Given the variety of family and relationship forms already in existence today, perpetuating and enforcing the nuclear family ideal and the sex-based relationship norms that underlie it may be seen as at best unnecessary and at worst directly harmful. In the context of parenting and the question of which parenting combinations are permitted, supported or legally recognized, it places restrictions on reproductive choice that are not necessarily justified in terms of the usual stated reason for limiting reproductive choices, namely the interests of the child. More broadly, outside the reproductive context, the persistent fiction of the nuclear family both de-legitimizes alternative relationship modes, and generates social pressures and expectations that are sometimes unrealistic, may go unfulfilled and in doing so, create dissatisfaction and unhappiness amongst those who cannot or do not wish to conform to their strictures.

As we have noted, existing variants in family structure already challenge the nuclear/sexual family norm. Some of these have achieved a degree of recognition as legitimate family forms that attract legal and political support: for example, shared parenting in the absence of a continuing sexual relationship between estranged co-parents is acknowledged legally and socially as a valid, though not preferable, structure for child-rearing (though this varies between countries; for example, it seems to be much more accepted in Scandinavian countries than anywhere else in Europe). Others continue to be under-recognized.

Poly-parenting often occurs as a result of the dissociation of the original nuclear family, which may then reform into multiple units with varying degrees of similarity to the nuclear ideal, resulting in there being more than two adults who desire parental rights and bear parental responsibilities. Nevertheless, the law has steadfastly refused to recognize more than two legal parents for any one child (see also Lotz in this volume), and poly-parenting *de novo* (where more than two people may deliberately set out to embark on a project of parenthood together, in whatever various capacities) is scarcely acknowledged socially, let alone legally.

There is thus a need for greater recognition of the diversity of relationship forms and their validity, and for a critical reconsideration of what have been termed 'relationship normativities... expectations within the heterosexual relationship order – or what might be called, heterorelationality – of co-residence, romantic love, monogamy and the primacy of the conjugal couple' (Budgeon and Roseneil 2004). The endpoint of such a critique, it has been suggested, may be to deprivilege the sexual family: to 'render all sexual relationships equal with each other and all relationships equal with the sexual' (Fineman 1995: 230). Such a shift would represent a radical reconfiguration of the family and a drastic departure from the nuclear family ideal. Constructing and supporting alternatives to the nuclear family will require changes to both regulation and socio-cultural understandings of the family – changes that, some may argue, are long overdue.

The chapters: An overview

The chapters in this volume have been selected to provide a broad and cross-disciplinary perspective – philosophical, ethical, legal and sociological – on the challenges that threaten, or promise, to 'explode' the ideal of the nuclear family today. Through these, we hope to demonstrate how contemporary realities and practices are already contributing to reshaping current understandings of the family; to examine the philosophical and ethical underpinnings of the norms surrounding families and relationships, and how these intersect with reproductive technologies that perturb such norms; and to explore ways in which reconfigured notions of the 'post-nuclear' family might find expression in future policy debate and the development of jurisprudence in this area.

In Chapter 2, Julie McCandless examines the development of the concept of legal parenthood within English law, arguing that recent legislative and policy changes (in particular the 2008 amendments to the Human Fertilisation and Embryology Act 1990), while prompted by reproductive technologies that 'dismantle the seemingly axiomatic two-parent connections of sexual reproduction', nevertheless reinscribe essential elements of the nuclear family paradigm even as they enable non-conformity. McCandless suggests that broader legal understandings of parenthood and family are necessary to account adequately for the range of parent-child relationships that are already possible and that may occur in the future.

Continuing on the theme of legal parenthood, in Chapter 3, Mianna Lotz presents a critique of one particular aspect that is almost universally entrenched in law: the stipulation that a child may have no more than two legally-recognized parents. She argues that such a limitation is unjustified by reference to the interests either of children or potential parents, and that in the context of social and technological changes that create increasingly complex family and reproductive structures, an expansion and diversification of the legal as well as social concept of parenthood will be required.

Chapter 4 broadens the focus from parenthood to 'familyhood', in terms of 'what social configurations should be recognized as a potentially fitting context for children to enter into'. Christian Munthe and Thomas Hartvigsson propose the term 'reproductive caring units' (RCUs) to describe such contexts, and go on to evaluate the arguments regarding children's best interests that are often raised as a criticism of certain forms of RCU – particularly those that diverge from the nuclear family ideal. On this analysis, they conclude that the interests of children do not provide a justification for disallowing RCUs that differ from the nuclear ideal, nor for discriminating wholesale against these RCUs in favour of others that conform to it.

Chapters 5 and 6 explore issues involved in donor conception from differing perspectives. Joanna Scheib and Paul Hastings, in Chapter 5, draw together a considerable breadth of sociological research examining the development and welfare of donor-insemination (DI) children raised in lesbian-couple families, and compare this with studies of DI in heterosexual families. These findings indicate that children of DI-lesbian couple families experience at least as positive, or perhaps better, outcomes than children in conventionally-conceived heterosexual families (the 'nuclear family' ideal), and that heterosexual DI also results in positive family outcomes. They identify, however, openness about donor origins as a major point of difference between lesbian DI families (in which the absence of a father promotes and facilitates openness at an early stage) and heterosexual DI families (in which the child's donor origins can more easily be, and indeed often are, kept secret) and highlight lack of openness as a potential 'risk factor'; evidence drawn from lesbian families about the benefits of early disclosure might thus support an argument for openness and provision of information about donors across all forms of DI family.

In Chapter 6, David Gurnham explores the experiences of *parents* in donor conception families, analysing the narratives that parents construct around their own roles and that of the donor in order to establish the priority of their own parental relationship over the genetic connection represented by the donor. He examines the way in which the fragmentation of reproductive roles entailed by donor conception can lead to 'linguistic ambivalence' in how parents describe both themselves and donors in relation to their children, in deploying concepts such as 'father' and 'fatherhood' and the ambiguous notion of the 'real' parent. The language selected by DI parents to narrate their 'reality' of parenthood may thus, Gurnham argues, reflect parents' own anxieties about their status relative to that of the donor. He draws an analogy between Rousseau's 'dangerous supplement' that masquerades as what is 'true', 'real' or 'natural', and the potential for gamete donors to intrude into the narratives of parents and usurp the role of 'real' or 'natural' parent, thereby illustrating the reconfiguration of the 'ethical and linguistic contours of society' that the revisioning of the nuclear family might necessitate.

In Chapter 7, Susanna Graham builds on research by herself and others in order to outline some perhaps less expected aspects of elective single motherhood. Whereas we may be tempted to think that elective single motherhood illustrates a choice against the model of the nuclear family, the women represented in Graham's research portrayed their choice as a back-up solution when building the nuclear family did not seem to work. Moreover, for these women, embarking upon this choice does not necessarily mean that they have given up their aspirations to build a family as close to the nuclear family ideal as possible: on the contrary, they describe it as giving them more time to find the right partner. Thus rather than assuming the mantle of 'single-motherhood' entirely by choice, the women in Graham's study are choosing between two aspects of the nuclear family that are not, for them, simultaneously attainable: that is, they choose to become mothers, but within a broader context of being single by chance or by necessity, whilst some of them still hope eventually to 'complete' the family with a male partner, and thus re-attain nuclear conformity.

Mary Shanley and Sujatha Jesudason, in Chapter 8, consider the practices and policies surrounding reproductive surrogacy. They contend that traditional social and legal frameworks for understanding and regulating surrogacy are inadequate both to capture the complexity of relationships created by surrogacy arrangements and to protect the interests of potential surrogate mothers and children. Instead, they argue, a new paradigm of collaborative caregiving may emerge to characterize the relationships created through surrogacy. This will require an active disruption of the expectations engendered by the nuclear family model in order to pave the way for the recognition of new relationships that fall outside its scope.

The willingness to recognize and acknowledge the complexity of relationships that extend beyond traditional nuclear family boundaries is an important feature of Adrienne Asch's concept of 'parental fitness', in Chapter 9. Asch revisits the idea of licensing parenthood, particularly in relation to the provision of assisted reproductive technologies (ARTs), and argues that parental responsibility, rather than procreative liberty, is a better criterion upon which to base access to assisted reproduction. The creation of children via the use of ARTs has implications for the special responsibilities imposed upon parents in this situation, including obligations of openness about children's origins.

Chapters 10 and 11 deal with polygamy and polyamory from the perspectives of political philosophy and criminal law, respectively. Simon May, in Chapter 10, considers the ethics of polygamy in the context of liberal feminist critiques. He distinguishes two possible moral objections to polygamy as such, first in terms of the harmful or iniquitous impact of polygamous marriages, and second in terms of the sexist social meaning of polygamy as a social practice. He argues that although the first objection is not made out, the asymmetry of the polygamous marital ideal plausibly presupposes stereotyped gender roles in a way that symmetrical marital ideals do not, and that this represents a potential point of moral difference of some significance in ethical analyses of polygamy.

These issues are illustrated in practice by Maura Strassberg's critique of Mormon polygyny practices (Chapter 11). Strassberg writes about polygamy (with a focus on polygyny) and polyamory and, relying on previous work in these areas by herself and others, indicates the fundamental distinctions between the two. According to Strassberg, the inherently coercive nature of Mormon polygyny practices and the problematic, patriarchal social structures they create and support, justify the ban put upon them. Polyamory, she argues, does not share those characteristics: although there is still the potential for coercive and unequal power dynamics to arise within polyfidelitious groups, particularly where polyfidelity is used as a communal organizing principle, these properties are not inherent to polyfidelity as it is commonly practised.

Chapter 12 represents a departure from the academic approaches of previous chapters, but is, we believe, an important perspective to recognize and include. Dossie Easton is an ardent advocate of recognizing alternative relationship structures and has herself played an important role in the development of polyamorous identity and culture, notably through outputs such as her co-authored book *The Ethical Slut* (Easton and Hardy 2009). In this chapter, she makes a plea for un-demonizing sex and embracing it as an enriching part of our lives. She does this by way of illustrating the constraints that social norms about sex, and in particular the sexual foundation of the nuclear family and its associated normativities, place upon us. Her first-hand account of the experiences of someone who has, both professionally and personally, been actively and for many years 'exploding' the nuclear family, gives us a glimpse of one possible 'post-nuclear' future from an insider's perspective – a reminder that in parallel with the critical theorizing and scholarly discourse that will be required to mediate this transition, socially, politically and legally, these issues are already being negotiated in multiple ways through the lived experiences of many people.

The last two chapters address a form of reproductive technology that is not yet in human use: reproductive cloning. Kerry Macintosh, in Chapter 13, considers ethical objections to human cloning as a mode of reproduction and concludes that principled objections are invalid; she contends, moreover, that through forcing a re-examination of assumptions about reproduction and the family, cloning may promote a wider acceptance of diverse family forms. While in many cases human cloning might well be used to 'approximate the nuclear family', in others it will be used to generate other forms of family. In either case, she argues, the availability of asexual reproduction in the form of cloning will provide a challenge to the biologically-grounded nuclear family ideal.

In Chapter 14, Melinda Roberts uses the case of human reproductive cloning to address the philosophical problems posed by basing the acceptability of reproductive choice on accounts of harm to future children. The difficulty of establishing harm in the case of selecting between children has often been a sticking-point for ethical arguments that seek to justify limiting the exercise of certain reproductive choices, for example those that would result in the creation of a disabled child. On Roberts' analysis, the harm of being brought into existence as a genetic multiple can in some cases justify an argument against human cloning.

Note

1 *Contra* Archard (2010) we use the notion of *family* to also cover modes of organization of private life that do not include children.

References

Archard, D. (2010), *The Family: A Liberal Defence*, London: Palgrave Macmillan.

Budgeon, S. and Roseneil, S. (2004), 'Beyond the Conventional Family', *Current Sociology*, 52: 127–134.

Cutas, D. (2011), 'On Triparenting: Is having three committed parents better than having only two?', *Journal of Medical Ethics* doi: 10.1136/jme.2011.043745.

Cutas, D. and Bortolotti, L. (2010), 'Natural versus Assisted Reproduction: In Search of Fairness', *Studies in Ethics, Law and Technology*, 4: 1–18.

Diduck, A. and Kaganas, F. (2006) (second edition), *Family Law, Gender and the State: Text, Cases and Materials*, Oxford: Hart Publishing.

Fineman, M.A. (1995), *The Neutered Mother, the Sexual Family, and other Twentieth Century Tragedies*, London: Routledge.

Fineman M.A. (2009), 'The Sexual Family', in M.A. Fineman, J.E. Jackson and A.P. Romero (eds), *Feminist and Queer Legal Theory: Intimate Encounters, Uncomfortable Conversations*, Farnham: Ashgate.

Houlihan, A. (2011), 'When "No" Means "Yes" and "Yes" Means Harm: HIV Risk, Consent and Sadomasochism Case Law', *Law & Sexuality: A Review of Lesbian, Gay, Bisexual, and Transgender Legal Issues*, 20: 31–59.

McCandless, J. and Sheldon, S. (2010), 'The Human Fertilisation and Embryology Act (2008) and the Tenacity of the Sexual Family Form', *Modern Law Review*, 73:175–207.

Nicholson, L. (1997), 'The Myth of the Traditional Family', in L. Nicholson (ed.), *Feminism and Families*, New York: Routledge.

Stacey, J. (2011), *Unhitched: Love, Marriage, and Family Values from West Hollywood to Western China*, New York: New York University Press.

White, C. (2006), 'The Spanner Trials and the Changing Law on Sadomasochism in the UK', *Journal of Homosexuality*, 50:2–3, 167–187.

European Commission, Directorate-General for Employment, Social Affairs and Inclusion & Eurostat 2011, *Demography Report 2010* (Commission Staff Working Paper). Available at http://epp.eurostat.ec.europa.eu (accessed November 2011).

United Nations Economic Commission for Europe 2005, *Families and Households*. Available at http://www.unece.org (accessed November 2011).

R v Brown, [1994] 1 A.C. 212.

2

The Role of Sexual Partnership in UK Family Law

The case of legal parenthood

Julie McCandless[1]

Introduction

The question 'What makes someone the parent of a child?' is at once straightforward and complex. Straightforward because we often have what we feel to be a 'common sense' or 'intuitive' response. This might be with respect to individual parent-child relations – 'Z and Y are X's parents' – or it might relate to a more generalized normative standard – 'the woman who gives birth to you is your mother'. However, if we collected a number of these 'common sense' or 'intuitive' responses, we are likely to find variation and contradictions within, signalling that our notions about parenthood are rather more complex than we might first envisage. In this chapter, I set about exploring this complexity through the lens of legal parenthood in the UK. It should be noted from the outset that I am not suggesting law to be somehow representative of how people understand parenthood: this is an empirical question far beyond the scope of this short chapter. Instead, what I am interested in are the various grounds upon which a person may be regarded as a *legal* parent at the moment of a child's birth in the UK. When we investigate this closely, we see that while these grounds have arguably shifted and expanded over recent decades, the notion that a child has two 'real' parents has remained constant. This is reflected in the strict two-parent model for legal parenthood (see also Lotz, this volume).

Although legal parenthood has primarily developed through the common law, specific statutory provisions have been enacted in response to a number of assisted reproduction techniques, namely donor insemination, IVF using donated gametes and certain surrogacy arrangements.[2] While clearly these provisions affect a relatively small proportion of births in the UK, the extent to which assisted reproduction generates controversy and captures the social imagination renders related legislation highly significant and symbolic. Moreover, Part 2 of the Human Fertilisation and Embryology Act 2008 ('the 2008 Act') provides the most recent formal statement and codification of legal parenthood in the jurisdiction. That this codification reaffirms the strict two-parent model for legal parenthood is important, not least because the parenthood provisions apply to reproductive techniques which very directly dismantle the seemingly axiomatic two-parent connections of sexual reproduction which conflate bio-genetic ties with socio-legal roles and responsibility in most, if not all, Western societies (Boyd 2007; Diduck 2007; Dolgin 1997; Franklin 1997; Strathern 1992). What purpose does reaffirming the two-parent normative model serve and what does it say about our understandings of parenthood and family more generally? What tensions does it present for how legal parenthood is determined in the context of sexual reproduction where bio-genetic ties are increasingly determinative, especially for fatherhood? Did the law-makers involved really engage with the question of *who* counts as a parent and on *what* basis? Or were their deliberations primarily informed by 'common sense' and intuitive ideas of what a family *should* look like, rather than reasoned consideration and analysis of different reproductive contexts?

In this chapter I first provide some background to the 2008 Act, explain its role in the determination of legal parenthood and set out the significance of the parenthood provisions for the normative family ideology signalled by the legislation. I then introduce Martha Fineman's analytical concept of the 'sexual family' (1995) as a framework for explaining the changes introduced by the 2008 Act, analysing how they reconfigure but retain this family model in part 3 of the chapter. While Fineman's definition of the sexual family is similar to the definition of the nuclear family used by this collection, I have adopted her term as a way of highlighting the centrality of adult sexual partnership for legal regulation of familial relationships. The final part of the chapter questions the extent to which this family model can continue to maintain normative force for legal regulation.

The 2008 Act

The 2008 Act is a piece of amending legislation to a 1990 Act of the same name. The legislation deals with a number of controversial issues in the field of human genetics, reproduction and embryology. My focus in this chapter relates to Part 2 of the legislation, which provides for the attribution of legal parenthood following certain assisted reproductive techniques. In short, these provisions are determinative for legal motherhood in all cases of licensed treatment, while for fatherhood they are determinative when donated sperm is used[3]. When a man's own sperm is used in the legal mother's treatment, legal fatherhood is not governed by the 2008 Act, but falls to the common law. This effectively means that it is determined by the genetic link[4]. Unlike the 1990 Act, the 2008 Act also provides for legal parenthood to be attributed to a second female parent. Although the determination of female parenthood is similar to fatherhood, one key difference is that when a woman donates an egg to the legal mother, the parenthood provisions remain determinative and she cannot be attributed parenthood on the basis of her genetic link. This will be discussed further in part 3.

The decision to have amending legislation was deliberately taken by the Department of Health in order to ensure that Parliamentary debate was not reopened on questions such as the general permissibility of research on human embryos (McCandless and Sheldon 2010a: 180). Although Part 2 completely replaces the corresponding portion of the 1990 Act – so that while reference is usually given to 'section X of the 1990 Act, as amended', any reference to the parenthood provisions reads as 'section X of the 2008 Act' – this should not be taken as an indication that the provisions relating to parenthood were fundamentally re-countenanced. While a number of important changes did occur, not least the possibility of recognizing two women as the parents of a child from the moment of birth, the 2008 Act left undisturbed many of the key assumptions of the original legislation, most particularly the notion that a child should have no more than two legal parents. With the extension of parenthood to a second female parent, the two-parent family model has clearly been reshaped. However, the insistence in the 2008 Act on a normative model of two 'real' parents is crucial in shoring up several assumptions relating to appropriate parenting and family form. Before moving to a more thorough discussion of this, I want here to set out the significance of the parenthood provisions in the new legislation.

In academic scrutiny relating to how the 1990 Act attempted to maintain and impose the heterosexual nuclear family model on reproductive practices that in very direct ways challenged such a paradigm, it seems fair to say that the parenthood provisions, although present, have been in the background of such commentary (for notable exceptions see Jones 2006; Smith 2006). I suggest, however, that in analyses of the family ideology signalled by the 2008 Act, they must be brought to the fore. This is for two main reasons. First, they are highly significant in and of themselves. This will be discussed further in part 3. Second, developments relating to the typically more talked about means of imposing normative family values in the original legislation – donor anonymity and the statutory duty imposed on clinicians to consider the child's welfare, including his or her need for a father, before offering a woman treatment (s. 13(5), 1990 Act) – render the parenthood provisions increasingly important. Together, donor anonymity and the welfare clause have attracted extensive academic commentary. This may be because they were seen as responding to particularly heightened anxieties about the role of fatherhood and masculinity in the associated reproductive practices (Cooper and Herman 1991; Haimes 1993; McCandless and Sheldon 2010b; Millns 1995; Sheldon 2005; Thomson 2008: 97–126). Moreover, in contrast to the rather technical nature of the parenthood provisions, which run to several pages of legislation and may have been regarded as necessary but complicated 'legal jargon' relating to status, donor anonymity and the welfare clause perhaps had a more direct appeal and polarizing force.

While it is beyond the scope of this chapter to address donor anonymity and the welfare clause in depth, I want to outline a couple of developments which push their significance from the fore. First, there is no longer a policy of donor anonymity in the UK, following the HFEA (Disclosure of Donor Information) Regulations 2004. The removal of donor anonymity is a complex phenomenon with associated debates being highly gendered (Haimes 1993; Thomson 2008: 97–126). However, the crucial point for my purpose is that while donor anonymity was a key method of shoring up the two-parent family form in the 1990 Act, this is no longer the case. There was no serious discussion throughout the reform process of implementing legislation that would entail going back to a policy of donor anonymity. Indeed, while a statutory duty to inform a child that they are donor conceived was rejected, concern was apparent regarding the role of the state in 'deceiving' a child about their parentage (McCandless 2011). It would seem, therefore, that there is considerably less contemporary concern about a gamete donor threatening the security of the child's family unit. While this has clearly been influenced by discourses relating to the significance of so-called 'genetic identity' (for a critical exploration of such, see Fortin 2009; McCandless 2011; Smart 2009; Wallbank 2004), we might also want to suggest that it reflects a sense of confidence in the security of the parental ties formed by law, at least from those charged with making the law (on the continuing sense of insecurity felt by parents with donor-conceived children, see Nordqvist and Smart 2011; and Gurnham, this volume).

Moving now to the welfare clause, described as one of the 'twin pillars' of the 1990 Act (Sheldon 2006). Agreed upon as a compromise measure, its origins lay in an attempt by some parliamentarians to limit access to fertility treatment to married women (McCandless and Sheldon 2010b: 203; see also Lee and Morgan 2001: 159–167). Given that the 1990 Act technically allowed for a child to have only one legal parent (mother) (s. 28(6)), the inclusion of the words 'need for a father' in the welfare clause were a highly significant way of signalling a normative preference for a child to have both a mother and a father and be located within the heterosexual family paradigm. However, as I have discussed elsewhere, the interpretation of the welfare clause in regulatory and clinical practice (as opposed to political and patient interpretation more generally: see respectively Millns 1995 and Harding 2010: 130–4) was becoming increasingly liberal, both in relation to welfare assessments coming to be seen as 'risk assessments' and in light of developments in equality law relating to sexual orientation (McCandless and Sheldon 2010b). Originally then, the Department of Health proposed to retain the welfare clause but remove the words 'the need for a father' from it (2006: paras 2.23 and 2.26;

Human Tissues and Embryo (Draft) Bill 2007, s. 21(2)(b)). This suggestion, however, proved highly controversial and after extensive scrutiny and debate, the original wording was instead replaced with 'the child's need for supportive parenting' (2008 Act, s. 14(2)(b); on the interpretation of this phrase, see further McCandless and Sheldon *Ibid.*).

While it remains an empirical question how the phrase 'supportive parenting' will be interpreted and applied in practice, there is nothing implicit in the phrase which demands that a child be located within the hetero-nuclear family. However, there seems plenty of scope to argue that the two-parent family paradigm certainly underpinned political understandings of the phrase (McCandless and Sheldon 2010b). Note the following indicative statement made during the parliamentary debates:

> If we follow the provisions of the [legislation], we stand to guarantee supportive parenting. We are almost assured that that child will have two parents. Not only that, but should anything happen to one of those parents, there will be another clearly identified parent with parental rights to look after the child. I can see nothing wrong with that: it is entirely logical. (Per Dr Turner, HC Debs, Vol 476, Col 183 (20 May 2008))

To what extent then will those family units which do not centre on dyadic parenting be considered as supporting child welfare? In addition, although there is nothing in the legislation to require two adults to be in an intimate relationship for the parenthood provisions to apply,[5] the consistent use of the word 'partner' throughout the parliamentary debates and in the Human Fertilisation and Embryology ('the HFEA') Code of Practice Guidance (2009) on the 2008 Act indicate that this is how the provisions will be understood. As I discuss further in part 3, several other aspects of the parenthood provisions in the 2008 Act indicate a strong normative preference for the two parents to be a sexually intimate couple. What I turn to next, however, is an elaboration of the sexual family concept, which I will then use to help analyse the parenthood provisions of the 2008 Act.

The Sexual Family

Writing 15 years ago in the context of American law and policy relating to the family, Fineman bemoaned the hold of what she termed the 'sexual family' model. She argued that 'our societal and legal images and expectations of family are tenaciously organized around a sexual affiliation between a man and a woman' and that beyond biological imperatives, this has important ideological ramifications regarding perceptions of the 'natural' for the social and cultural organization of intimacy (1995: 143, 145–76). The historically privileged position enjoyed by married couples in relation to family law and policy in most common law legal systems identifies what Fineman describes as the 'pure' form of the sexual family: the formally celebrated (i.e. married) heterosexual couple living with genetically related children (*Ibid*: 143; on the construction of marriage as a site for reproductive sex, see further Collier 1995). Clearly this is similar to the definition of the nuclear family adopted by this collection. However, I have adopted her term in order to highlight the central role of adult sexual partnership in Western socio-legal ideas about family form.

A number of social and demographic realities have significantly challenged the normative value of this family form, such as the increasing numbers of births outside of marriage and fragmentation of genetic families across households, as well as the greater visibility of families headed by single and/or same sex parents (McCandless and Sheldon 2010a: 187–188). Indeed, even in 1995 Fineman was prepared to accept that the pure form of the sexual family was not an 'untarnished icon' given moves to relax the formality of marriage (1995: 156). However, in response to calls for the recognition of the familial relationships of heterosexual couples not formally celebrated through marriage, as well as same sex partnerships and parenthood, Fineman argued that 'by duplicating the privileged form' the legal recognition of alternative relationships 'merely affirms the centrality of sexuality to the fundamental ordering of society and the nature of intimacy' (*Ibid*: 143, 1–2). In other words, in many mooted reforms to family law the conjugal couple remains valorized as the core unit around which families should be recognized and regulated, as opposed to other organizing concepts such as care, (inter)dependency, vulnerability or even child welfare. Family relationships and forms are only rendered legitimate if they can be assimilated under the rubric of a dyadic sexual partnership.

If we return to our context of assisted reproduction, it is well documented how reproductive technology and collaborative reproductive techniques offer to challenge socio-legal ideas about family form and relatedness (Dolgin 1997; Franklin 1997; McCandless 2009: chpt 3; Mykitiuk 2002; Strathern 1992). The 2008 Act therefore represents a very appropriate site to test the 'tenacity' of Fineman's conceptual offering, as if the model was going to buckle, it would be likely to do so first in the context of the reproductive situations covered by the legislation. A primary way in which assisted reproduction offers to reconfigure the sexual family model is its ability to disassociate reproduction and parenting from heterosexual intercourse (McCandless *Ibid*; Nordqvist 2008). While clearly the potential for such a deliberately transformative political exercise is there (Firestone 1970), the more usual reason why people engage in assisted reproduction is as a reaction to the inability of their sexual relationship(s) to produce biologically related children, whether for medical or social reasons. Despite this, and as we will see below in relation to the 2008 Act, an adult sexual partnership often 'rescues' (Whitehead 2008) the formal legality of the 'assisted' family unit and the parent-child connections therein, whether or not there is a formally celebrated relationship between the adults and/or bio-genetic connections with the child(ren). In agreement with Fineman, I argue that this reflects the extent to which the 'sexual-family-as-natural imagery' (1995: 147) has become ingrained in our socio-legal thinking, drawing our attention to the persistent centrality of sexuality and adult sexual partnership in the legal ordering of family life.

Understanding the changes in the 2008 Act

Framing the parenthood provisions

I have elsewhere explored in depth the 'tenacious hold' of the sexual family model on the parenthood provisions in the 2008 Act (McCandless and Sheldon 2010a), observing that the fundamental question of who counts as a parent and on what basis was not particularly high on the legislative reform agenda which culminated in the 2008 Act. Instead, discussions relating to parenthood appeared to be informed by three main concerns. First, building on previous legislative measures relating to the recognition of some same sex partnerships and parenting relationships (Civil Partnership Act 2002 and Adoption and Children Act 2004), as well as the direction in the HFEA's Sixth Code of Practice on the 1990 Act that patients should not be unfairly discriminated against on the grounds of sexual orientation (HFEA 2003: para G.3.2.2), the Government was concerned that the 2008 Act should signify formal equality for families headed by a same sex couple. There was also concern that single-parent families should not be discriminated against by the legislation, with the possibility of single women accessing treatment seemingly proving less objectionable than in the debates leading up to the 1990 Act (McCandless and Sheldon 2010b). However, as I discuss below, this (formal) equality and non-discrimination agenda did not play out in any straightforward way in the final legislation.

Second, there was not only concern, but often anxiety regarding the general use of the reproductive techniques governed by the legislation and specifically what they mean for the position of men and masculinity within the family. For example, in response to the suggestion that the phrase 'need for a father' be removed from the welfare clause, Baroness Deech, a previous chair of the HFEA, asserted the following:

> It is where the Bill crosses over into the organization of family life that I have more concerns. There is a risk in the unfolding of IVF and the consequent science that our humanity and the respective roles of men and women are ignored. It would be extraordinary if this House were to ignore the contribution made by half of the human race towards the upbringing of the next generation. It is important that this House should reaffirm the importance of parenting; both mothering and fathering. (HL Debs, Vol 696, Col 672-3 (19 November 2007))

While such strongly termed assertions were typically challenged with equal passion by other parliamentarians and commentators, they do reflect the controversy surrounding fatherhood throughout the passage of the legislation. Although concerns mostly played out in discussions relating to the welfare clause (McCandless and Sheldon 2010b), the parenthood provisions were also evoked. The strategy here appeared to be twofold: either attack was made on the extension of legal parenthood to a second female parent, or suggestions were made which attempted to reassert the male involvement in reproduction. For example, a significant portion of the time spent debating the parenthood provisions in Parliament was dedicated to an amendment which sought to remove the provisions for posthumous female parenthood, with no similar discussion for the pre-existing posthumous fatherhood provisions (see HL Debs, Vol 698, Cols 475-9 (28 January 2008)), while some parliamentarians went as far as suggesting that parenthood – or more accurately, fatherhood – could not be separated from genetic procreation and that all genetic fathers should be legal fathers accordingly (see for example per Lord Patten, HL Debs, Vol 697, Col 30 (10 December 2007); see further McCandless 2011: 195–7).

My third point is less a 'concern' and more of a foundation on which several of the provisions relating to parenthood proceeded: 'common sense'. For example, that the legislation should provide for two legal parents was generally accepted, with only one consultation response and two parliamentarians questioning whether legal parenthood should be extended to three (or more) legal parents in certain situations (AHRC Research Centre for Law, Gender and Sexuality 2005; per Baroness O'Neill and Baroness Barker, HL Debs Vol 696, Col 358-61 (21 November 2007) – note, however, that they did not table any amendments to this effect). Other prominent examples include the attribution of legal motherhood on the basis of gestation alone (1990 Act s. 27; 2008 Act s. 33); the newly inserted provisions relating to prohibited degrees of relationship between persons seeking to avail of the 'agreed parenthood provisions' (2008 Act ss. 37 and 44) and the parental order provisions (s. 54); as well as the explicit prohibition of legal motherhood, or indeed female parenthood, on the basis of the genetic link alone (2008 Act, s. 47). At no stage during the passage of the legislation were these provisions and their formulation seriously questioned or scrutinized.

Elsewhere I have offered two explanations for this lack of attention (McCandless and Sheldon 2010a: 188). The first relates to the politically sensitive nature of the legislation, which resulted in many key assumptions of the original legislation being left undisturbed in order to secure the passage of other prioritized reforms. The second relates to provisions not being questioned because they reflected a strong normative and seemingly 'intuitive' understanding of family. In other words, various provisions relating to parenthood were not discussed because they were regarded as uncontroversial and as 'not needing to be discussed' given that they reflected a sense of adherence and continuity with how family is 'intuitively' understood. Such continuities are detailed further below. The general analytical point to be made is that such an approach resulted in a fairly assimilative piece of legislation which does little to answer the opening question of 'what makes someone a parent'. The tensions in relation to different tests for legal parenthood in different contexts are therefore not sufficiently explained. This is not to say that there is anything intrinsically problematic with having different grounds for legal parenthood in different situations. However, without any explanatory work for these differentiations, the legislation is less an engagement with empirical variety or reasoned conceptual consideration and more an exercise in shoring up the continuing ideological preference for a certain family form in UK family law and policy: a family form which may be 'rescued' by adult sexual partnership when other familiar fault-lines dissipate. I turn now to an explanation of the parenthood provisions in the 2008 Act and how they remain significantly informed by the sexual family model.

The 2008 Act and the Sexual Family

The ongoing significance of the formally recognized adult couple
The 2008 Act maintains the hierarchical structure of the 1990 Act, whereby husbands – and now female civil partners – are given 'first shot' at legal parenthood along with the gestational mother, to include surrogacy arrangements (see further Horsey 2010). Only when there is no father or female parent by virtue of this formally recognized relationship (ss. 35 or 42 respectively) are the courts directed to consider whether there is a father or female parent under the 'agreed parenthood provisions' (ss. 37 and 44 respectively), which provide for the attribution of legal parenthood to a second parent who is not in a formally recognized relationship with the legal mother. As such, while marriage may no longer be the only means of legally recognizing an adult couple, it retains considerable importance and the extension of the marital presumption of parenthood to civil partners in this context[6] can be seen as assimilation to this marital ideal rather than any radically new way of legally recognizing parent-child ties.

A further distinction between formally recognized and other partnerships is that while legal parenthood is presumed for husbands and civil partners in both licensed and self-arranged 'artificial insemination' (ss. 35 and 42), the provisions for other partnerships only confer legal recognition in the context of licensed treatment and only where the agreed parenthood provisions are satisfied. While procedures such as IVF can only occur in a medical setting, practices such as donor insemination do not necessarily require medical assistance. The 2008 Act can be seen therefore to respond to the un-governability of donor insemination by again reverting back to the traditional underpinnings of the sexual family model and 'closing the circle' on those reproductive situations which challenge it the most (see further Donovan 2006).

Maintaining this distinction between formally recognized and other adult relationships is noteworthy given the widespread erosion of the relevance of this distinction elsewhere in family law since the original legislation. We see this trend most recently in the Welfare Reform Act 2009 which provides for compulsory joint birth registration (unless an exemption applies) and with it, the automatic conferral of parental responsibility under the Children Act 1989 to virtually all unmarried fathers (Probert 2011; Sheldon 2009; Wallbank 2009). While part of the explanation for retaining and building on this distinction lies in the 2008 Act being an amending statute, the result is a piece of legislation which is now significantly out of line with broader family law principles. This distinction can be explained as a legislative attempt to entrench the sexual family model in reproductive contexts which drive clear inroads into the ideals associated with the model.

The two parent model

Despite the lack of cultural and political consensus on what grounds parents should be recognized, there seems to be widespread acceptance of the notion that we can have two – and only two – 'real' parents. As has been noted elsewhere in this volume (Lotz), claims of authenticity through exclusivity appear to have outlived any inevitable relationship between legal parenthood and either biological connections or marital convention. While the reform of the welfare clause ensured that there was sustained attention to the question of whether a child could flourish equally well without a father, either in a single parent family or a family headed by a female same sex couple, there was no corresponding discussion of whether having more than two parents might benefit children.

As Lotz's contribution in this volume shows, there are many good reasons for moving beyond the two parent family model for legal parenthood by reference to the interests of would-be parents and children, as well as families and society more generally, marking the silence and lack of scrutiny on this issue as particularly noteworthy. Moreover, it stands in contrast to the increasingly flexible and creative ways in other UK family law contexts of recognizing a range of adults as significant to a child. To take just two examples: parental responsibility can be awarded to any number of adults and current adoption practice seeks to maintain links with birth parents alongside those with social/legal parents (Children Act 1989; Ball 2002). It also stands in contrast to developments and discussions in a limited number of other common law jurisdictions, namely Canada and New Zealand (see further Lotz, this volume).

While the possibility of recognizing more than two parents was countenanced early in the reform process by the Department of Health, including such a proposal in the menu of legislative reforms was explicitly rejected on the basis that the consequences of this change would be too far reaching and controversial, with the potential to 'hijack' the overall process

(McCandless and Sheldon 2010a: 191). The Department may well have been right, given that the issue was not seriously raised throughout the process by any parliamentarian involved and indeed, indirect possibilities for such to happen were explicitly excluded in relation to two women contributing biologically to the reproductive process (s. 47), leaving open the possibility that a third party may try to claim fatherhood or female parenthood through the parenthood provisions (see below). This indicates that the idea that a child may benefit from having more than two parents was seen as too radical, with reformers reverting to the two parent model as the default position without any real explanation seemingly either needed or demanded.

While it is possible for a child to have only one legal parent under the 2008 Act (legal mother), it is important to locate this in the strong normative preference in the legislation for two parents. The possibility of this playing out in interpretations of the welfare clause was mentioned earlier. What I additionally want to refer to here are the parental order provisions for surrogacy arrangements.

As a type of fast-track adoption, a parental order effectively transfers legal parenthood from the birth mother (and her partner, if she has one and he/she is considered the second legal parent) to the persons who commissioned the surrogacy arrangement. To be able to apply for a parental order and thus bypass the full adoption procedure, a number of criteria have to be met. For example, age, residency and time-since-birth requirements, and there must be at least a partial genetic link between the child and the persons applying for the order (s. 54). Under the 1990 Act, only married couples could apply for a parental order (s. 30). The 2008 Act extends the eligibility criteria to couples in a civil partnership and other couples 'who are living as partners in an enduring family relationship' and who are 'not within prohibited degrees of relationship to each other' (see further below). It is not clear from the legislation whether the two persons must be living together in the same household, but the underlying assumption certainly seems to be there. However, what is more important for my purposes is that a person cannot apply for a parental order without a (potentially sexual) partner. When asked why single persons were excluded from this part of the legislation, the then Minister of Health responded that:

> The Government are still of the view that [because of] the magnitude of what [surrogacy] means that it is best dealt with by a couple. (Per Dawn Primarolo, HC Debs, Vol. X, Col. 249 (12 June 2008))

The matter was not pressed further and her explanation appears to have been deemed sufficient. However, it is hard to reconcile this with the Government's determination not to discriminate against single-parent families, as evidenced by their earlier rejection of the recommendation by the Joint Committee of the House of Lords and House of Commons (which closely scrutinized the original Bill) that the words, 'the child's need for a father' should be replaced by 'the child's need for a second parent' (Department of

Health 2007: para 57). Several questions emerge here. For example, why is a single-parent family acceptable in some contexts, but not others and does this differentiation relate to uncertainty about the acceptability of surrogacy as a reproductive technique, or the creation of families with only one parent? Given the reluctance of various UK governments to properly regulate surrogacy (Gamble and Ghevaert 2009), we may be inclined to point towards surrogacy as the chief difficultly not least because, as previously mentioned, the issue of single women accessing treatment was deemed significantly less problematic than in previous legislative debates. However, I am not convinced that the explanation of 'surrogacy is difficult' is sufficient here. Single parent families remain heavily stigmatized in society (see Graham, this volume) and while marriage and civil partnership are 'protected characteristics' under equality legislation in the UK (Equality Act 2010), status as a single person is not[7]. As a result, all restrictions placed on single persons in the legislation fall to be governed by the rather nebulous concept of child welfare. Given the clear preference for the two-parent family model in the 2008 Act, as well as other recent legislation such as the Welfare Reform Act 2009, we should not be complacent that single parenthood has become any less objectionable than in years previous.

Parental dimorphism: One mother plus one father/female parent

While UK law has become increasingly open to the idea that a child can have two parents of the same gender, the sexual family model still continues to resonate in a steadfast resistance to the possibility that a child can have two 'mothers' or two 'fathers'[8]. The two parent model thus also appears to encompass an assumption of what Sheldon and I have previously referred to as 'parental dimorphism', meaning that the two parents are seen as occupying complementary yet different legal roles. This can be seen in the fact that a second female parent is not to be legally recognized as a 'mother' but as a 'female parent'. Legal motherhood is reserved for gestational mothers (s. 33), with gestation holding a significance *per se* given the prohibition of attributing motherhood (or female parenthood) on the basis of the genetic link (s. 47), while female parenthood is attributed on grounds which closely parallel those by which men achieve fatherhood (ss. 35–40 and 42–46).

While Fineman was more concerned with the gendered imagery of the sexual family in relation to care-work and dependency rather than the attribution of parental status *per se*, this sense of complementarity appears to be an implicit part of the sexual family model, whereby each parent occupies a distinctive role in the family unit: a role which somehow relates to their part in the (sexual) reproductive process. The explicit refusal of the possibility that motherhood might be grounded in genetic links, rather than emphatically through gestation, serves to emphasize the distinction between how motherhood and fatherhood are countenanced. What then of female parenthood? It is interesting here to recall an earlier point relating to when the parenthood provisions apply. I noted that when a man donates sperm to his female partner for treatment, his parental status is determined by the common law and not the 2008 Act. In contrast, when a woman donates an egg to her female partner, s. 47 explicitly prohibits her obtaining parental status on the basis of the genetic link. Instead, she must fall within the female parenthood provisions, either as the civil partner of the woman receiving treatment, or by satisfying the 'agreed parenthood conditions', similar to non-genetic fathers. This not only holds the potential for problematic and unequal legal scenarios relating to the use of female and male bio-genetic material (McCandless and Sheldon 2010a: 195–6); it also highlights the difficulty of assimilating family forms which resemble, but are clearly different from, the pure form of the sexual family model into legislation which continues to privilege and retain this family model (Diduck 2007).

To have allowed for the recognition of a second female parent on the basis of a bio-genetic tie appears to have been a step too far for the legislators, either on the basis that it would somehow compromise the certainty of who a child's birth mother was – perhaps casting doubt over who had primary responsibility for the child – or leave open the possibility that a third person might attempt to assert legal parenthood (McCandless and Sheldon 2010a: 194–6). We should also note here that the parenthood provisions are not extended to male same sex partnerships. Although two men can now apply for a parental order following a surrogacy arrangement (if they satisfy the above-mentioned criteria), the possibility of two men being recognized as legal parents from the moment of birth seems not to have been considered throughout the passage of the legislation. To do so would have involved either moving beyond the idea that the birth mother is a legal mother or alternatively, recognizing three parents from the moment of birth. Again, this can be explained by the hold of the two-parent, sexually dimorphic family model on the socio-legal imagination. While reforms which 'compromise' this family model may be allowed, those which fundamentally reconfigure its commitment to gender complementarity and the centrality of adult sexual partnership are either rejected or not deemed worthy of discussion. Indeed, a further possibility – that of a gender-neutral category of legal parent, rather than legal mother, father and female parent – was also rejected early in the reform process by the Department of Health, for reasons similar to the noted rejection of the possibility of a child having more than two recognized parents: that it would simply prove too controversial[9].

The potentially sexual couple

As noted above, husbands and civil partners have 'first shot' at obtaining legal parenthood along with the child's legal mother. Although there is no consummation requirement in the Civil Partnership Act 2004 (see further Barker 2006), it is assumed that married and civilly partnered couples will normally be in a sexually intimate relationship and must, at least, be lawfully permitted to be so (Marriage Act 1949, as amended and Civil Partnership Act 2004). While the 'agreed parenthood provisions' were clearly designed to cater for couples not in a formally recognized relationship, they are not explicitly restricted to those in an intimate relationship. However, as mentioned above, legal recognition under these provisions cannot be accorded to those who fall within the prohibited degrees of relationship with the child's mother (as defined by 2008 Act, s. 58(2)). The same provision appears in the eligibility criteria for parental order applications. There is nothing in the published deliberations regarding the rationale for including this prohibition and no significant discussion in any associated debates, suggesting its inclusion to be completely uncontroversial and thus to require no scrutiny or elucidation. Such a prohibition is unlikely to be grounded in eugenic considerations, given the reproductive context. Rather, to recognize as legal parents two people who ought not to be involved in a sexual relationship because of existing kinship relationships would, it appears, offend some deeply held but unstated value, confusing our ideas about appropriate family relationships and form. Thus, while the two-parent family model might be seen as having outlived its moorings in the heterosexual couple, the sexual family continues here to frame socio-legal understandings of family in so far as the couple at the heart of the family remains a sexual one.

I have elsewhere paused to consider the self-evident necessity of this provision, in light of various kinds of collaborative inter-familial parenting arrangements which occur as a matter of social fact, and which in many instances are seen as the ideal arrangement, such as where a mother and father raise a child with their own daughter who has become pregnant at a young age (McCandless and Sheldon 2010a: 198–9). If these circumstances are acceptable, what then is different about allowing individuals in these kinds of relationships to choose to create a child together, especially if we accept that legal parenthood does not always follow genetic links or that it is dependent in some way on a marital (or formally recognized) relationship between the parents (see also Lotz, this volume)? Is there a solid ethical underpinning for refusing to extend legal parenthood to two (or more) individuals who are already in a close kinship relationship? Reading the prohibition alongside the current HFEA Code of Practice guidance, which advises clinics that where they have concern about a woman's ability to provide 'supportive parenting' they may take into account support offered by family and friends (2009: para 8.11), it appears that while it is acceptable – possibly even desirable – for a woman's family to help her raise a child, it is not similarly acceptable for family members to seek to create a child together, or at least not in a way that is formally recognized through law. Furthermore, the prohibition perhaps also stands in contrast to the permissibility of intra-familial gamete donation – such as when a mother or sister donate eggs to a daughter or sister – the practice of which is currently under consideration by the HFEA, but which looks set to continue in certain circumstances (HFEA 2011).

As well as the incest prohibition in the parenthood provisions and the underlying assumption that those seeking to prevail of the provisions will be in a sexually intimate relationship, we could pose further questions about how partners in non-monogamous intimate relationships will be regarded. Would being explicit about the non-exclusive nature of an intimate relationship raise concerns relating to the welfare of the child and possible refusal of treatment? We currently have very little idea of how clinicians do or might regard such relationships. However, there is anecdotal evidence from the context of fostering that being explicit about the non-exclusive nature of even a long-term and formally recognized partnership will adversely affect an application on the basis of child welfare[10]. While non-monogamy is practiced by same and opposite sex couples alike, it is perhaps more prevalent in same sex relationships, rendering again as problematic the directly parallel treatment of same sex parenthood with opposite sex parenthood. Although I wish to avoid drawing direct parallels between the different contexts of assisted reproduction and fostering, it would seem that despite the decline of marriage as a life-long permanent commitment to one person, and greater fluidity in how people partner and re-partner, the pure form of the sexual family arguably reasserts itself by presupposing the couple at the heart of it as being exclusive.

Concluding discussion

What we see above is a reshaping of the sexual family form in the legislation pertaining to human fertilization and embryology. In the 1990 Act, there was a very explicit acceptance of the separation of genetic parenthood from social and legal parenthood and a formal recognition that the heterosexual couple (and legal parents) at the heart of the family unit need not be the genetic parents. There was also a step-away from the need for the parenting couple to be in a marital relationship. In the 2008 Act, these shifts are extended further to countenance a second female parent. However, as was discussed above, several possibilities were rendered as steps too removed from the sexual family ideal, stretching the current socio-legal imagination too far. Indeed, several new insertions into the 2008 Act further entrench the sexual family model in UK legislation, such as the incest prohibition and the silencing of the female genetic link for determinations of motherhood and female parenthood.

While these provisions will make sense for a great number of people who seek to avail of them, for many others they will prove problematic. An obvious example is the reproductive possibilities that are now open to transgender parents and several scholars have started to analyse how the explicitly gendered parenthood provisions of the 2008 Act will struggle to accommodate such possibilities (McGuinness and Alghrani 2008; McCandless 2009: chpt 5; McCandless and Sheldon 2010a: 200–3). Just as the parenthood provisions of the 1990 Act were challenged by various scenarios not countenanced by the legislators (see for example *X, Y and Z v UK*; *Leeds Teaching Hospital NHS Trust v A and B*; *Blood v UK*; *Re D/Re R*) it is highly likely that the provisions in the 2008 Act will come under similar challenge. This was surely easy to predict. However, the legislation is in no way 'future-proofed' for scenarios that fall out-with the provisions offered, meaning that the persons involved will simply fall outside legal recognition or have to turn to other child law provisions under the Children Act 1989, such as residence orders (Diduck 2007; McCandless 2005). If we are to accept that it is in the best interests of children, parents and families more generally for legal parenthood to exist (see further Lotz, this volume), we need to be slightly more imaginative in how this is attributed if some of the more vulnerable parent-child relationships are to be fully protected. Highly prescriptive legislation, which relies on an arguably outdated family model, does not sufficiently serve this need.

We saw above how the 2008 Act relied on dyadic adult sexual partnership to 'rescue' certain family relationships, marking the paradox whereby non-sexual reproduction becomes regulated firmly around adult sexual partnership. This seems in contrast to the increasing emphasis placed on vertical bio-genetic ties between adults and children in the context of sexual reproduction, especially for fathers (Collier and Sheldon 2008). Such contrasts illuminate two things: first, that we have now accepted as legitimate a range of grounds for attributing parenthood; and second, that there are ideological motives behind status recognition, in the sense that the different tests for parenthood in different circumstances often serve to shore up common ideals and assumptions about family. While it is generally argued that law represents an *informal* kinship system (Mykitiuk 2002) in contrast to the more *formal* kinship ties inherent in connections formed through shared bio-genetic substance, it could be argued that in today's increasingly bureaucratic society law holds a formative power that is as significant as 'blood ties'. This is not to say that only those ties recognized through law matter, but just that to provide for legal recognition is a powerful way of signalling a relationship as deserving of socio-political recognition. While legal recognition and socio-political acceptance do of course not always neatly follow from each other, law can act as a powerful state-sanctioned discourse (Sheldon and Collier 2008: 15), which sends clear normative indications on 'who' and 'what' counts as family. Extending the legal parenthood provisions to a second female parent in the 2008 Act provides an example of how law can be innovative. However, this innovative move has proceeded without really tackling the bigger question of 'why'? To answer this question in the context of legal parenthood we need to move beyond the various components of the sexual family model and probe more deeply the question that I opened this chapter with: 'what makes someone a parent?' This would be a much more beneficial exercise, rather than simply shifting boundaries that will inevitably need to be redrawn in a short space of time.

There is already a growing body of legal scholarship which provides thoughtful schemas for how relationships between adults and children might be recognized, beyond centring legislation on a linchpin of adult sexual partnership. For example, legal parenthood could be governed primarily by intent (Horsey 2010; Shultz 1990; Zanghellini 2010) or we could look at the potential of relational theory (Boyd 2010) or functionality (Whitehead 2008). Others still, in the context of relationship recognition between adults, have focussed on the realities of care and interdependency as a way of moving beyond 'conjugality' (Barker 2006; Boyd and Young 2005). This important scholarship can be developed further by drawing on research from other disciplines, such as sociology and social anthropology, to better understand how people experience and live their intimate lives. For example, anthropological work which seeks to explain how people understand their kinship connections and disconnections, especially in those contexts where the biological processes of (sexual) reproduction mean very little (Carsten 2004; Franklin 2006; Thompson 2005), or sociological work which examines how people live their personal and intimate lives and their understandings of concepts such as care, interdependency and responsibility. My analysis in this chapter has demonstrated that while the sexual family model continues to retain a powerful hold on UK family law and policy, various social, demographic and even legal developments have strained and undermined the future credibility of this model for law. It is therefore important that legal research and scholarship continues to rethink the role of this model, so that policy and law makers can be convinced of the value of measures that on the surface appear 'too controversial' for law reform.

Notes

1 This chapter draws on research conducted with Sally Sheldon, Kent Law School, and I am grateful for her permission to draw on this work here. My thanks to the editors of this collection for their very helpful comments on previous drafts of this chapter.

2 This process began with the Family Law Reform Act 1987, which provided for the attribution of legal parenthood to the husband of a woman receiving donor insemination, providing he consented to the treatment (s. 27). The Human Fertilisation and Embryology Act 1990 ('the 1990 Act') extended this legal recognition to other fertility procedures such as IVF and to unmarried male partners (s. 28). It also provided for the transferral of parenthood following certain surrogacy arrangements (s. 30). The Human Fertilisation and Embryology (Deceased Fathers) Act 2003 further extended the parenthood provisions to men who had died before their female partner's treatment and/or the birth of the child, for the purposes of birth registration only. The Human Fertilisation and

Embryology Act 2008 provides for the recognition of a second female parent along similar lines as fatherhood (ss. 42–47) and for a relaxation of the criteria for parental order applications (s. 54). Note that the Surrogacy Arrangements Act 1985 makes no provision for legal parenthood.

3   As will be made clear here, this is mostly in the context of licensed treatment. However, the provisions relating to husbands and civil partners also apply in the context of self-arranged donor insemination.

4   To say this is not to deny the continuing operation of the common law presumption *pater est*, but to observe that this presumption can now be rebutted through DNA evidence establishing the genetic link between a man and a child. On the increased willingness of the courts to determine legal fatherhood on the basis of the genetic link, even when the child might otherwise be located within a marital family unit, see Fortin (2009) and Sheldon (2005).

5   Note that this was also the case under the 1990 Act in relation to a man and woman who sought treatment together and wanted to avail of the parenthood provisions.

6   Note that there is no presumption parallel to the *pater est* presumption in common law for people who enter into a civil partnership and that the extension here is limited to this specific context.

7   Neither is it clear that the Human Rights Act 1998 could be used in legal challenges by single persons in such contexts, given that the state can interfere with a person's rights to privacy and family life so long as the interference is proportionate (ECHR, Art 8). Indeed, that some European states explicitly prohibit single women from accessing fertility treatment would indicate the likely failure of such a challenge.

8   Although same-sex couples have been able to adopt a child together since changes in the Adoption and Children Act 2002 were implemented, the gendered semantics of parenthood were avoided as adoptive parents have always been recorded gender neutrally as 'parent' rather than as 'mother' and 'father'.

9   This information was conveyed in an interview with representatives from the Department of Health, as interviewed by me and Sally Sheldon on 19 January 2009 (transcript on file with author). Those interviewed were: Edward Webb, Deputy Director for Human Tissue Transplantation, Embryology and Consent; Gwen Skinner, the policy manager responsible for the development of the legal parenthood provisions in the 2008 Act; and Katy Berry, who was responsible for the implementation of the 2008 Act.

10   This story was conveyed to me in a personal communication. As the couple involved are still in dispute with the local authority over the matter, it is not possible to give any further detail about the situation.

References

Arts and Humanities Research Council, Research Centre for Law, Gender and Sexuality (2005), *Response to the Public Consultation on the Human Fertilisation and Embryology Act*, available at http://www.kent.ac.uk/clgs/documents/pdfs/clgshfearespfianl.pdf (last accessed September 2011).

Ball, C. (2002), 'Regulating Inclusivity: Reforming Adoption Law for the 21st Century', *Children and Family Social Work*, 7: 285–96.

Barker, N. (2006), 'Sex and the Civil Partnership Act: The Future of (Non) Conjugality', *Feminist Legal Studies*, 14: 241–259.

Boyd, S. (2007), 'Gendered Legal Parenthood: Bio-genetic Ties, Intentionality and Responsibility', *Windsor Yearbook of Access to Justice*, 25: 55–85.

Boyd, S. and Young, C. (2005), 'From Same-Sex to No Sex?: Trends Towards Recognition of (Same-Sex) Relationships in Canada', in B.A. Crow and L. Gotell (eds), *Open Boundaries: A Canadian Women's Studies Reader*, Toronto: Prentice Hall, 217–229.

Carsten, J. (2004), *After Kinship*, Cambridge: Cambridge University Press.

Collier, R. (1995), *Masculinity, Law and the Family*, London: Routledge.

Collier, R. and Sheldon, S. (2008), *Fragmenting Fatherhood: A Socio-Legal Study*, Oxford: Hart.

Cooper, D. and Herman, D. (1991), 'Getting "the Family Right": Legislating Heterosexuality in Britain, 1986–91', *Canadian Journal of Family Law*, 10: 41–78.

Department of Health (2007), *Government Response to the Report from the Joint Committee on the Human Tissue and Embryo (Draft) Bill*, Report Cm 7209.

Diduck, A. (2007), '"If only we can find the appropriate terms to use the issue will be solved": Law, Identity and Parenthood', *Child and Family Law Quarterly*, 19: 458–80.

Dolgin, J. (1997), *Defining the Family: Law, Technology and Reproduction in an Uneasy Age*, New York: New York University Press.

Donovan, C. (2006), 'Genetics, Fathers and Families: Exploring the Implications of Changing the Law in Favour of Identifying Sperm Donors', *Social and Legal Studies*, 15: 494–510.

Fineman, M. (1995), *The Neutered Mother, the Sexual Family and Other Twentieth Century Tragedies*, New York: Routledge.

Firestone, S. (1970), *The Dialectic of Sex: A Case for Feminist Revolution* (originally published in 1970), New York: William Morrow and Company, Inc; reprinted in 2003: New York: Farrar, Straus and Giroux.

Fortin, J. (2009), 'Children's Right to Know their Origins – Too Far, Too Fast?', *Child and Family Law Quarterly*, 21:336–55.

Franklin, S. (1997), *Embodied Progress: A Cultural Account of Assisted Conception*, London: Routledge.

Franklin, S. (2006), 'Origin Stories Revisited: IVF as an Anthropological Project', *Culture, Medicine and Psychiatry*, 30: 547–555.

Gamble, N. and Ghevaert, L. (2009), 'Moving surrogacy law forward? The Department of Health's consultation on parental orders', *Bionews*, 532.

Haimes, E. (1993), 'Issues of Gender in Gamete Donation', *Social Science and Medicine*, 36: 85–93.

Harding, R. (2010), *Regulating Sexuality: Legal Consciousness in Lesbian and Gay Lives*, London: Routledge.

Horsey, K. (2010), 'Challenging presumptions: legal parenthood and surrogacy arrangements', *Child and Family Law Quarterly*, 22: 449–74.

Human Fertilisation and Embryology Authority (2003), *Code of Practice*, Sixth Edition, London: HFEA.

Human Fertilisation and Embryology Authority (2009), *Code of Practice*, Eighth Edition, London: HFEA.

Human Fertilisation and Embryology Authority (2011), *Donating Sperm and Eggs: Have your say*, London: HFEA.

Jackson, E. (2006), 'What is a Parent?', in A. Diduck and K. O'Donovan (eds), *Feminist Perspectives on Family Law*, Abingdon: Routledge-Cavendish, 59–74.

Jones, C. (2006), 'Parents in Law: Subjective Impacts and Status Implications around the Use of Licensed Donor Insemination', in A. Diduck and K. O'Donovan (eds), *Feminist Perspectives on Family Law*, Abingdon: Routledge-Cavendish, 75–100.

Lee, R. and Morgan, D. (2001), *Human Fertilisation and Embryology: Regulating the Reproductive Revolution*, London: Blackstone Press Limited, Second Edition.

McCandless, J. (2005), 'Recognising Family Diversity: The "Boundaries" of *Re G*', *Feminist Legal Studies*, 13: 323–336.

McCandless, J. (2009), *Reproducing the sexual family: law, parenthood and gender in assisted reproduction*, thesis submitted for the Degree of Doctor of Philosophy in Law, Keele University.

McCandless, J. (2011), 'The Changing Form of Birth Registration?', in F. Ebtehaj, J. Herring, M. Johnson and M. Richards (eds), *Birth Rites and Rights*, Oxford: Hart, 187–204.

McCandless, J. and Sheldon, S. (2010a), 'The Human Fertilisation and Embryology Act (2008) and the Tenacity of the Sexual Family Form', *Modern Law Review*, 73:175–207.

McCandless, J. and Sheldon, S. (2010b) '"No Father Required"? The Welfare Assessment in the Human Fertilisation and Embryology Act 2008', *Feminist Legal Studies*, 18: 201–225.

McGuinness, S. and Alghrani, A. (2008), 'Gender and Parenthood: the Case for Realignment', *Medical Law Review*, 16: 261–283.

Millns, S. (1995), 'Making social judgements that go beyond the purely medical: The Reproductive Revolution and Access to Fertility Treatment Services', in J. Bridgeman and S. Millns (eds), *Law and Body Politics: Regulating the Female Body*, Aldershot: Dartmouth, 79–104.

Mykitiuk, R. (2002), 'Beyond Conception: Legal Determinations of Filiation and the New Reproductive and Genetic Technologies', *Osgoode Hall Law Journal*, 39: 771–815.

Nordqvist, P. (2008), 'Feminist heterosexual imaginaries of reproduction: Lesbian conception in feminist studies of reproductive technologies', *Feminist Theory*, 9:273–292.

Nordqvist, P. and Smart, C. (2011), 'Relative closeness: situating donor conception in family relationships', conference paper at 'Proximities', Morgan Centre for the Study of Relationships and Personal Life, University of Manchester.

Probert, R. (2011), 'Recording Births: From the Reformation to the Welfare Reform Act', in F. Ebtehaj, J. Herring, M. Johnson and M. Richards (eds), *Birth Rites and Rights*, Oxford: Hart, 171–86.

Sheldon, S. (2004), '*Evans v Amicus Health Care*: Revealing Cracks in the "Twin Pillars"?', *Child and Family Law Quarterly*, 16: 237–52.

Sheldon, S. (2005), 'Fragmenting Fatherhood: the Regulation of Reproductive Technologies', *Modern Law Review*, 68: 523–53.

Sheldon, S. (2009), 'From "absent object of lame" to "fathers who take responsibility": Reforming Birth Registration Law', *Journal of Social Welfare and Family Law*, 31: 373–89.

Shultz, M. (1990), 'Reproductive Technology and Intent-Based Parenthood: An Opportunity for Gender Neutrality', *Wisconsin Law Review*, 2: 297–398.

Smart, C. (2009), 'Family Secrets: Law and Understandings of Openness in Everyday Relationships', *Journal of Social Policy*, 38: 551–67.

Smith, L. (2006), 'Is Three a Crowd? Lesbian Mothers' Perspectives on Parental Status in Law', *Child and Family Law Quarterly*, 18: 231–52.

Strathern, M. (1992), *Reproducing the Future: Essays on Anthropology, Kinship and the New Reproductive Technologies*, New York: Routledge.

Thompson, C. (2005), *Making Parents: The Ontological Choreography of Reproductive Technologies*, Cambridge, MA: The MIT Press.

Thomson, M. (2008), *Endowed: Regulating the Male Sexed Body*, New York: Routledge.

Wallbank, J. (2004), 'The Role of Rights and Utility in Instituting a Child's Right to Know her Genetic History', *Social and Legal Studies*, 13: 245–64.

Wallbank, J. (2009), '"Bodies in the Shadows": Joint Birth Registration, parental responsibility and social class', *Child and Family Law Quarterly*, 21: 1–18.

Whitehead, D. (2008), 'Regulating diversification in family life: to recapture the old or to recognise the new?', conference paper at 'Family Responsibility, Gender and Legal Change', University of Sussex.

Zanghellini, A. (2010), 'Lesbian and Gay Parents and Reproductive Technologies: The 2008 Australian and UK Reforms', *Feminist Legal Studies*, 18: 227–51.

Case list

Blood and another v UK [1 March 2003] High Court (unreported).
Leeds Teaching Hospital NHS Trust v A and B [2003] 1 FLR 412.
Re D (A Child) (IVF treatment) [2001] 1 FLR 972.
Re R (A Child) (IVF: Paternity of Child) [2003] EWCA 182.
X, Y and Z v the UK [1997] 24 EHHR 143.

Legislation list

Adoption and Children Act 2002.
Children Act 1989.
Civil Partnership Act 2004.
European Convention on Human Rights and Fundamental Freedoms 1950.
Equality Act 2010.
Family Law Reform Act 1987.
Human Fertilisation and Embryology Act 1990.
Human Fertilisation and Embryology Act 2008.
Human Fertilisation and Embryology Authority (Disclosure of Donor Information) Regulations 2004 (SI 2004/1511).
Human Fertilisation and Embryology (Deceased Fathers) Act 2003.
Human Rights Act 1998.
Human Tissue and Embryos (Draft) Bill 2007.
Marriage Act 1949.
Surrogacy Arrangements Act 1985.
Welfare Reform Act 2009.

3

The Two-Parent Limitation in ART Parentage Law

Old-fashioned law for new-fashioned families

Mianna Lotz

Introduction

The expanding opportunities and increased acceptance of assisted reproductive technology (ART) have brought significant 'new modalities' of reproduction (Leckey 2009: 78) and along with those the seeds of potentially profound challenges to traditional assumptions about what constitutes a 'family' and 'parent'. Widespread legislative reforms around same-sex marriage, parenting and adoption rights have transformed family law in a range of states, countries and continents. The role of gamete donors and surrogates, along with the increase of 'blended' families and open adoptions, stretch traditional conceptions of the family well beyond the dominant paradigm of the heterosexual, biologically-grounded and 'exclusive' nuclear family (Young 1998: 519).

Yet the undeniable social progressiveness of these reforms can obscure a recalcitrant fact: namely that what continues to prevail in law is, in key respects, a deeply traditional conception of the family as a *two-parent* nuclear construct. Furthermore, Kelly (2009) and Millbank (2008) point out that legal developments around ART parentage have in a number of cases served to protect or advance the claims of biological fathers at the *exclusion* of, rather than in addition to, those of lesbian co-mothers. This potentially entrenches traditional ideals of the family as biologically-grounded, rather than facilitating a more 'inclusive' and pluralistic revisioning of the family that more adequately reflects the realities of ART families.

This chapter considers the moral validity of maintaining adherence to a two-parent legal family construct, as assessed by reference to the interests of would-be parents and children as well as of families and society more broadly. The arguments presented here support a more inclusive legal conception of the family than currently prevails in most jurisdictions that have sought to develop a legal framework for assigning parentage in the ART context.

ART parentage law: Key aspects
in international legislation

While the complexity and breadth of current ART-related legislation and recent reform processes make an exhaustive summary impossible here, key aspects of the legislative context prevailing in at least the Commonwealth and the United States can be highlighted.

Worth observing at the outset is a notable shift away from legislation assuming what McCandless and Sheldon (2010) refer to as 'parental dimorphism' (that is, a view of mothers and fathers as necessarily occupying distinct and complementary legal roles). As McCandless's contribution to this volume also shows, the 2008 revisions to the Human Fertilisation and Embryology Act made it possible for the first time in the United Kingdom for lesbian partners accessing ART to *both* be recognised as legal 'parents' of a resulting child: the birth mother as 'mother' and her consenting female partner as 'parent'[1]. As a result, the UK's ART parentage law now aligns with that which prevails in many other jurisdictions – including Australia[2], New Zealand[3] and some provinces of Canada[4]. Of notable exception to these reforms is the fact that in no United States statute can legal parenthood status be allocated to the same-sex partner of a woman who conceives using ART, where the partner is not biologically related to the child (VCLR 2007: 11). At best (and only in some States) legal parenthood status can be achieved for a lesbian partner only via adoption, even where she consents to the ART and fully intends to co-parent the child. The US lags well behind the other countries considered here in terms of reforms to same-sex marriage and adoption law; reforms to ART parentage law in relation to legal parent recognition of same-sex non-birth partners are unlikely to be imminent.

In addition, the status of ART sperm donors, and of gestational surrogate mothers, is uniform across most of these legislatures in two key respects. First, a sperm donor is generally *not* recognised as the legal father[5]. In the context of a heterosexual couple using donor sperm, the man married or in civil union with the woman treated will everywhere presumptively be regarded as the 'father'. If a woman is single, there will generally be no father recognised, with some exceptions (including Delaware, New Mexico, Texas, and New Zealand) allowing a donor who intends to take on the role of a parent to be recognized as a legal parent (though that status may not necessarily attract the full rights and liabilities of fatherhood). Second, while *genetic* contribution is deemed insufficient for parent status in the case of ART 'fatherhood' (because overridden by the marital status of a heterosexual ART treatment couple), in all jurisdictions it is *gestation* that counts for purposes of legal recognition as 'mother'. Commissioning parents have no legal status with respect to the child in a legal surrogacy arrangement, even where they have provided the gametes for the conception. The child is legally recognised as the child of the gestating woman and, if she is in a marital or civil union relationship, her male partner. This can only be altered post-birth, via a parenting order attained through the courts or by means of adoption. There exists no provision for the egg-donor (who may also be the contracting woman who intends to parent the child) to be given presumptive legal parenthood status, irrespective of the wishes and intentions of all parties.

What is particularly striking, and the main focus of the rest of my discussion here, is that these widespread reforms regarding *who* may count as a legal parent in the ART context, have not been accompanied by changes to *how many* may count. There is a *prima facie* oddity in this phenomenon, given that lesbian couples accessing ART will be using donor sperm (and perhaps even donor egg or donor embryo). Thus legal recognition of same-sex family structures has not prompted legal acknowledgment of the new context of ART parenthood as one in which there can be multiple contributors to a procreative project. Potentially, an ART-conceived child could result from an arrangement whereby a couple contracts to use the donated sperm of a third person and the donated ovum of a fourth person, to be fertilized using IVF and implanted to be gestated by a fifth person, with the consent of a sixth person (the surrogate's partner). While likely to be rare, in such a scenario we could have up to *six* persons with some grounds – genetic, gestational, contractual, intentional and/or social – for a claim to parenthood status, three (or even more) of whom could potentially advance a claim to 'mother' status: the ovum donor; the woman who gestates and gives birth to the child; and any woman or women – whether single, partnered, or indeed part of a would-be parental group; and whether gay, bisexual or heterosexual – who form the original intention to become parent(s) and to raise the child.

Yet in spite of the real prospect of procreative projects between at least three would-be parents, provisions almost universally preclude recognition of more than two legal parents. This *exclusivity* of the family paradigm underpinning ART parentage law becomes apparent when we consider that generally speaking, no sperm donor (or any male partner) is able to be recognised as a *second* 'father', or indeed as any kind of third legal parent, no matter how willing all parties might be. Likewise, if a lesbian couple uses ART and the female partner *is* registered as a parent, parentage law either explicitly or implicitly precludes any man from being identified as 'father' for purposes of birth registration[6]. The possibility that the grounds for recognition of two mothers might *coexist* with grounds for *also* recognising a man as 'father' or 'co-parent' is thus expressly excluded.

One significant implication of this plays out in situations in which the relationship of the original ART treatment couple breaks down. The two-parent legal limitation means that legal recognition of any new partner – who might occupy fully the social role of an additional parent in the child's life – is *incompatible with* the continued legal status of one of the original parents: granting of parent status to someone additional would have to extinguish the legal parent status of one of the original two parents[7]. Yet there is no reason to expect that an existing legal parent, who – as per ART parenthood eligibility requirements – fully intended to undertake parenthood, would subsequently desire to alter her status, even (or perhaps especially) following relationship breakdown.

Lack of access to legal parent status for more than two co-progenitors has in some cases precipitated legal proceedings in which originally-intending parents (typically sperm donors) have sought greater recognition and security following deterioration of relationships with the other parties to the ART arrangement (often a lesbian couple)[8]. While courts have found in favour of custodial and guardianship entitlements for sperm donors in a number of these cases – usually on grounds of the child's best interests – the granting of legal status at the outset of a child's life to all consenting parties to an ART conception, would obviously establish their entitlement to continued involvement in the child's life and obviate the need for legal proceedings of this kind.

To summarize, a range of 'failures of recognition' result from the prevailing legal paradigm of the two-parent ART family. A considerable number of people are either unable to receive *de jure* recognition as the parents that, in terms of actual parenting practice, they *de facto* are; or are in a sense legally *misrecognised* as the parent of a child with whom they intend and have no active parenting role or relationship. In addition, nowhere is it possible for a friend or family relative of a single woman who accesses ART, to be registered as a legal co-parent of the child, even though they may undertake custodial and care-giving responsibilities equivalent to those of a parent. Kinship-based parenting is excluded as falling within what in UK law is termed 'prohibited degrees of relationship'; and both kinship and friendship-based co-parenting is precluded by a persistent commitment to the legal construct of the family as a fundamentally *sexual* unit. Accordingly McCandless and Sheldon (2010: 198) point out that '[while]… the two parent model might be seen to have outlived its moorings in the heterosexual couple, the sexual family model continues… to frame our understanding in so far as the couple at the heart of the family remains a sexual one' (see also McCandless, this volume). Yet it is far from obvious that to be raised collectively by people in a close kinship relationship – such as sisters, or a single woman supported by her parent(s) – or indeed by any persons not sexually intimate with each other, is necessarily incompatible with a child's best interests[9].

One notable departure from the two-parent limitation has occurred in the Canadian case of *A.A v B.B*[10]. In this case 'A', the long-term female partner of an ART birth mother, sought a court declaration legally recognizing her as a mother of the resulting child *in addition to* his birth mother *and* his biological father (the sperm donor, a close male friend of the couple who agreed to assist them to start a family, be actively involved in the child's life, and be recognised legally as his father). Importantly, all parties wanted 'A' to be granted equal legal status *without that extinguishing 'B"s legal parental status*, as would of necessity have occurred had 'A' pursued the available alternative of seeking to adopt the child. While initially dismissed on technical grounds, ultimately the Ontario Court of Appeal unanimously voted in favour of a *non-excluding* extension of legal recognition to 'A' as the then five-year-old child's mother, their decision resting on a judgment of the child's best interests. It is that moral consideration – of the interest of the ART-conceived child – to which I first turn in analysing the moral considerations in favour of what might be referred to as a 'three-parent-plus permission' in ART parentage law.

Moral considerations favouring legal inclusivity

While the idea that a child's best interests ought to be paramount in decisions affecting their welfare is now ubiquitous, nevertheless they are not the only interests directly at stake in this matter. Parents (and would-be parents) have distinguishable interests in legal parentage status, and these warrant consideration even if they are not fully separable from the child's interests once s/he comes into existence. Finally, a consideration of the interests of children and parents (prospective and actual) should be supplemented by a broader assessment of the impact of reforming current legal parentage provisions, not just for those individuals but for families and social practices more broadly.

Importantly, the moral considerations that follow speak at most in favour of greater *permissiveness* in regards to legal parentage recognition. I do not intend any of my arguments to support a claim that the various parties to ART conception should be morally or legally *obligated* to be registered as parents. Nor, importantly, are the arguments here intended to designate any *specific* correlation between recognition of legal *parentage* status, on the one hand, and attribution of *parenting* rights and responsibilities, on the other. Legal parentage recognition need not and does not entail equal and full legal parenting rights and responsibilities. The specific (and potentially highly variable) distribution of parenting rights and responsibilities that will be appropriate for specific families is a matter for determination on a case-by-case basis; and while differentiated parenting rights and responsibilities *may* track differentiated grounds for legal parentage (for example social versus biological), that need not be the case, and should not be assumed *ab initio*.

Interests of the child

The Victorian Law Reform Commission (2007: 112) has pointed out that the assignation of legal parental status 'is principally intended to protect children', conferring powers on parents to enable them to provide due care. Accordingly, several considerations support the claim that in a significant class of cases an

ART-child's best interests would be served by allowing recognition of three or more legal parents, where that is the univocal wish of all parties.

First, a child's *financial security* stands to be significantly enhanced from permitting 'three-parent-plus' legal families. Legal parent status protects a child by ensuring that from the very outset of their life, readily-identifiable adults have stable ongoing responsibilities of care towards them as well as the authority to make decisions about significant matters in their life. Importantly, as noted by the New Zealand Law Commission (2004: 16), '... the rules regulating succession on intestacy, family protection, citizenship, and child support stem first and foremost from the status of "legal parent", not from guardianship'. Moreover, the provisions and corresponding rights and obligations of legal parent status endure beyond childhood, unlike in the case of guardianship. And of particular importance is the fact that both automatic inheritance upon intestacy, and the ability to make a claim against a deceased estate, is in every jurisdiction available only to legally-recognised children of a person who dies without a will. Furthermore, if an ART birth mother should die, her partner will not be legally recognized as having status or custodial rights in relation to the child unless a parenting or guardianship order has been obtained or she has adopted the child. Millbank (2009: 15) also notes that a lack of parental status disadvantages lesbian co-mothers in child-related legal disputes with the birth mother, potentially causing significant loss of contact between a child and a co-mother after relationship breakdown. Thus, while in many lesbian relationships the female partner *will* be appointed as a guardian, it is clear that neither parenting orders nor guardianship status are equivalent to full legal parent status; for that reason they are widely regarded as inadequate for fully recognizing the *de facto* status of the female partner in the child's life.

In most jurisdictions additional sources of financial security are likewise precluded in the absence of legal parent status, such as the ability to seek compensation for a parent's accident, death or injury. Finally, in the event of relationship breakdown anyone not legally recognised as a child's parent is not automatically liable for child support, a fact with the potential to significantly disadvantage a child. Given that the availability of ongoing financial support for a child is of critical importance where there is a relationship breakdown between parents, or where a parent becomes very ill or dies, expanding the range and number of legally recognisable parents to permit inclusion of same-sex partners of birth mothers, and potentially *also* sperm donors (where that is desired by all parties) would only further secure a child's financial position.

Of course, in order to be justified by reference to the best interests of the child, the financial provisions effected by legal parent status would need to apply only to financial benefits and not to financial burdens; accordingly only assets and protections, and not debt and liabilities, should be able to be incurred by the child. This imperative, however, is in line with existing practice in most jurisdictions, and its extension to ART-families with more than two legally recognized parents presents no distinct problems or risks.

Beyond financial security, a child's *sense of psychological security* is also likely to be significantly enhanced by expanding legal recognition to all of those who *in fact* parent the child. Where three or more persons are fulfilling the roles and responsibilities of parent in relation to a particular child, it is surely not in a child's best interests to have any of those persons deprived of legal recognition as a parent. Endorsing a Supreme Court ruling in a relevant Canadian case, Bouchard (2007: 467) points out that 'the recognition of multiple parents would be in a child's best interests, regardless of number, provided they are actually acting as parents', namely because it will enable them to be able to count on the parental relationship continuing. Bouchard also notes that where legal recognition is bestowed on persons acting in the role of parent, that declaration of parentage brings a child's family 'out of the shadows', giving both practical and symbolic recognition to all of the most important relationships in the child's life (468). And as Young (1998: 517) points out, to deny legal parentage beyond two parents is in many cases simply misrepresentative, failing to 'reflect the multiple roles and [persons] involved in a child's life'. It is this misrepresentativeness that, for Young, constitutes the central normative objection to the exclusive two-parent family legal paradigm.

In considering a child's interests we must also acknowledge important lessons drawn from evidence and testimony in the adoption and, more recently, anonymous gamete donation context. A significant concern emerging from research studies is that widespread practices of secrecy and non-disclosure in relation to biological family history, can produce serious negative outcomes for child welfare (Turner and Coyle 2000; Lycett *et al.* 2004, 2005).[11] As noted by the New Zealand Law Commission (NZLC 2004: 5), '[l]aws that create fictional parenthood and extinguish the child's ties with the genetic parents' are increasingly under scrutiny. ART parentage law's insistence on presumptively recognising only male *partners* of women receiving ART, and on precluding coextensive recognition of sperm donors in any case in which two legal parents are already recognized, seems to create a legal fiction that is in considerable tension with our best evidence concerning the importance of full and independent access to information about one's familial history. In addition to enabling provision of full medical-genetic history and the ability to avoid consanguineous relationships, a significant benefit of legal parentage recognition for all consenting ART contributors is the protection that full disclosure of biological parentage offers against the possible identity-development challenges that confront many adoptees and other children resulting from alternative modes of family formation, including gamete donation and surrogacy (see also Shanley and Jesudason in this volume). Extensive research indicates that even where adoptees enjoy considerable legal safeguarding and support of their entitlements to information about their adoption and birth parents, nevertheless there remains a discrepancy between adoptees' and adoptive parents' perceptions as to level of interest in and desire for contact with biological parents, and also levels of anxiety about disclosing interest in biological parentage (Hawkins *et al.* 2008; Jones and Hackett 2008; Brodzinsky 2005, 2006; Stein and Hoopes 1985). Importantly, I am not here arguing for *mandatory* full disclosure or genetic testing of biological parentage, nor for the prohibition of anonymous gamete donation. The arguments here apply exclusively to cases in which *there is known willingness to be identified* on the part of procreative contributors. In such cases, the potential benefits for the resulting child of having all parties legally registered as parents, and of therefore having independent, unmediated access to potentially important identifying information, strongly support legal permissiveness towards three-parent-plus families. To acknowledge this, however, is not to suggest that legal parenting status is necessary or morally mandated on these grounds. There clearly exist alternative mechanisms sufficient for achieving the goal of providing independent, unmediated parentage information.

Before turning to parental interests, one potential child-welfare-related concern about the proposed legal inclusivity warrants attention: namely, that permitting more than two legally-recognized parents will increase the risk of harm to children, either by predisposing them to increased stigmatization, or by predisposing multi-parent families to increased intra-familial conflict. Both concerns are significant, and deserve closer consideration than I can here give them. Yet three quick points can be made.

First, one highly efficacious way in which to de-stigmatize a given phenomena is precisely by according it legal standing. As McNair (2004: 9) points out, '[i]nadequate representation of diverse families in the public arena increases the already stigmatized nature of ART, infertility, surrogacy, and lesbian and gay families'. Enabling the formal sanctioning of diverse family forms that we know already exist in reality, could only assist with normalizing such families, helping to reduce stigma and the negative child outcomes associated with that.

Second, the potential for increased conflict arising from multi-parent families will not be eliminated by a refusal to legally recognize more than two parents. Relationship breakdown and re-partnering presents considerable challenges for families, and parental conduct sometimes falls well short of the ideal. Yet *all* families encountering post-separation conflict have full legal recourse through family courts and their instruments. Even if we accept the possibility that legal recognition of three-parent-plus ART families could increase the frequency or intensity of such conflict, families experiencing such conflict can avail themselves of the existing dispute resolution mechanisms that arbitrate on matters of custody and access. Indeed, weighing against concerns of a greater likelihood of intra-familial conflict, the New Zealand Law Commission (2004: 242) has noted that the fact that ART-family arrangements will typically have been the subject of extensive planning, thought and deliberation between all intending parents prior to conception and birth, may well predispose these families to *reduced*, rather than increased, conflict.

Finally, it can be argued that it is in fact the *current* legal system – with its tenacious commitment to an exclusive, two-parent family paradigm – that exacerbates grounds for conflict. As Young (1998: 546) has pointed out, the fact that current law treats claims for legal parentage as a zero-sum game – namely by requiring extinguishment of an existing parent's legal status as a condition of the extension of legal status to any additional persons – creates a system of 'winners and losers' which 'fails to encourage the seeking of common ground'. Indeed it might be noted here the extent to which currently-prevailing and highly adversarial systems of post-separation family law arbitration likewise embody a 'zero-sum' model in which one party's gain is necessarily another's loss. Young notes that in many of the cases that have come before courts, lesbian couples have sought to exclude sperm donors from attaining or retaining legal status and from playing any role in the child's life, principally for the reason that such a status for the sperm donor is incompatible with legal recognition of both women as parents, and therefore threatens the lesbian relationship itself. The result of this is that '... the child, and the family as a whole, must forego certain relationships that could be complementary to, and supportive of, the core unit' (548). Thus a significant potential source of the very conflict that we are here concerned about, is in fact an artefact of prevailing parentage law itself (see also Scheib and Hastings, Graham, and McCandless, all in this volume).

Interests of parents

Notwithstanding the intimate co-dependence of children's and parents' interests, it is at least *conceptually* possible to distinguish parental interests that will be promoted by a greater permissiveness and inclusivity in ART parentage law.

The first of these is the interest in *equality of access to the 'goods' of legal family founding*. It is my view that the central goods of family founding are bound up not primarily with securing a realm of privacy or relations of intimacy (*contra* Schoeman 1980) but with the enhancement of individual flourishing, autonomy and self-realization. Founding a family offers the opportunity to pursue one's own conception of the good – one's own freely-chosen 'experiment in living' – not just within one's purely self-regarding sphere but amongst a sphere of intimates. This constitutes the building of a family as an inherently creative and self-expressive activity. As Brighouse and Swift (2006: 92) note, the relationships that adults have with the children they parent 'have a different moral quality, make a different kind of contribution to their flourishing, and so are not interchangeable with other [intimate] relationships'. Citing Callan (1997: 142), Brighouse and Swift argue furthermore that parents have 'a non-fiduciary interest in playing this fiduciary role', based on the fact that parenting develops capacities and self-knowledge that (for many) are central to a flourishing life (95).

If we accept this account of the important goods of parenthood and family-founding, then the equality argument establishes a moral imperative for law to ensure that *all* individuals are accorded equal opportunity to access these goods; and that any family-related legislation that is – in intent or effect – discriminatory, is removed. For many individuals (especially gays and lesbians) contributing sperm or ova to an ART conception represents the *only* opportunity they have to play a role in creating and parenting a child and founding a biologically-related family (which is, rightly or wrongly, currently highly valued in most societies). Claims of inequality and discrimination gain a footing wherever a person's unchosen attributes curtail their equal access to important personal or social goods. Any barriers to legal parenthood status that impact disproportionately and negatively upon same-sex couples or individuals are *pro tanto* discriminatory.

The second parent-centred argument for permitting three-parent-plus legal families in at least some cases concerns a *parent's interests in de facto/de jure parity*. Legal recognition or not, we know that there are, and will be, families of a less traditional composition in which the social roles and responsibilities of parenting are undertaken by three or more people. Yet access to child welfare support and carer entitlements of various kinds, and to employment entitlements such as parental leave, are limited to legal parents. Other restrictions similarly prevent full participation in a child's life, such as the ability to obtain a passport and citizenship for one's child, to register a child in school, to grant consent to medical treatment and in some cases to obtain medical information about a child. Only a legal parent can grant consent to a child's future adoption (a fact which may become relevant if a sole remaining parent faces terminal illness, for example); and as we have already noted, without a declaration of parentage or an adoption or guardianship order, a surviving partner is not entitled to make important decisions for a child whose birth mother has died.

In view of these significant impediments to full parental participation in a child's life, considerations of fairness suggest that those who *de facto* contribute to raising a child – and who may well have been involved in planning their conception – are entitled to equivalent *de jure* recognition, not least of all where that is required for access to significant entitlements and capabilities. Legal recognition is certainly in the *economic* interests of those who have committed to parenting a child; however, it is also a matter of the *symbolic recognition* of the significance of the person's role in the child's life. This symbolic recognition has the power to enhance both parents' and children's welfare, as expressed by one submission reported in A.A. v B.B, (ONCA 2, 2007: 6):

> [L]egal recognition of our role as parents to our children is essential for their safety and social well being. It is critical to children that they have reflected back to them the value and integrity of their lives, including the legitimacy of their families ... Equal familial status sends a powerfully positive message to all social institutions that have an influence on our children's lives. It obliges them to acknowledge and respect the families our children live in.

Moral imperatives of social transformation

A final moral consideration in favour of increased inclusivity in existing ART parentage law is motivated not in the first instance by the direct interests of ART-conceived children or their progenitors, as central as these are, but by socio-political objectives more broadly conceived. A loosening of the two-parent family paradigm reflected in law embodies the potential to promote acceptance of diversity and pluralism more widely within our communities, increasing tolerance and enhancing welfare well beyond individual ART families.

Perhaps contrary to initial expectations, it also has the potential to weaken the grip of the biologically essentialist ideals underpinning traditional conceptions of family and parenthood, which might be thought to be enjoying something of a reification with the expansion of technological opportunities for people to contribute biologically to the creation of a child (Levy and Lotz 2005; Lotz 2008). However, enabling consenting families to register three or more legal parents would challenge traditional assumptions that 'real' or 'true' families comprise exclusively one mother and one father, united by a sexual bond, producing biologically related offspring. While a more inclusive parentage law can allow for increased recognition of biological or genetic contributors – in particular gamete donors – what is crucial is that enabling such persons to legally count as parents need not come at the cost of the parent status of any existing parent. Thus, expanding the legal model of the family beyond persons with biological grounds for parentage recognition, will serve the interests of same-sex partners, both male and female, who have no biological or genetic relationship to the child, and who occupy an exclusively *social* parental role. Greater inclusivity will ultimately promote equality and non-discrimination for all persons, regardless of sexual orientation, and will formally communicate acknowledgement of the significance of social parenting. In turn, increased acceptance of non-genetically-based parent-child relationships – such as are found within adoptive families – is also promoted via formal acknowledgement of the many diverse yet normatively equivalent foundations upon which parent-child relationships are built.

There might appear to be something paradoxical in the suggestion that an expanded legal parentage law – which will *inter alia* facilitate increased recognition of *biological* parents – is to be supported on the grounds that it will serve to promote more inclusive *non-biologistic* conceptions of parenthood and family. Commenting on judicial decisions that have granted limited custody and guardianship to gay male donors where lesbian couples use ART, Legge, Fitzgerald and Frank (2007: 20) note the tension that exists in the fact that in such cases, biological kinship 'is being prioritized in a manner which reflects the contemporary biologization of kinship ties, while at the same time… [providing] legal recognition to a wider and non-traditional family unit of three homosexual parents'. However, rather than exclusively entrenching biological kinship ideals, recognising three-parent-plus families at law in fact provides 'simultaneous reinforcement *and destabilization* of the traditional family unit' (Legge *et al.* 20, emphasis added). Thus it helps to *confound* traditional conceptions of parenthood and family, creating the space in which a much wider diversity of families can flourish and thereby loosening the grip of narrow genetic and biological conceptions of what constitutes a family and a parent.

The apparent paradox is further removed by re-calling attention to the point, made earlier, that legal parental *recognition* need not and does not entail equal and full legal parental *rights and responsibilities*. On the contrary, the distribution of parental rights and responsibilities both can and should track *differentiated* forms of parenthood. Thus a child's birth registration might distinguish *amongst* the legal parents those that stand in the *social* relation of parent to the child as opposed to those who do not, signifying different degrees and spheres of parental entitlement and obligation accordingly. Such delineation can also assist, where applicable, in the appropriate and equitable distribution of financial and social entitlements and obligations between eligible parties. Importantly, I suggest, what should in *every* case determine the allocation of legal parent *rights* and *responsibilities* (as distinct from mere legal parental *status*) is the *actual social role* that a person plays, or intends to play, in the child's life. The claims here are therefore not to be taken to support automatic recognition of gamete donors as legal parents, nor claims of a child's need for a biological father, nor any arguments seeking to secure legal status on grounds of an alleged moral significance of biological or genetic contribution alone. Just as it might be appropriate to *limit* the scope of parental rights and responsibilities for some genetic or biological contributors, so too might it be appropriate to *extend* rights and responsibilities to more than two social parents. Thus an expanded conception of what it means to be a 'parent' can fruitfully ground a diversification of the types of rights and responsibilities accorded to 'parents'; and the fact that one is a 'parent' is to be understood as under-determining matters of rights and responsibilities. I take these to be, in principle and in practice, fully achievable legal determinations and demarcations.

Conclusion

A substantial body of research now demonstrates that welfare outcomes for children in diverse family compositions cannot be linked to method of conception, the absence or presence of genetic or gestational link in parent-child relationships, parental sexual orientation, or family form; and that what matters above all else are factors such as the level of family functioning, stability and harmony, and openness of communication (Golombok 2006, 2004, 2002, 1999, 1996; McNair 2004; Brewaeys 2001; Wise 2003). Family structure in itself is not predictive of parenting quality, and is 'an inadequate proxy measure for child outcomes due to the huge variation in levels of functioning within any one family form' (McNair 2004: 19). Yet while legislative progress has been achieved to remove some discriminatory aspects of law in relation to matters of family, marriage, adoption and even ART parentage, the family construct that continues to prevail in law is one that is out of alignment with reality, and poorly suited to accommodating changed and changing family forms. Removing the two-parent limitation so as to allow a broader range of consenting contributors to a child's conception and parenting to potentially gain legal parentage recognition has the potential to substantially promote the welfare of children, parents, families and society more broadly. As Young (1998: 555) argued over a decade ago:

> ... [A]t a time when fewer and fewer children live with two parents, when more and more children live in strained economic conditions, and when the state appears to be less and less likely to provide support, the 'channeling function' of law could be deployed to encourage and support the creation and maintenance of more connections with those who may have special interests in a particular family or child, and a particular inclination to contribute... From this perspective, social policy should be contemplating ways of encouraging more people to feel greater levels of responsibility for more children.

Removal of the two-parent limitation in ART parentage law would make a significant contribution towards fulfilling that moral objective.

Notes

1   By Sections 33(1) and 42(1) of the HFE Act (2008).

2   In Australia reforms have progressed through State legislatures since 2002 with the final legislation (in South Australia) due to come into effect later this year. For a comprehensive overview of Australia's legal developments in same-sex parenthood see in particular Millbank (2009) and the Victoria Law Reform Commission Final Report (2007), hereafter cited as (VCLR 2007).

3   NZ Law Commission Occasional Paper (2004), hereafter cited as (NZLC 2004).

4   Namely Newfoundland, Quebec and the Yukon, with British Columbia achieving this via Human Rights Tribunal ruling. See Leckey (2009).

5   Though a man who assists reproduction by means of sexual intercourse *is* a legal parent, and indeed *cannot be removed* as such.

6   Per HFE Act (2008) section 45(1).

7   Ibid, per section 44(1).

8   Including in New Zealand the case of P v K ([2003] 2 NZLR 787); P v K and M ([2004] NZFLR 752); and P v K ([2004] 2 NZLR 421); and in Australia of Re Patrick (An Application Concerning Contact) [2002] FamCA 193 (5 April 2002).

9   McCandless and Sheldon (2010: 199) refer to a 2005 BBC report on the IVF arrangement between a married woman (infertile following chemotherapy), her consenting husband (who donated the sperm), and her two sisters – one of whom contributed the egg while the other gestated the baby. See 'Sisters make baby with three mums'.

10 A.A. v. B.B., 2007 ONCA 2 Date: 20070102 Docket: C39998. Court of Appeal for Ontario.

11 An excellent meta-analysis is provided in VLRC (2007), especially chapters 2 and 12, and Appendix 1.

References

Bouchard, D. (2007), 'The Three-Parent Decision: A Case Commentary on *A.A v. B.B*', *Saskatchewan Law Review*, 70: 459–478.

Brewaeys, A. (2001), 'Review: Parent–Child Relationships and Child Development in Donor Insemination Families', *Human Reproduction Update*, 7: 38–46.

Brighouse, H. and Swift, A. (2006), 'Parents' Rights and the Value of the Family', *Ethics*, 117(1): 80–108.

Brodzinsky, D. (2005), 'Reconceptualizing Openness in Adoption: Implications for Theory, Research and Practice', in D.M. Brodzinsky and J. Palacios (eds), *Psychological Issues in Adoption: Research and Practices*, Westport, CT: Praeger.

Brodzinsky, D. (2006), 'Family Structural Openness and Communication Openness as Predictors in the Adjustment of Adopted Children', *Adoption Quarterly*, 9(4): 1–18.

Callan, E. (1997), *Creating Citizens*, Oxford: Oxford University Press.

Golombok, S., Murray, C., Brinsden, P. and Abdalla, H. (1999), 'Social versus Biological Parenting: Family Functioning and the Socioemotional Development of Children Conceived by Egg or Sperm Donation', *Journal of Child Psychology and Psychiatry*, 40 (4): 519–527.

Golombok, S., Brewaeys, A., Cook, R., Giavazzi, M.T., Guerra, D., Mantovani, A., van Hall, E., Crosignani, P.G. and Dexeus, S. (1996), 'The European Study of Assisted Reproduction Families: Family Functioning and Child Development', *Human Reproduction*, 11(10): 2324–2331.

Golombok, S., Brewaeys, A., Giavazzi, M.T., Guerra, D., MacCallum, F. and Rust, J. (2002), 'The European Study of Assisted Reproduction Families: The Transition to Adolescence', *Human Reproduction*, 17(3): 830–840.

Golombok, S., Murray, C., Jadva, V., MacCallum F. and Lycett, E. (2004), 'Families Created Through Surrogacy Arrangements: Parenting Relationships in the 1st Year of Life', *Developmental Psychology*, 40(3): 400–411.

Golombok, S., Murray, C., Jadva, V., Lycett, E., MacCallum F. and Rust, J. (2006), 'Non-Genetic and Non-Gestational Parenthood: Consequences for Parent-Child Relationships and the Psychological Well-Being of Mothers, Fathers and Children at Age 3', *Human Reproduction*, 21(7): 1918–1924.

Hawkins, A., Beckett, C., Rutter, M., Castle, J., Groothues, C., Kreppner, J., Stevens, S. and Sonuga-Barke, E. (2008), 'Communicative Openness About Adoption and Interest in Contact in a Sample of Domestic and Intercountry Adolescent Adoptees', *Adoption Quarterly*, 10:(3 & 4): 131–156.

Jones, C. and Hackett, S. (2008), 'Communicative Openness Within Adoptive Families: Adoptive Parents' Narrative Accounts of the Challenges of Adoption Talk and the Approaches Used to Manage these Challenges', *Adoption Quarterly*, 10(3&4): 157–178.

Kelly, F. (2009), 'Producing Paternity: The Role of Legal Fatherhood in Maintaining the Traditional Family', *Canadian Journal of Women and the Law*, 21(2): 315–351.

Leckey, R. (2009), 'Where the Parents Are Of the Same Sex: Quebec's Reforms to Filiation', *International Journal of Law, Policy and the Family*, 23: 62–82.

Legge, M., Fitzgerald, R. and Frank, N. (2007), 'A retrospective study of New Zealand case law involving assisted reproduction technology and the social recognition of "new" family', *Human Reproduction*, 22(1): 17–25.

Levy, N. and Lotz, M. (2005), 'Human Reproduction and a (kind of) genetic fallacy', *Bioethics*, 19(3): 232–49. Reprinted in *Readings in Health Care Ethics* (second edition), Broadview Press: Calgary, Alberta (forthcoming).

Lotz, M. (2008) 'Overstating the biological: Geneticism and essentialism in social cloning and social sex selection', in J. Thompson and L. Skene (eds), *The Sorting Society: The Ethics of Genetic Testing and Therapy*, Cambridge: Cambridge University Press.

Lycett, E., Daniels, K., Curson, R. and Golombok, S. (2004), 'Offspring Created as a Result of Donor Insemination: A Study of Family Relationships, Child Adjustment and Disclosure', *Fertility and Sterility*, 82(1): 172–9.

Lycett, E., Daniels, K., Curson, R. and Golombok, S. (2005), 'School-aged Children of Donor Insemination: A Study of Parents' Disclosure Patterns', *Human Reproduction*, 20(3): 810–819.

McCandless, J. and Sheldon, S. (2010), 'The Human Fertilization and Embryology Act (2008) and the Tenacity of the Sexual Family Form', *The Modern Law Review*, 73(2): 175–207.

McNair, R. (2004), 'Outcomes for Children Born of ART in a Diverse Range of Families', Victorian Law Reform Commission *Occasional Paper*, Melbourne.

Millbank, J. (2008), 'The Limits of Functional Family: Lesbian Mother Litigation in the Era of the Eternal Biological Family', *International Journal of Law, Policy and the Family*, 22(2): 149–77.

Millbank, J. (2009), 'De facto relationships, same-sex and surrogate parents: Exploring the scope and effects of the 2008 federal relationship reforms', *Australian Journal of Family Law*, 23: 1–34.

New Zealand Law Commission (2004), Preliminary Paper 54, 'New Issues in Legal Parenthood', Wellington, New Zealand. Available online at http://www.lawcom. govt.nz/project/status-parenthood-0?quicktabs_23=preliminary_paper#node-545 [accessed October 2011].

Phillips, C. (2007), 'Case Note: Reforming the laws governing parenthood', *Family Law Journal*, 4: 240.

Schoeman, F. (1990), 'Rights of Children, Rights of Parents, and the Moral Basis of the Family', *Ethics*, 91(1): 6–19.

Stein, L.M. and Hoopes, J.L. (1985), *Identity Formation in the Adopted Adolescent*, New York: Child Welfare League of America.

Turner, A.J. and Coyle, A. (2000), 'What Does it Mean to be a Donor Offspring? The Identity Experiences of Adults Conceived by Donor Insemination and the Implications for Counselling and Therapy', *Human Reproduction*, 15(9): 2041–2049.

Victorian Law Reform Commission (2007), Final Report: 'Assisted Reproductive Technology and Adoption', Melbourne, Victoria: Victorian Law Reform Commission, March 2007. Available at http://www.lawreform.vic.gov.au/projects/ art-adoption/art-and-adoption-final-report [accessed October 2011].

Wise, S. (2003), 'Family structure, child outcomes and environmental mediators: An overview of the Development in Diverse Families Study', *Australian Institute of Family Studies*, Research Paper No. 30, Commonwealth of Australia, Melbourne. Available at http://www.aifs.gov.au/institute/pubs/wise5.html [accessed October 2011].

Young, A.H. (1998), 'Reconceiving the "Family": Challenging the Paradigm of the Exclusive Family', *American University Journal of Gender and Law*, 6: 505–555.

4

The Best Interest of Children and the Basis of Family Policy

The issue of reproductive caring units

Christian Munthe and Thomas Hartvigsson

Introduction

The notion of the best interest of children figures prominently in family and reproductive policy discussions and there is a considerable body of empirical research attempting to connect the interests of children to how families and society interact. Most of this research regards the effects of societal responses to perceived problems in families, thus underlying policy on interventions such as adoption, foster care and temporary assumption of custodianship, but also support structures that help families cope with various challenges. However, reference to the best interest of children can also be applied to a more basic issue in family policy, namely that of *what is to be considered a family in the first place*. This issue does not raise any questions regarding the proper conditions for when society should intervene in or change the family context of a child. Rather, it is about what social configurations should be recognized as a potentially fitting context for children to enter into and (if all goes well) eventually develop into adulthood within. Any social configuration so recognized constitutes what we will call a *reproductive caring unit* (RCU). An RCU is a social configuration such that society's default institutional arrangements allow it to have (by sexual and artificial reproduction, adoption, and combinations of these), care for and/or guard children – the approved RCUs thereby being the basic 'menu' of what families with children there may be in society. Opinions on what should be allowed to be an RCU will frame any further discussion of the questions already mentioned, but also policies having further implications for, for example, the practices of adoption and reproductive technology, as well as regulation of custody in the event of separation or parental disagreement.

There is a communicative problem involved in talking about this issue in terms of the word 'family', however. Due to a combination of biological necessities, socio-economic and developmental circumstances, prejudice and custom, people around the world tend to associate this term with the presence of romantic or sexual relationships (between adults) and/or genetic links (between adults and children). However, the question indicated above does not necessarily imply such things to be in place in the case of a legitimate RCU. What should be awarded the standing of a family in *this* sense, then, may be something that many people find strange to *call* a family. At the same time, if you ask the question whether a single mother and her adopted child, or four adult siblings living together and caring for a foster child could constitute fitting social arrangements for children to enter and develop within, people would not (we presume) rule out this question as empty just because the word 'family' seems odd to apply to them. Rather, we suggest, social configurations within which children are raised are called 'families' as we tend to view them as legitimate RCUs. Thus, to the extent that there are reasons to allow RCUs not involving the ingredients of romantic/sexual relations or genetic linkage, this will be a reason to change linguistic practice.

The question we want to address, then, is about what is implied by arguments in terms of the best interest of children for the issue of what should be allowed to be a family *in the sense of an RCU*. This is a question not about particular cases, but about general institutional arrangements. Society needs policies as to what RCUs to allow and within these frames, any single initially legitimate RCU may be found unfitting for serving this purpose, just as in the case with dysfunctional 'nuclear families'. Arguments about what is in the best interest of the concerned children in such cases can (and should) be brought to bear on this issue. However, as will be seen, these arguments involve quite different considerations compared to when assessments in terms of the best interest of children are applied to the issue of RCUs.

The best interest of children as a moral notion

An evident starting point for this investigation is to recognize the importance and standing of the formulation in the UN Convention on the Rights of the Child (CRC), that:

> In all actions concerning children, whether undertaken by public or private social welfare institutions, courts of law, administrative authorities or legislative bodies, the best interests of the child shall be a primary consideration. (United Nations 1989)

This sentence signals the idea that, when making social decisions or policy, considerations about what is in line with or goes against the interest of children should be given special attention and weight. Over and above that, however, it is not very informative. It does not explain *why* children's interests should be accorded this standing, for example. Is it because there is something morally special in itself about children or their interests, or is it due to some instrumental reason? Neither does it explain what the term 'interest' is supposed to include. It is, furthermore, unclear what the expression 'primary consideration' is supposed to imply. For instance, the fact that the interests of a child may conflict with both the interests of other people (some of them children) and with other valid moral considerations cannot plausibly be ignored (Archard 2011; Blustein 1982; Brock and Buchanan 1989; Dawson 2005; Downie and Randall 1997; Kopelman 1997; Miller 2003). The notion of *best* interest can hardly mean that the satisfaction of children's interests must always be maximized (Archard 2010; Brock and Buchanan 1989; Goldstein *et al.* 1996; Kopelman 1997; Lindemann and Lindemann 2008). A maximization requirement would imply, for example, that no matter the cost, society has reason to find the *best possible* guardians of children also in cases where there is no apparent dysfunction to be found in the child's close social environment, or that all societal resources spent on care for the elderly should be transferred to activities aimed at the care of children. Both these latter points seem especially easy to accept in relation to questions about basic institutional arrangements. From this overarching standpoint, there are many interests that need to be looked after, and there has to be some sort of division of responsibility between the state and citizens, implying a limit to how far the state should go to promote various interests. None of this invalidates the general idea of CRC, however. Giving the interests of children special consideration in societal decision-making can, if nothing else, be motivated as a precautionary measure to protect an especially fragile and vulnerable class of people.

This leaves two issues of clarification: what are the interests of children and what underlies the ethical importance of these interests? The answer to the latter question has a bearing on the extent to which (and, if so, why) CRC can be supported on the basis of ethical theory. On this matter, we may note that there are three major ethical traditions that appear to have some difficulty affirming the presence of ethically important interests in the case of children, at least very young ones. First, some theories combine the ideas that (a) especially powerful moral claims are those of autonomous/rational/self-aware beings to have the plans flowing out of their autonomy/rationality/self-awareness respected by others and (b) the conditions that have to be met for being autonomous/rational/self-aware are such that children, or at least very young and some disabled ones, cannot be ascribed interests of the relevant sort.[1] Second, the contractarian tradition has peculiar problems of accommodating the interests of beings that do not (yet) live up to the conditions imposed on those agreeing to a 'social contract' that determines the content of justified moral rules[2].

The explanation for why these traditions have difficulties supporting the notion of children as (especially) morally important is that they both represent a general idea about the nature of morality as a collection of reciprocal constraints between rational or autonomous beings[3]. In effect, just as Kant once observed regarding our obligations to non-human animals, our reasons for paying attention to other beings become purely instrumental: we have reason to care about the interests of (young or particularly disabled) children only to the extent that this furthers (or is required to respect) the interests of some autonomous/rational beings. This justification, however, fails to supply what is needed in the form of moral reasoning, since it implies that consideration of children's interests is not available to sound moral thinking in exactly those cases where it would seem to be most apt; namely when grown-ups act against or ignore these interests to further their own.

The third tradition that runs into problems with regard to the core idea of CRC is that of classic natural law ethics – especially variants explicitly embracing the main tenets of abrahamic religion regarding family and reproduction (Donagan 1977; The Vatican 1968, 1987). One reason for this is that this type of ethics is made up of absolute bans (such as the Ten Commandments), where promotion of the interests of children does not figure. Another reason is that this form of religiously grounded ethics tends to consider children important mainly due to their role in the realization of a divine procreative plan. How children *fare* is considered important mainly from the point of view of instrumental considerations of having the human species multiply in the prescribed way. To be sure, for example, as within many branches of Christian ethics, these ideas may be complemented by virtue ethical ideals of compassion with and sensitivity to the vulnerability of people, that may give children a special position. However, those latter ideas are logically independent of the natural law ethical stance or the notion of our duty to realize a divine procreative plan, and thus need a separate theoretical underpinning. Our comment here only regards the core natural law elements.

In this chapter, we will proceed on the assumption that these ethical traditions, rather than providing reasons to doubt the idea of CRC, should be seen as seriously challenged by their implications with regard to the moral status of children and the ethical importance of considering their interests.

So, assuming that children do have morally weighty interests, what are these? And how can they be related to the issue of RCUs? Regarding the former question, earlier discussions have distinguished between an *objective* and a *subjective* interpretation (Archard 2011; Dawson 2005). The latter notion signifies a strategy to overcome problems faced by ethical theories that want to keep the basic rationale of ethical claims connected to autonomy/rationality, but still acknowledge that people with no or diminished autonomy/rationality have morally valid interests. The trick employed to accomplish this is a hypothetical 'ideal observer' formula according to which, for example, a child's interests are identical to what this child would have wanted or preferred had he or she been a fully competent adult (Rawls 1999). The basic problem of this idea is that it does not (even in theory) seem to imply definite answers to the question of what children's interests are. Different adults believe and prefer different things and what a child would prefer as an adult is in part determined by childhood experiences (Archard 2011)[4]. The trick thus failing, there remains the idea of having the wants of non-autonomous/non-rational people still deserve some moral consideration in their own right. However, besides the idea that children have some interest in not being subjected to needless coercion, this suggestion seems to ignore the challenges facing an autonomy/rationality based account of the morally valid interests of children (Dawson 2005).

The 'objective' take on the interests of children, in contrast, is basically to identify these interests with the furthering of the child's *quality of life* (Archard 2011; Kopelman 1997). Since there are many competing notions on what determines quality of life, there has been some debate on what this idea implies for children (Archard 2011; Brock and Buchanan 1989; Degrazia 1995; Miller 2003[5]). We will here set out and use a suggestion that combines a number of ideas in this debate, with the overt ambition of including rather than excluding ideas about what may be in a child's interest:

1. *Experiential interests*: the interest of having enjoyable experiences and avoiding unpleasant ones.

2. *Developmental interest*: the interest of having one's development into a well-functioning adult promoted as far as possible.

3. *Basic interests*: the interest of being provided with such material, mental and social resources that are a prerequisite for experiential and developmental interests to be satisfied.

This list implies that there are different aspects of children's interests that may, in particular cases, pull in opposite directions. Such conflicts are familiar to any parent or caretaker of children. A complete ethical theory on the interests of children would thus need to say something about how to handle such conflicts. In the present case, however, we will take another route and investigate if any of the listed types of interests can be shown to tell against any particular suggestion regarding the issue of RCUs.

We also propose that, based on this list, the CRC-idea that children's interests should be given special attention and consideration is warranted. One reason for this claim is the weak ability of children to promote and protect their own interests – their *incapacity*. Another reason is that, often and potentially, children have more to lose than adults in terms of future detriment if their interests are not met properly – they are more *vulnerable*. A third one is that children are in many respects simply easier to harm – they are *fragile*[6]. Some may want to interpret these reasons as instrumental, others as pointing to more basic moral considerations. In any case, in case of conflicts, children's interests need to be balanced against the interests of other parties. In the following, however, we will limit our analysis to looking at some suggested types of RCUs from the point of view of the interest of the child.

Are some types of RCUs better for children?

Before we move on to this – the main – question, some initial observations need to be made in connection to the debate on the best interest of children in relation to family policy. It is a recurring pattern of this debate to take the case of a heterosexual couple whose members are involved in a romantic/sexual relationship with each other, and bring up children to whom they are genetically linked, as being the default initial RCU. Questions regarding justifiable state interventions in the name of the best interest of children are then addressed on the basis of that (Archard 2011; Dawson 2005; Kopelman 1997; Goldstein *et al.* 1996). This, we want to underline, is *not* the discussion we are undertaking in the present chapter. We acknowledge the need for policies regarding societal intervention in RCUs from the point of view of children's interests. However, as mentioned at the outset, such policies need to operate within a framework set by a policy as to *what is to be allowed to be an RCU in the first place*. It is this latter issue that we are focusing on.

This focus implies that the considerations that may be mustered in support of the claim that *changing or breaking up* a child's initial RCU always brings important downsides in terms of this child's interest (although these may be balanced by benefits in particular cases, see further below) – important as they are – have *no* bearing on the question that we are considering. Similarly, the fact that these downsides seem to imply a bias in favour of not breaking up or disturbing 'nuclear family' RCUs has no relevance for the question if also other social configurations should be allowed as RCUs. Rather, this apparent bias merely reflects the contingent fact that not many other configurations are presently allowed as RCUs. Had other configurations been dominant as *de facto* RCUs (for example, single fathers of adopted children), the evidence about the problems for children's interests of breaking up or disturbing RCUs would have implied a bias for *that* sort of RCU.

Something similar can be said about the sort of communitarian interpretation of children's developmental interests found in, for example, debates about confessional religious education, or parents' rights (or lack of rights) to apply culturally specific disciplining methods that deviate from those tolerated in general society, and so on. The claims made in these contexts are that children may have important interests of being socialized into a specific socio-cultural environment. It may be challenged if this is really the case in different concrete instances, but making that claim is not our business here. We merely want to highlight that even a *supposed* interest of children to be integrated in a specific socio-cultural environment is no argument in favour of having them so integrated with regard to *one particular socio-cultural environment rather than another*. If socio-cultural integration and belonging bring an important good to children, they do so no matter which RCUs we allow, as long as these are capable of providing *some* such environment for the child[7].

What *would* be relevant, however, is if there were reasons to think that some particular types of social configurations have clear downsides in terms of the concerned children's interests compared to others, were they to be allowed as RCUs. So, are there any correlations between the composition of social configurations into which children may enter and develop, on the one hand, and on the other, how well the child can be expected to fare in terms of having its interests met? In particular, is the sexual orientation, gender or relationship of and between the adults of the RCU, the number or relative age of these adults and the degree of genetic connection between adults and children linked to how well a child's interest may be met?

According to the predominant view in developmental and child psychology, one of the RCU's most important functions is to provide the child with a secure *attachment*. Attachment is a special relation that the child develops through interacting with certain people in its proximity. Regardless of the extent to which the attachment that the child develops is secure, a prolonged separation from the persons to whom the child is attached will have severe consequences for the child's social and emotional wellbeing (Cassidy 2008). The nature of the attachment depends on several things, some of them outside the direct control of the RCU, such as socio-economic circumstances, but the most important factor seems to be how attentive and responsive the attachment figures are to the child's emotional signals[8].

The child becomes attached to its primary caregiver when it is about six months old and it is the pattern of that attachment which is most predicative of its future development. The child may also become attached to other people (which is not uncommon), although there seem to be no findings of a child having more than four attachment figures. The attachment figures are ordered hierarchically and the loss of the primary attachment figure may not be fully compensated by the others (Cassidy 2008).

A secure early attachment is connected to several beneficial traits for the child at a later age. A securely attached child is more likely to have more and better relationships with its peers. The relationships will not only be more stable but also have fewer conflicts. The child is also likely to be substantially more confident in and knowledgeable about coping with and identifying its own emotions and those of others. A secure attachment is also connected to better cognitive functioning (Thompson 2008; Berlin *et al.* 2008) as well as protection from risk factors associated with clinical mental illness (DeKlyen and Greenberg 2008). The connection between the child's early attachment and its adult relationships is more complex, although it is believed that it matters. It is clear that later relationships are important and affect a person's basic attachment pattern throughout life, and that influences from outside the RCU, for example from friends and teachers, may change a child's basic attachment pattern. However, an insecurely attached child is particularly vulnerable to ending up in a vicious circle, where its insecure pattern generates responses which further consolidate this tendency.

The child's primary attachment figure has most commonly been found to be its mother (Cassidy 2008). However, this can probably be explained by the facts that mothers in many societies tend to spend more time with their children than the fathers (Golombok 2000) and that the amount of time spent and social cues are two of the factors which determine who the child's primary attachment figure will be (Cassidy 2008). There is nothing in the ways in which fathers can and do interact with their children that could explain that they more seldom become the primary attachment figure (Golombok 2000).

Since attachment relationships are organized hierarchically and the attachment to the primary caregiver is the most predicative, it seems to follow that there is little risk involved in letting RCUs consist of a single adult raising children. Now, research does indicate that children in 'nuclear families' fare better than children of single mothers and also that the presence of an involved father does have positive effects on a child's cognitive and emotional development. However, there seems to be no reason to believe that this is due to the presence of a father *per se* – it is more likely that it is the presence of an adult person in addition to the first, who is engaged in the child's life, that explains the difference (Golombok 2000; Graham in this volume). Although the amount of research that has been done is not so abundant, what has been done further supports the idea of the father's role as just an extra adult. For instance, there is no difference in developmental problems of children raised by lesbian couples as compared to children of nuclear families. In fact, the evidence suggests that lesbian parents are better than heterosexual couples in terms of emotional regulation and cognitive capacities (Golombok 2000; Gartrell and Bos 2010; Graham's, and Scheib's and Hastings' respective chapters in this volume). This difference could be explained by several factors such as the economic situation of lesbian parents, their parenting style and other things mentioned. Lesbian families also plan for the child in much the same manner as adoptive parents do and this might make the parents more motivated to adapt their lives to the needs of the children, a factor that has been identified as important for how children fare in the adoption case (Golombok 2000; Hamilton, Cheng and Powell 2007)[9]. A further difference between single adult RCUs and the nuclear family is that single adult RCUs only have one source of income. Financial strain may affect the caregiver's capacity to be emotionally responsive towards the child due to stress and time spent apart. Thus when the nuclear family is compared to single mothers with a good income and a supportive social network, there are no indications that the child would suffer from being raised in a single adult RCU (Golombok 2000; Graham in this volume).

Another question relevant for our topic regards the importance of a (perceived[10]) genetic link between children and their parents for facilitating the bonding between them. Many studies suggest that adopted children are more susceptible to harm than children raised by biological parents, but most of these children have been adopted after they have formed attachments to their biological parents, i.e. after six months (Golombok 2000). Nevertheless, the studies mentioned above regarding parental investment and commitment seem to indicate that these, rather than genetics, are primary explanatory factors. If, in addition to being committed, the RCU is open about the child's origin, then it seems likely that there would be no difference between the development of adopted and non-adopted children[11] (Golombok 2000; Hamilton *et al.* Gurnham, and Scheib and Hastings in this volume).

Child development is complex and attachment is not the only factor that affects it. For example, the child's genetic make-up, the relationship between the adult members in the RCU and the wider social context of the child are also important factors. Poverty is an obvious example of this and may, as previously said, be stressful for the adult members of the RCU and affect their ability to parent well. Poverty may also place the child in a social context, for example high crime rates and bad schools, which might prevent it from developing its potential.

In any case, it seems clear that available evidence suggests that – with two exceptions[12] – there is no particular *type* of RCU – in terms of the gender, sexual orientation or identity of, the nature of the relationship between, the age-mix or the number of adults, or (perceived) genetic links between adults and children – that stands out as potentially better or worse at meeting the interests of children compared to the present default of heterosexual couples with children to which they are (or believe themselves to be) genetically linked. In single cases, of course, any particular RCU may turn out to be, or be strongly suspected to become, dysfunctional in a way detrimental to the interests of their children and, with regard to such cases, society should be prepared to intervene in some way as well as create tools and structures for prevention[13]. However, none of that supports any resistance against expanding the class of allowed RCUs to include many social configurations beside the nuclear family default.

If this safeguard seems insufficient, one may be attracted to the idea that RCUs – regardless of kind in the terms addressed above – should not be permitted *by default* to have and raise children. LaFollette (1980, 2010) has proposed the idea of parenting licences, where any RCU needs to demonstrate that it meets certain requirements regarding its ability to provide the child with emotional stability and responsiveness, as well as meeting its physical needs. Besides the case of very elderly or sick people already mentioned, such demands would also discriminate against RCUs where domestic abuse is present, as well as RCUs where the adult(s) have a sexual interest in children. Again, though, while this suggestion weakens the legal default position of RCUs (they are not *a priori* assumed to be fitting contexts for children to enter and develop within), it does not imply that any particular *type* of RCU in the terms discussed earlier should be denied this status.

This leaves two arguments in terms of the best interests of children that may be brought to bear on the issue of RCUs. The first argument attempts to turn the uncertain evidence regarding the significance of (the perception of) a genetic linkage between (some of) the adults of an RCU and the children of that RCU into an argument in favour of RCUs where such linkage exists[14]. Such an argument *may* be read into the reasoning of, for example, Archard (1993) that the uncertainty regarding the importance of (perceived) genetic links should make society more hesitant to move children out of RCUs where such links are present[15]. Expanding on such a line of thought, the idea in the RCU discussion would be that, in the spirit of a 'better to be safe than to be sorry' approach to decision-making, we should hesitate to allow RCUs lacking a genetic linkage between adults and children[16]. This argument has several flaws, however. First, it assumes that we have evidence supporting the claim that, due to genetic links between adults and children, RCUs with such links are capable of meeting children's interests better than those without. However, the evidence collected so far seems equally compatible with the hypothesis that children of such RCU's enjoy such chances *in spite of* the genetic link. That is, lacking evidence about a *causal* link, mere statistical correlation between some factor and how outcomes score on some scale of desirability works both ways when it comes to providing hypotheses regarding the actual impact of this factor. Second, as a consequence, it does not imply much of sensible caution to assume the effect of the factor in question to be more positive (or less negative) than other factors. Such a commitment to *status quo* rather seems to reflect a sort of 'simplistic conservatism' that for no good reason blocks access to alternative options that might very well *better* secure the desirability of the outcome. In plain language, present evidence suggests that genetic links between adults and children of an RCU may just as well harm as they may benefit the children. A morally responsible precautionary thinking would then rather imply a need to look out for other ways of classifying RCUs, where evidence about typical factors actually promoting the interests of children is provided (which is what we have done above)[17].

However, a more pragmatically sensitive argument can be made in terms of caution. Suppose that, in a given societal context, social configuration type A is an established and much accepted RCU. Then requests arise also to allow type B as RCU, although being in several ways markedly different from A with regard to those features that people use to identify A. We can then expect that configurations of type B that become RCUs will initially be viewed with scepticism, prejudice and open dislike. This social response to type B RCUs can be assumed to create some risks in terms of the interests of children of type B RCUs.

We concede this point, but want to highlight two things about it. First, the argument is in itself unbiased as to what type of social configurations that should be allowed as RCUs. Although many readers of the preceding paragraph may have spontaneously identified type A with a 'nuclear family' and type B with some radically different type of RCU, this is not assumed by the argument. That is, if the initial position of a society would be that the dominant RCU type is a single male parent with adopted children, the argument would imply that there are risks in terms of children's interests to introducing nuclear or single female parent families as RCUs. Second, the argument is unable to ground any wholesale opposition to the idea of allowing RCUs different from the nuclear family default, even if present realities are assumed. What it supports is the idea of a reformative rather than a revolutionary view on how changes with regard to which RCUs are allowed are to be implemented. Although this may frustrate some adult persons eager to become parents in configurations presently not recognized as RCUs, there are reasons to make such changes in a moderate pace that allows people in general to adjust their attitudes and responses[18]. At the same time, however, we find *strong* moral reasons to be wary of the danger of allowing such 'moderate conservatism' to take a rigid, simplistic form. Giving in to prejudice and unfounded hostility is not much different from succumbing to blackmail – a strategy well confirmed as both irrational and morally objectionable (regardless of what basic ethical outlook that is applied) and would, in the present case, mean allowing policy to be directed by confirmed *bad* reasons (a similar point is argued by Macintosh in this volume).

Concluding discussion

Based on the facts and research findings so far available, we have failed to find weighty reason in terms of the best interest of children to refrain from widening what is allowed as RCUs from the present 'nuclear family' paradigm to include variations as regards either the sexual orientation/identity/relationship or number of adults, or the genetic connection between adults and children. Consideration of children's interests may, as before, provide reason for societal intervention in particular RCUs or even support a licensing system of the sort proposed by LaFollette, but neither of those undermine our main thesis. While we concede the need for some pragmatic caution when changing existing RCU paradigms, we have also noted that the very same pragmatism supports the idea that refraining entirely from such changes for fear of social dislike would mean supporting and affirming views that deny children to have what is in their best interest.

It is notable that some well-established ethical traditions face difficulties in justifying what we have proposed as an obviously plausible understanding of the best interest of children statement of the CRC. In spite of this, proponents of these traditions often figure strongly in societal debates on family and reproductive policy.

Notes

1   Famous arguments to these effects can be found in rights-based ethical argumentation (Tooley 1984), certain qualified versions of consequentialist thinking (Singer and Kuhse 1985), as well as attempts of mixing the two (Warren 2000). Similar arguments have been used to deny that non-human animals have any morally valid claims on us to be treated in any particular way (Frey 1980). The most well-known example of this sort of general theory is the one set out in the peculiar ethics of rights of Nozick (1974).

2   There are differences between different variants of contractarian ethics with regard to this. David Gauthier (1986) sees this conclusion as a major result of his theory. Rawls (1971), in contrast, struggled with the question of whether or not the formula of what self-interested, rational parties would agree to had they been unaware of whether or not they are really rational beings is a coherent (denied in Brandt 1972) or morally valid notion. Rawls eventually solved the problem by an ad hoc assumption that the parties to the contract all feel obliged to consider the interests of posterity. In the real world, of course, this is many times not the case.

3   This notion (represented by such diverse thinkers as Aristotle, Hobbes, Locke and Kant) usually employs a rather rigid, binary (in addition to demanding) idea of what it means to be autonomous/rational. It is unclear to what extent it could be accommodated to a more enlightened and gradual view of how these features appear and develop in human beings as they grow up. In any case, we concede David Archard's point (1993) that any serious account of the moral status of children needs to be consistent with such an accommodation.

4   These problems of the hypothetical ideal observer solution are very similar to those afflicting similar solutions to similar problems in other areas, for example the idea of hypothetical consent and the so-called substituted judgment standard as a guiding principle for clinical decision making in the case of incapacitated adult patients. See, for example, Broström *et al.* 2007 and Wrigley 2011.

5   The case of Richard Miller is a bit ambiguous. Miller's literal suggestion is to use a 'thin theory of the good' for identifying children's interests. That is, children's interests are to be identified with what Rawls (1971) called *primary goods*. However, Rawls offer two distinct and different explanations of what a primary good is. One explanation is in terms of what 'every rational man is presumed to want' (Rawls 1971: 62, 93) and that idea would rather seem to place Miller in the 'subjective' hypothetical ideal observer theory camp. Another idea of Rawls, however, is to conceive of primary goods as resources *that will often be of use whatever one's more exact plans, wants and needs* (Rawls 1971: 92–93), which is how we assume Miller's idea to be meant in the present context.

6   As Archard (1993) notes, as children overcome these impediments to self-sufficiency, we attain stronger and stronger reasons to treat them as adults – i.e. our reasons for applying the rule of extra attention and consideration disappears. Also, piece by piece, new interests may enter the picture, for instance, the interest of having one's wants respected.

7   This point echoes the argument (Kymlicka 1989) with regard to the importance of cultures: the fact that people need a cultural context to fare well does not in itself speak in favour of any particular cultural context, as long as it is capable of delivering that which makes our cultures contribute to the value of our lives.

8   Thus, the difference between secure and insecure attachment patterns is about the quality of these responses, for example regarding recognition, support and consistency.

9   The longing for parenthood and the complicated process necessary to attain that end tend to make parents to invest more commitment in their children. This is common to all 'alternative' RCUs, such as lesbian mothers, DI and IVF mothers and adoptive parents (Golombok 2000; Hamilton *et al.* 2007; Graham, and Scheib and Hastings in this volume).

10   This is to indicate a general source of uncertainty regarding all opinions, arguments and studies on the possible connection between actual genetic links between parents and children and children's wellbeing. Lest we were to systematically use genetic testing technology to actually reveal it, we presently do not know the extent of such linkage within actual 'nuclear' families. Nevertheless, most people *believe* such linkage to be in place.

11   This apparent fact seems to be of particular importance for how to assess new possibilities of having children without any genetic connection to the adults of the RCU made possible by reproductive technological developments, such as gamete or embryo donation and surrogacy, that may be used by homosexual people, single adults or groups of adults who are not sexually involved albeit wanting to form a family (see, further, Macintosh's chapter in the present volume).

12   The exceptions are, first, the single adult RCU, which is more vulnerable to disturbances that may affect the child negatively – although much of this vulnerability can be compensated for through economic support and well-developed social support structures (such as publicly funded daycare). However, it may be observed that the same factors making single parenthood more risky for the child seems to suggest that 'nuclear' families are worse for children than RCUs made up of more than two adults (cf. Cutas 2011). The few studies there are, as we saw, suggest that two person homosexual RCUs function just as well as their heterosexual counterparts from the point of view of the child's interests. Second, if all of the adults of the RCU are very old (or for some other reason likely to die before the child has developed enough of self-sufficiency and security to fare well as an adult) this would seem to be a clear downside. Since such potential RCUs could have children only through adoption or the use of reproductive technology, this may be a reason for society to deny them access to such means.

13   As we have noted, this may imply that some heterosexual couples that today are allowed as RCUs by default, would not be so allowed in a system focusing on the interests of children, for example in the case of documented paedophiles.

14   There is no space in this short chapter to account for the complex mass of suggested evidence for rivalling opinions on this topic, where arguments range from speculations in evolutionary biology, over data of the sort considered earlier in this chapter, to official statistics on abuse of children within families. Some of it is considered when Archard (1993) ponders the issue of the importance of genetic linkage, when Hamilton, Cheng and Powell (2007) speculate about evolutionary mechanisms that may explain parental investment in children – and for Golombok (2000) it is one of many contenders in the debate on what explains a family situation that is beneficial for the children. However, we do think that some of the evidence considered earlier (such as the apparent importance of parenting style and socio-economic context) puts the onus rather heavily on anyone pursuing the idea that genetic linkage as such is a vital factor for successful parenting.

15 It should be mentioned, though, that *literally* this claim implies nothing with regard to the question of what social configurations should be allowed as RCUs.

16 This argument, it must be emphasised, is *not* made by Archard.

17 Cf. the theory about morally responsible decision-making on the basis of uncertain evidence presented and defended in Munthe 2011.

18 An example might be that allowing homosexual couples as RCUs should be precluded by a development towards increased social acceptance of homosexual love, at least enough to shield children from serious bullying. As a matter of fact, this was an important part of the reasoning underlying the acceptance in Sweden of homosexual couples as eligible as adoptive parents, in 2003 (one of the authors of this chapter took part in this process as member of the National Council for Medical Ethics).

References

Archard, D. (1993), *Children, Rights and Childhood*, London: Taylor & Francis.

Archard, D. (2011), 'Children's Rights', *The Stanford Encyclopedia of Philosophy* (Summer 2011 Edition), Edward N. Zalta (ed.), http://plato.stanford.edu/archives/sum2011/entries/rights-children/ [accessed March 2011].

Berlin, L., Cassidy, J. and Appleyard, K. (2008), 'The Influence of Early Attachments on Other Relationships', in J. Cassidy and P.R. Shaver (eds), *Handbook of attachment: Theory, research, and clinical applications (second edition)*, New York: Guilford Press.

Blustein, J. (1982), *Parents and Children: The Ethics of the Family*, Oxford: Oxford University Press.

Brandt, R. (1972), 'The Morality of Abortion', *The Monist*, 56 (4): 503–526.

Brock, D. and Buchanan, A. (1989), *Deciding for others*, Cambridge: Cambridge University Press.

Broström L., Johansson M., Nielsen M.K. (2007), 'What the patient would have decided: A fundamental problem with the substituted judgment standard', *Medicine Health Care and Philosophy*,10(3): 265–78.

Cassidy, J. (2008), 'The Nature of the Child's Ties', in J. Cassidy and P.R. Shaver (eds), *Handbook of attachment: Theory, research, and clinical applications (second edition)*, New York: Guilford Press.

Cassidy, J. and Shaver, P.R. (eds) (2008), *Handbook of attachment: Theory, research, and clinical applications (second edition)*, New York: Guilford Press.

Cutas, D. (2011), 'On Triparenting: Is Having Three Committed Parents Better Than Having Only Two?', *Journal of Medical Ethics*, online first, doi: 10.1136/jme.2011.043745.

Dawson, A. (2005), 'The Determination of "Best Interests" in Relation to Childhood Vaccinations', *Bioethics*, 19 (2): 188–205.

Degrazia, D. (1995), 'Value Theory and The Best Interest', *Bioethics*, 9(1): 50–61.

DeKlyen, M. and Greenberg, M. (2008), 'Attachment and Psychopathology in Childhood', in J. Cassidy and P.R. Shaver (eds), *Handbook of attachment: Theory, research, and clinical applications (second edition)*, New York: Guilford Press.

Donagan, A. (1977), *The Theory of Morality*, Chicago: University of Chicago Press.

Downie, R. and Randall, F. (1997), 'Parenting and the Best Interest of Minors', *Journal of Medicine and Philosophy*, 22(3): 219–231.

Frey, R.G. (1980), *Interests and Rights: The Case Against Animals*, Oxford: Clarendon Press.

Gartrell, N. and Bos, H. (2010), 'US national longitudinal lesbian family study: Psychological adjustment of 17-year-old adolescents', *Pediatrics: Official Journal of the American Academy of Pediatrics*, 126: 28–36.

Gauthier, D. (1986), *Morals by Agreement*, Oxford: Oxford University Press.

Goldstein, J., Solnit, A., Goldstein, S. and Freud, A. (1996), *The Best Interest of the Child: The Least Detrimental Alternative*, New York: Free Press.

Golombok, S. (2000), *Parenting: What Really Counts*, London: Routledge.

Hamilton L., Cheng S. and Powell, B. (2007), 'Adoptive Parents, Adaptive Parents: Evaluating the Importance of Biological Ties for Parental Investment', *American Sociological Review*, 72: 95–116.

Kopelman, L. (1997), 'The Best-Interests Standard as Threshold, Ideal and Standard of Reasonableness', *Journal of Medicine and Philosophy*, 22: 271–289.

LaFollette, H. (1980), 'Licensing Parents', *Philosophy and Public Affairs*, 9 (2): 182–197.

LaFollette, H. (2010), 'Licensing Parents Revisited', *Journal of Applied Philosophy*, 27 (4): 327–343.

Lindemann, J. and Lindemann, H. (2008), 'The Romance of the Family', *Hastings Center Report*, 38(4): 19–21.

Miller, R. (2003), *Children, Ethics & Modern Medicine*, Bloomington: Indiana University Press.

Munthe, C. (2011), *The Price of Precaution and the Ethics of Risk*, Dordrecht, Heidelberg, London & New York: Springer.

Nozick, R. (1974), *Anarchy, State and Utopia*, Oxford: Basil Blackwell.

Rawls, J. (1971), *A Theory of Justice*, Oxford: Oxford University Press.

Singer, P. and Kuhse, H. (1985), *Should the Baby Live? The Problem of Handicapped Infants*, New York & Oxford: Oxford University Press.

Thompson, R. (2008), 'Early Attachment and Later Development: Familiar Questions, New Answers', in J. Cassidy, and P.R. Shaver (eds), *Handbook of attachment: Theory, research, and clinical applications (second edition)*, New York: Guilford Press.

Tooley, M. (1984), *Abortion and Infanticide*, New York & Oxford: Oxford University Press.

United Nations (1989), *Convention on the Rights of the Child*, Geneva: United Nations. http://www2.ohchr.org/english/law/crc.htm [accessed October 2011].

The Vatican (1968), *Humanae Vitae*. Available at http://www.vatican.va/holy_father/paul_vi/encyclicals/documents/hf_p-vi_enc_25071968_humanae-vitae_en.html [accessed October 2011].

The Vatican (1987), *Instruction of Respect for Human Life in its Origin and On the Dignity of Procreation*. Available at http://www.vatican.va/roman_curia/congregations/cfaith/documents/rc_con_cfaith_doc_19870222_respect-for-human-life_en.html [accessed October 2011].

Warren, M.A. (2000), *Moral Status: Obligations to Persons and Other Living Things*. Oxford: Oxford University Press.

Wrigley, A. (2011), 'The Problem of Counterfactuals in Substituted Judgement Decision-Making', *The Journal of Applied Philosophy*, 28 (2): 169–187.

5

Donor-conceived Children Raised by Lesbian Couples

Socialization and development in a new form of planned family

Joanna E. Scheib and Paul D. Hastings

As a family structure, a two-mother, lesbian-parented family is not a new or recent construction. However, the way in which lesbian families typically form has been evolving. In the past, many lesbian mothers had their children through heterosexual relationships prior to recognizing their lesbian identity. The ability of publically 'out' single and partnered lesbians to conceive children was limited to a small number of progressive donor insemination (DI) programs that used anonymous donors or known donors, such as male friends or relatives. In recent years, lesbians have gained greater access to assisted reproduction technologies and more opportunities to build their families without the direct involvement of male partners. It is likely that multiple factors led to this change.

Perhaps foremost is the fact that attitudes towards sexual minorities have changed, leading to greater public acceptance of lesbian families (Bos and Gartrell 2010; Goldberg 2010). Social policies have changed accordingly. For example, in the UK, the phrase 'need of [the] child for a father' was dropped from section 13(5) of the Human Fertilisation and Embryology Act in 2008. Similar changes were recommended earlier by the American Society for Reproductive Medicine's Ethics Committee in 2006. Such changes officially opened access to assisted reproductive technologies to single women and lesbian couples. In addition, many infertile heterosexual couples now choose improved reproductive techniques over DI that preserve genetic links between father and child. In North America, this left a consumer void in DI programs, such that some clinics began to actively solicit lesbian couples and single women as clients. Not surprisingly, these populations now constitute the majority of DI clients in the US (Amato and Jacob 2004; Ehrensaft 2008). The net result is that there are now more lesbian-headed families raising children conceived through DI than ever before.

An outcome of this change in user-demographics is that more children are learning about their donor origins. Among lesbian couples, there is no male infertility to hide, nor a need to keep the family's origins a secret. In addition, the children likely question how their family came to be, and why, unlike many of their classmates, they have no father. Thus, the majority of lesbian parents will be open with their children about the family's donor origins from early on. Further, because many lesbians may have experienced secrecy and its repercussions as related to their sexuality, they may be even less willing to keep secrets again (Ehrensaft 2008). Consequently, lesbians may be the most open among DI parents about using a donor to build their families (Brewaeys *et al.* 1993; Gartrell *et al.* in press).

Some parties have raised concerns that we are now engaged in an unguided social experiment that increases the rights of sexual minorities to become parents, to the detriment of the children's wellbeing (Somerville 2003, 2010). It is not the case, however, that we are lacking in knowledge regarding children's development in diverse family structures (Patterson and Hastings 2007). More specifically, research into lesbian parents' socialization practices, family processes and the development of children conceived through DI actually predates the recent changes in attitudes, social policy, and DI clinic practices. Patterson, Gartrell, Golombok and their colleagues initiated ground-breaking programs of study with lesbians who were successful in accessing DI programs in the 1980s in order to examine the development of children in DI-conceived lesbian families. Thus, there is a considerable body of well-designed, cross-sectional and prospective longitudinal research that speaks directly to these concerns. What is less clear is whether developmental outcomes of children differ depending on whether they are raised in relative openness about their family's donor origins. What we know about DI family functioning primarily comes from heterosexual-couple families who used anonymous donors and maintained secrecy about their donor origins both within and outside their families. We now also need to look at how children fare when raised in relative openness and, as adults, can sometimes even contact their donor through open-identity DI programs. In this chapter, we will review this research and draw conclusions regarding the development of children in DI lesbian families and the factors that promote their positive growth and wellbeing.

What happens to children who are raised in DI lesbian-couple families?

Differences in child outcomes across family types

Can lesbian couples parent their children in a way that supports a child's positive adjustment, development and wellbeing? Findings from the earliest studies on small samples of DI lesbian-couple families indicated a preliminary yes. Steckel (1987) conducted the first systematic comparison of eleven children (aged three to four years) raised by lesbian couples to eleven same-age children who were conventionally-conceived and raised by heterosexual couples. Using structured interviews with the mothers and children, and both parental and teacher reports, she found healthy, normal separation-individuation in both groups of children. In addition, the girls of lesbian couples showed no more androgynous or masculine behaviour than expected, whereas the boys of lesbian couples appeared slightly less aggressive than those raised by heterosexual couples. The latter finding has been replicated in a larger sample of children who were on average ten years old (range seven to seventeen; Vanfraussen *et al.* 2002). Overall, keeping in mind the small sample sizes, these initial findings indicated that having a co-mother rather than a father did not appear to negatively affect a child.

In the early 1990s, Patterson (1994, 1996) conducted the Bay Area Family Study – the first to examine psychosocial development in elementary-school age children (four to nine years) being raised by lesbian parents. All but three of the thirty-seven children were donor-conceived. Whereas the results did not distinguish between coupled (70 per cent) and single parents, the study's strengths included using standardized measures with norms to which the children's scores could be compared, score cut-offs to identify clinically problematic behaviour, and reports from sources outside the family, such as teachers. Findings suggested that children raised by lesbian parents were developing normally. The children's adjustment levels – as measured through social competence, closeness with peers, numbers of behavioural problems, and most areas of self-concept – fell within normal, non-clinical ranges, as did their gender-role preferences. However, children reported experiencing more reactions to stress (for example, feeling angry, upset), but also a greater sense of wellbeing (for example, feeling comfortable with themselves, joyful) as compared to normed reports from similar-age children of heterosexual parents. Patterson interpreted this as either the children experiencing a higher number of stressful events, but having the skills to cope with them, or being more open to expressing their feelings, both negative and positive. This last finding has yet to be replicated.

A series of studies followed that used the same methodology – interviews, standardized and normed measures (most commonly the Child Behavior Check List, CBCL; Achenbach and Edelbrock 1983, 2000), and outsider reports. Additionally, they included comparative groups of heterosexual-couple and single-mother families who were demographically matched on parental age, education, socioeconomic status, relationship length, and child age. Optimally, DI heterosexual-couple families were also included, but this was less common due to recruitment difficulties. (These couples often maintain complete secrecy about using DI and fear that participating in a study will expose their family's origins to their children.) Using a comparative approach allowed investigators to address questions about the effect of parental sexual orientation, absence of a father, and number of parents in the household, and this continues to be the dominant study paradigm to date. (For the little research available on single-mother DI families see Murray and Golombok 2005; Landau *et al.* 2008; Landau and Weissenberg 2010.) A common feature among all these families was that the parents tended to be somewhat older (starting families in their thirties), well-educated, financially secure, and established in their relationships. Risk factors, such as divorce, poverty, lack of education, and instability were relatively rare, giving the children an advantage from the start. In addition, among the DI families clearly these were wanted children; their parents intentionally underwent a personally intrusive and somewhat costly procedure to have them. In turn, the children appear to have benefited.

In the first of this next wave of studies, Flaks *et al.* (1995) compared a sample of fifteen DI lesbian-couple families to fifteen matched heterosexual-couple families (conventional conceivers, CC) with three to nine year old children. Results of standardized measures based on parental and teacher reports again indicated no differences between the children on the CBCL's measures of social competence and behavioural adjustment, and on Wechsler's (1974, 1989) measures of cognitive functioning. With the exception of an average Performance IQ among boys of heterosexual couples, in all areas the children in both groups scored in the well-functioning ranges of the standardized samples for the measures used.

Golombok and her colleagues in the UK (1997) reported similar findings. They compared thirty three to nine year old children from lesbian families (combined couples and singles) to children in forty-one CC heterosexual-couple families and thirty single-mother families and found that overall the children were developing normally. Only a small number of differences emerged among the family types. The children in father-absent homes had greater attachment security than children in heterosexual-couple families. The children themselves reported no differences in being accepted by peers (see also Gartrell *et al.* 2000), but children in the lesbian and single-parent families reported feeling less cognitively and physically competent than children from the families with fathers. However this finding was not maintained in a follow-up of twenty-five of the lesbian families when the children were age twelve (MacCallum and Golombok 2004; see also Vanfraussen *et al.* 2002). In addition, as young adults – the only study so far of adult-outcomes from DI lesbian families (eighteen adults, twenty mothers) – they reported the opposite: young adults with lesbian mothers or single heterosexual mothers reported higher levels of self-esteem and lower levels of depression, anxiety and hostility compared to young adults from CC heterosexual families (Golombok and Badger 2010). Furthermore, contrary to suggestions that children raised by lesbians might identify as lesbian or gay themselves, all but one young adult identified as heterosexual.

Further findings continued to support the idea that the adjustment of children is remarkably similar – or by some measures, better – in DI lesbian-couple families as compared to heterosexual-couple families. In a European study (Belgium and the Netherlands), Brewaeys and colleagues (1997b) assessed the gender role development and emotional and behavioural problems in four to eight year olds from families headed by thirty lesbian couples and sixty-eight heterosexual couples, including thirty-eight DI and thirty CC families. Study participants were recruited from university hospital fertility and obstetrics departments. All lesbian couples agreed to participate, making the findings representative of lesbian-couple families who had used DI during that time period. Additionally, including all three family types allowed Brewaeys and colleagues to test whether DI families in general differed from CC families (i.e. the two DI groups versus the CC group) and provided a better test of the effects of parental sexual orientation in comparing the two DI families who were matched on using assisted conception, having a donor, and having a child who was not genetically related to one of her/his parents[1]. As before, parental and teacher reports on the CBCL indicated that children from lesbian-couple families did not differ from the two heterosexual-couple groups in their adjustment, and their scores looked similar to Dutch norms. No differences were found in gender role development (see also Bos and Sandfort 2010). Later, more extensive assessment of the children's wellbeing at age ten indicated much the same pattern of development, with the exception that teachers reported more attention problems in the lesbian couples' children than in the children of CC heterosexual couples (a DI heterosexual couple group was not included). However, the level of these problems was still within the normal range and the groups did not differ on either mother- or child-reported attention problems. In addition, children of lesbian couples reported fewer aggression and anxiety problems than children of CC heterosexual couples (Vanfraussen *et al.* 2002).

Brewaeys *et al.*'s (1997b) study of the younger, four to eight year old children, was one of the first to include a comparison sample of DI heterosexual-couple families. When results from the three family types (DI lesbian, DI heterosexual, CC heterosexual) were compared, children from DI heterosexual families experienced a higher incidence of behavioural and emotional problems than those from CC families, suggesting something problematic about the heterosexual – but not lesbian – couples using DI. One difference between the two DI family types (beyond sexual orientation) was their openness about using DI: all but one lesbian couple had told their children about their donor origins, whereas only one heterosexual couple had and few intended to. This was one of the first indications from a comparative study (in addition to case reports) that openness and secrecy could be associated with different outcomes for children. Clamar (1989) had earlier suggested that the challenge of keeping secrets negatively affected families. Whereas both DI lesbian co-mothers and fathers might have trouble accepting their non-genetically related children as their own, the additional challenge of hiding the father's potentially stigmatizing infertility might hinder family processes, such as communication quality, and negatively affect the child. Together, the facts that Brewaeys and colleagues found comparable or better outcomes for lesbian-couple families, that other research suggests better outcomes for disclosing over non-disclosing heterosexual-couple families (Golombok *et al.* 2002; Lycett *et al.* 2004; see section below on openness) and that DI fathers appear to differ little from adoptive and CC fathers in their relationships with their children (Golombok *et al.* 1995; Owen and Golombok 2009; see Golombok *et al.* 2002 for same pattern with one exception) suggests that it is the secrecy that is a problem for DI families (Daniels *et al.* 2011). Secrecy versus openness, and related family processes, may be more important determinants of child wellbeing than parental sexual orientation.

Chan, Raboy and Patterson's (1998a) findings provided strong evidence for the importance of family processes. Using the resources of one sperm bank, they recruited a representative sample of eighty matched families with five to eleven year old children conceived through the DI program. They then compared the children's adjustment, social competence and adaptive functioning across family types varying by sexual orientation (fifty-five lesbian, twenty-five heterosexual) and number of parents (thirty single, fifty couple). Again, family type was not associated with differences in most measures of child outcomes (see similar findings in Gartrell *et al.* 2005, 2011 in press; Bos *et al.* 2007). Based on reports from both parents and teachers, the results indicated that the children were developing normally, although co-mothers reported more internalizing and externalizing problems than fathers. It is noteworthy that this was not evident in the reports by the biological mothers and teachers, and fathers tended to report fewer problems and better adjustment than all other groups, suggesting that the finding reflected reporter differences rather than true child differences. What better predicted child outcomes were family processes, as we discuss below.

Differences in parenting and family processes across family types

Decades of socialization research have shown that how parents raise their children has important and lasting influences on children's development (Grusec and Hastings 2007). Studies have shown that it is as true for DI lesbian-couple families as it is for DI and CC heterosexual-couple families. Although children have not been found to differ in consistent or marked ways across these family types, it is still possible that their socialization experiences differ. In this section we examine the evidence for whether such differences in child-rearing practices exist across family types.

Paralleling the pattern of findings regarding children's characteristics, studies have identified few differences in parenting and family processes across family types. For example, Chan, Raboy and Patterson (1998a) found no differences between DI lesbian-couple families and DI heterosexual-couple families on measures of parental stress, self-esteem, depression and spousal relationship quality. With a smaller subset of these families (thirty lesbian and sixteen heterosexual), Chan and colleagues (1998b) found that lesbian mothers had a more equal division of child-care roles and responsibilities than did heterosexual parents, despite heterosexual mothers wishing that their husbands participated in child care more equally. Brewaeys and colleagues (1997b) also found that lesbian-couple families reported more equal co-parenting, or greater involvement of the non-biological parent in child care, than did heterosexual couples.

In their comparison of fifteen DI lesbian-couple families with fifteen matched DI heterosexual-couple families, Flaks and colleagues (1995) identified only one difference in parental socialization. Lesbian parents were more effective parenting problem solvers, meaning they were able to generate a greater variety of solutions to potential child-care problems, compared to heterosexual parents. This difference was mainly attributable to fathers in the heterosexual families, who scored lower on problem solving than all mothers.

Conversely, in an extensive study of 100 DI lesbian-couple families and 100 matched CC heterosexual-couple families of six year old children (Bos *et al.* 2004, 2007), heterosexual mothers and fathers, and lesbian genetically-linked mothers and co-mothers (not genetically linked) did not differ in their self-reported competence as parents. They also did not differ in feelings of parental burden, or access to social support outside the family. However, there were some parenting differences across the family types. Lesbian mothers (both types) reported stronger desires to have children, greater need to justify their roles as parents, and less concern for traditional child-rearing goals than did heterosexual parents, as well as greater couple and co-parenting satisfaction than heterosexual mothers. Lesbian genetically-linked mothers engaged in less structuring and limit-setting than heterosexual mothers, and compared to heterosexual fathers, all lesbian mothers were more emotionally involved, supportive and respecting of children's autonomy, and less power assertive.

Interestingly, longitudinal research has shown that some apparent differences in child-rearing and family processes change over time, indicating they may be tied to the family and parenting demands of specific developmental stages. In Brewaeys and colleagues' (1997b) study of four to eight years-olds in DI lesbian-couple, DI heterosexual-couple, and CC heterosexual-couple families, lesbian co-mothers reported more positive relationships with their children than did fathers in either of the heterosexual family types, although the children's reports of relationship quality did not differ for lesbian co-mothers and fathers. When families were seen again four years later, though, the researchers did not find any differences in parental socialization or parent-child relationship quality between heterosexual families and lesbian families (Vanfraussen *et al.* 2003b).

Similarly, comparing lesbian families (combined single and coupled parents) to single (combined DI and CC) and coupled CC heterosexual families, Golombok *et al.* (1997) reported only one difference, that single heterosexual mothers were more engaged with their six year-old children than were lesbian mothers. When these families were seen again six years later (MacCallum and Golombok 2004), however, this difference was not maintained. As had been noted when children were younger, there were also no differences across family types in parents' reports of warmth, affection, use of reasoning, parental monitoring and discipline. There were some differences in the parents' perspectives on family disputes. Single heterosexual mothers reported the highest levels of aggression during discipline, and all mothers in father-absent homes reported more serious disputes than mothers in father-present homes. Conversely, compared to children in father-present homes, twelve year old children in father-absent homes reported that their mothers were more available and dependable, and engaged in more activities with them.

It is interesting that these differences emerged when children were entering adolescence, when one would expect increases in the rate of parent-child conflicts due to normative adolescent individuation processes, but also a desire of youths to maintain family connectedness (Collins and Steinberg 2006). This would continue as children approached the end of adolescence. Correspondingly, when these children reached early adulthood (Golombok and Badger 2010), lesbian mothers reported less discipline, but more frequent and severe conflicts, than did single heterosexual mothers. However, their adult children did not perceive this difference, as the two groups reported similarly positive relationships with their mothers. Thus, at the beginning and end of adolescence, it might be the case that lesbian mothers are more attuned to or sensitive about the normative disputes that occur between parents and their maturing children. Reflecting the greater emotional involvement and concern reported by Bos and colleagues, lesbian mothers might perceive as potentially problematic what other parents, and what their own children, experience as the normal turmoil of adolescence.

Overall, then, the evidence suggests that the socialization experiences of children in DI lesbian-couple families are far more similar to those of children in heterosexual families than they are different. The families are similarly warm, engaged and involved, with positive parent-child and spousal relationships. Compared to heterosexual parents, lesbian mothers might be less likely to promote traditional child-rearing goals such as conformity and obedience. Children with lesbian mothers likely see their parents sharing child-care duties more equally than do children with heterosexual parents. They might also experience less assertive discipline and more emotional approaches to child-rearing. Lesbian mothers see their relationships with their adolescents as more tumultuous than heterosexual parents, but their children do not appear to share that perspective.

Relations between parenting, family processes and child outcomes

Only three of the studies of DI lesbian-couple families examined how parenting and family processes are associated with children's characteristics. Bos and colleagues (2007) found that in both DI lesbian and CC heterosexual families, couples who reported lower satisfaction with the partner's role as a co-parent had children with more internalizing and externalizing problems. (It is important to note, again, that the levels of children's problems were low and certainly within age-normed expectations for behaviour; the analyses did not predict clinically-meaningful levels of problems.) Similarly, across DI lesbian and DI heterosexual families, Chan and colleagues (1998a,b) found that when parents reported less satisfaction with the division of household labour, more parenting distress, and more dysfunctional parent-child relationships, children manifested (non-clinically) more behaviour problems. These studies also reported several correlations between parents' wellbeing and child-rearing behaviours and children's adjustment that were consistent with a large body of socialization research, such as children evidencing more internalizing or externalizing problems when parents were more depressed or used more power assertion (Bos *et al.* 2007; Chan *et al.* 1998a). However, these associations were not independent of the effects of spousal and parent-child relationship quality, and there is no clear evidence that parental sexual orientation is consistently linked with relationship quality.

Summary: Planned lesbian-couple family processes and outcomes

In summary, evidence available thus far suggests that the same family processes that support positive child adjustment in heterosexual families also function to the benefit of children in DI lesbian-couple families. Children fare best when their parents are satisfied with their spousal relationship and sharing of household and child-care tasks, when parents do not feel distressed by the challenges of child-rearing, and when parents and children share positive and close relationships. For the most part, lesbian- and heterosexual-couple families are quite similar on these characteristics, such that there should be no surprise that their children are similarly well-adjusted.

What is the outcome of children who are raised in openness about their family's donor origins?

Despite the remarkably similar and positive outcomes for children in DI heterosexual- and lesbian-couple families, the families differ dramatically in how open they are about having donor origins. Until recently, heterosexual couples rarely told their children about using DI to build their families (for example, anywhere from none to 30 per cent as reviewed in Brewaeys 2001; McWhinnie 2001; more recently 10 to 70 per cent as reviewed in Scheib *et al.* 2003; Paul and Berger 2007; Daniels *et al.* 2009). In contrast, virtually all lesbian couples tell their children, and almost all when children are quite young (Brewaeys 2001; Scheib *et al.* 2003; Beeson *et al.* 2011). Indeed, this openness is a major change that lesbian families bring to DI family-building. Yet we are now just starting to understand how openness affects child and later adult wellbeing. In addition, once the donor-conceived person knows about his or her origins, we have only preliminary findings on what offspring want or need to know about the donor and the significance he holds. We discuss this below.

Openness in DI families

Keeping a family's donor origins secret is becoming increasingly difficult with developing technologies in DNA and ancestry identification. The secrecy, risk of inadvertent disclosure, and perceived deception by one's parents is highly likely to damage family relationships and the psychological and medical wellbeing of the donor-conceived person (reviews in McGee *et al.* 2001; McWhinnie 2001; Ethics Committee ASRM 2004; Daniels and Meadows 2006; see also Hamilton 2002; Daniels *et al.* 2011). We expect then that being open within the family about having a donor will lead to better outcomes for the offspring and families more generally. But a major impediment to openness is that most families have an anonymous donor about whom little is known. Parents sometimes argue that living with the frustration of never being able to learn more about or meet the donor is likely to be worse than not knowing at all[2]. So unlike lesbian couples, heterosexual couples can and often do opt not to take this risk with their children.

Despite the risks, a growing number of parents beyond lesbian couples are choosing to be open with their children. Preliminary findings suggest either no association between disclosure and family outcomes or a positive association. In one of the first systematic comparisons, Brewaeys *et al.* (1997a) found no differences based on disclosure plans in the emotional and behavioural adjustment of four to eight year olds, although only eight out of thirty-eight heterosexual couples had told or planned to tell their child. Lycett and colleagues (2004) had a larger group of four to eight years olds in disclosing families (eighteen) and found more positive parent-child relationships among them than among the twenty-eight non-disclosing families. But they also emphasized that outcomes among the non-disclosing families were still good – the families scored within the normal ranges on standardized measures. In a qualitative study, Hunter and colleagues (2000) interviewed a sample of eighty-three heterosexual-couple parents who belonged to a support group for DI families who wanted to be open. Almost half had told their child (average age 3.5 years; range three months to fifteen years); the rest planned to tell (child average age 1.5 years; range eleven weeks to four years). No measures of wellbeing were used, but it is telling that the parents did not regret their decision to tell their child, nor did they regret using DI. They also found it easier if they disclosed when children were younger, and reported that children tended to respond neutrally and/or with curiosity (see also Rumball and Adair 1999; Lindblad *et al.* 2000; Mac Dougall *et al.* 2007). In Brewaeys and colleagues' (1997b) sample of thirty lesbian-couple families, where non-disclosure was unrealistic, the four to eight year olds (and later ten year olds; Vanfraussen *et al.* 2002) scored as well-adjusted, suggesting that knowing about the family's donor origins was not associated with negative outcomes. Among one of only two samples of adolescents so far, Scheib and colleagues found continued wellbeing across all family types – lesbian-couple, single-woman, and heterosexual-couple parented. This sample of twelve to seventeen year olds had open-identity donors who could be identified and potentially contacted when the youths reached age eighteen. Most youths reported having learned early, often so early that they could not recollect a time when they did not know about having a donor. In turn, their responses tended to be neutral or positive, with the vast majority expressing curiosity about the donor. While the researchers did not use standardized measures of wellbeing, reports from both the youths (Scheib *et al.* 2005) and their parents (Scheib *et al.* 2003) indicated that disclosure had either a positive or no effect on the relationships between parents and children, and that the youths remained comfortable and relatively open about their donor origins into adolescence. Many of these same youths had also participated in a study that measured their adjustment at age seven (range five to eleven years; Chan *et al.* 1998a; Fulcher *et al.* 2006). While not focused on the effects of disclosure, almost all the children knew about their origins. Measures of behavioural and emotional adjustment and social competence indicated that overall the children were well-adjusted, thus indirectly suggesting that disclosure was not negatively affecting families at that point in time.

The second sample of adolescents – at age seventeen – comes from a longitudinal study of lesbian families who were followed from before the children were born (Bos and Gartrell 2011). Whereas detailed information was not available about when the youths learned about their family's donor origins, most knew from an early age. Bos and Gartrell assessed psychological adjustment overall, as well as whether youth adjustment varied according to their type of donor – known from birth or currently anonymous. No differences emerged based on whether or not the youths knew their donor, and overall they evidenced positive wellbeing (see similar finding among four to eight year olds in Bos and Hakvoort (2007); re-analysis of Chan *et al.*'s (1998) sample by Scheib (unpublished) also indicates no difference in the adjustment of five to eleven year olds based on whether the donor was anonymous or open-identity). Knowing about one's origins and additionally donor type does not appear detrimental to donor-conceived youths' wellbeing. Similarly, Golombok and Badger's (2010) study of nineteen year old offspring of DI lesbian couple families suggested that positive development in open-origin families continues into early adulthood.

When individuals do not learn about their family origins until adolescence or adulthood, we see very different responses. It is important to emphasize that such late disclosure is rarely possible among DI lesbian-couple families. Most of what we know comes from individuals who were born to heterosexual DI couples and these individuals as yet do not form a representative study sample due to the secrecy common during their childhoods. No studies yet have included standardized measures of wellbeing and only one measured family functioning. Instead, feelings towards parents and attitude towards one's donor origins serve as proxies. Despite these caveats, findings remain crucial to understanding mental health outcomes among people with donor origins. Disclosure at such late stages often happens by accident and in difficult situations such as family arguments, divorce, and death. Donor-conceived people's responses – not surprisingly – include anger about being deceived, losing one's sense of trust, sadness, and genealogical bewilderment along with the disruption of one's sense of self and identity (for example, Hamilton 2002). Adolescents and adults also report discomfort with having donor origins and terrible frustration with having no access to donor information (Cordray 1999/2000; Turner and Coyle 2000; Hewitt 2002; Spencer 2007; Beeson et al. 2011; review in McWhinnie 2001; see also recent British Columbia, Canada Supreme Court decision based on this negative identity experience, Pratten v. British Columbia (Attorney General), 2011 BCSC 656). Even disclosure subsequently followed by avoiding the topic leads to poorer family functioning (Paul and Berger 2007). In a large sample of 165 donor-conceived adults, in which nearly 40 per cent had learned as teens or adults, late disclosure actually predicted more negative attitudes towards having donor origins (Jadva et al. 2009). But unlike earlier studies, age at disclosure did not predict feelings towards parents – some who learned late still felt positively towards parents, while others who learned early felt the opposite (but see Beeson et al. 2011). Although the researchers did not collect much information about the manner of disclosure, only a minority of participants had learned accidentally. This difference from earlier studies might partly explain why Jadva and colleagues found more positive feelings towards parents. In another study of eighty-five adults, the majority (66 per cent) had learned as teens or adults, and were told during planned conversations (64 per cent) (Mahlstedt et al. 2010). In this sample, no evidence was found for a link between age at disclosure and attitude towards one's donor origins, but instead attitude was better predicted by the quality of the relationship with their mother and viewing their (social) father as their 'real father'. In considering these relational and familial processes (for example, communication and relationship quality), as well as age at disclosure, these last three studies help to begin identifying what might be going on in families around openness and secrecy. Although overall findings suggest that donor-conceived individuals who learn early and are raised in openness will fare better than those who learn late, it is likely that the qualities of family communication and other processes will be similarly important predictors of wellbeing and comfort with donor origins.

On a final note, in studies in which children (or their parents; Rumball and Adair 1999; Lindblad *et al.* 2000; Vanfraussen *et al.* 2001, 2003a; Gartrell *et al.* 2005), adolescents (Scheib *et al.* 2005; Bos and Gartrell 2011) or adults (Cordray 1999/2000; Turner and Coyle 2000; Hewitt 2002; Spencer 2007; Scheib *et al.* 2008; Jadva *et al.* 2009; Mahlstedt *et al.* 2010; Beeson *et al.* 2011) were questioned about the donor, the vast majority expressed curiosity and wanting to know more about him. Among youths, degree of curiosity was not associated with their adjustment level (Vanfraussen *et al.* 2003a), much as interest in birth origins among adoptees is not associated with pathology (Howe and Feast 2000). Questions about the donor often centred around three main issues: what is the donor like as a person, what does he look like, and is he like me (for example, Scheib *et al.* 2005; Beeson *et al.* 2011). Donor-conceived adults also often had medical questions (for example, Jadva *et al.* 2010). Such questions appear motivated by the desire to learn more about oneself – about who you are – reflecting the normal developmental process of identity-formation (Benward, in press). When frustration was expressed about having donor origins, as commonly reported by adults, it went hand-in-hand with having an anonymous donor about whom little or nothing was known. Frustration was much less common and much less intense among adolescents with open-identity donors (we know nothing about any other age group with this type of donor), as seen when youths wanted their donor's identity sooner than at adulthood (Scheib *et al.* 2005; Bos and Gartrell 2011). While remaining preliminary, these findings suggest that having substantial information about a family's donor, and perhaps also an open-identity option, may lead to better outcomes among donor-conceived individuals and their families (Benward, in press). Based on the positive outcomes seen among children in DI lesbian families who learn early, the combination of early and honest disclosure, having information about the donor, and being open to children's questions about their family's origins may lead to the best outcomes yet observed for DI families.

Conclusion

In conclusion, the existing literature strongly indicates that children and parents in lesbian DI families are doing at least as well as those in heterosexual DI families, such that the DI literature mirrors the larger literature comparing children of lesbian and heterosexual parents. The sexual orientation of parents does not seem relevant. Rather, the family processes that support positive child development appear to be the same in DI heterosexual and lesbian-couple families. These include parents being satisfied with their spousal relationship and sharing of household and child-care tasks, parents feeling competent in their child-rearing skills, and parents and children sharing positive and close relationships. Given how similar lesbian- and heterosexual-couple DI families are on these characteristics, the similarly better-than-average adjustment and mental health of their children should come as no surprise.

Whereas family-building through DI often leads to positive outcomes for families, two major risk factors remain. First, it is becoming clear that donor-conceived people are at risk for psychological difficulties when they 'discover' their family's donor origins late, in adolescence or adulthood. Second, donor-conceived adolescents and young adults experience distress when they are unable to learn about their genetic and ancestral origins due to having anonymous donors, or being denied access to donor information. Notably, the former of these two risks would pertain most particularly to DI heterosexual-couple families. One of the few salient differences between heterosexual- and lesbian-couple families is with respect to the parents' degree of openness with their children about the family's DI origins. Children of lesbian-couple families are much more likely to learn about having a donor in early childhood, and to grow up knowing that in addition to their two mothers who are raising them, a man also made a biological contribution to their lives. Openness does not appear to harm children raised in lesbian families, as we see continued wellbeing into adolescence and young adulthood. With open and sensitive parents – whether lesbian or heterosexual – donor-conceived children will have the opportunity to develop a stable and healthy identity that includes this fact about their origins. However, if secrecy, shame, or concerns about the 'developmental appropriateness' of divulging the use of DI leads parents to delay informing their children of the donor until adolescence, after they have made considerable progress in their identity formation, then identity conflict, confusion, anger and distress could result (Beeson *et al.* 2011; Benward, in press).

With regard to the second risk, regardless of family structure, the vast majority of donor-conceived children, youths and adults who know about their origins are curious about the donor and their ancestry. If their attempts to obtain that information are blocked, at a minimum they are likely to be frustrated. This curiosity of donor-conceived individuals is normal, and when it cannot be fulfilled then risks for more substantive psychological distress or difficulties might also increase. This might become increasingly salient in adulthood, when concerns about their donor's genetic or medical conditions might affect their own family-planning or their own health, and when consolidation of the normative adolescent process of identity exploration should be resolved. This has important implications for health policies around the use of open-identity versus anonymous donors. If donor-conceived individuals want to be able to learn about their origins, then providing the means for them to access that information would seem to be supported on the grounds of psychological wellbeing.

Notes

1 See Golombok *et al.* 1995 for an effective study design to test the effects of using assisted conception and genetic asymmetry in heterosexual-couple families. Their groups included infertile, assisted conception families with genetic asymmetry (DI families), infertile, assisted conception families without genetic asymmetry (IVF families), infertile families without assisted conception and genetic asymmetry (adoptive families) and conventionally-conceived families.

2 It is noteworthy that adults who learn late about their donor origins often remark that it is better to know than not know (Kirkman 2003; Mahlstedt *et al.* 2010) and encouraging honesty in families appears to be a general theme among both those with and without donor origins (for example, Hamilton 2002; Kirkman *et al.* 2007; Jadva *et al.* 2009).

References

Achenbach, T.M. and Edelbrock, C.S. (1983), *Manual for the Child Behavior Checklist and Revised Child Behavior Profile*, Burlington: University of Vermont, Department of Psychiatry.

Amato, P. and Jacob, M.C. (2004), 'Providing fertility services to lesbian couples', *Sexuality, Reproduction and Menopause*, 2: 83–8.

Beeson, D.R., Jennings, P. and Kramer, W. (2011), 'Offspring searching for their sperm donors: How family type shapes the process', *Human Reproduction*, 26: 2415–2424.

Benward, J.B. (in press). 'Identity development in the donor conceived', in Juliet Guichon (ed.).

Blyth, E. and Frith, L. (2009), 'Donor conceived peoples' access to genetic and biographical history', *International Journal of Law, Policy and the Family*, 23: 174–91.

Bos, H. and Gartrell N. (2010), 'Adolescents of the USA National Longitudinal Lesbian Family Study: Can family characteristics counteract the negative effects of stigmatization?', *Family Process*, 49: 559–72.

Bos, H.M.W. and Gartrell N.K. (2011), 'Adolescents of the US National Longitudinal Lesbian Family Study: The impact of having a known or an unknown donor on the stability of psychological adjustment', *Human Reproduction*, 26: 630–7.

Bos, H.M.W., Gartrell, N., van Balen, F., Peyser, H. and Sandfort, T.G.M. (2008), 'Children in planned lesbian families: A cross-cultural comparison between the USA and the Netherlands', *American Journal of Orthopsychiatry*, 2: 211–9.

Bos, H.M.W., and Hakvoort, E.M. (2007), 'Child adjustment and parenting in planned lesbian families with known and as-yet unknown donors', *Journal of Psychosomatic Obstetrics and Gynecology*, 28: 121–9.

Bos, H.M.W. and Sandfort, T.G.M. (2010), 'Children's gender identity in lesbian and heterosexual two-parent families', *Sex Roles*, 62: 114–26.

Bos, H.M.W. van Balen, F. and van den Boom, D.C. (2004), 'Experience of parenthood, couple relationship, social support, and child rearing goals in planned lesbian families', *Journal of Child Psychology and Psychiatry*, 45: 755–64.

Bos, H.M.W., van Balen, F. and van den Boom, D.C. (2005), 'Lesbian families and family functioning: An overview', *Patient, Education, and Counseling*, 59: 263–75.

Bos, H.M.W. van Balen, F. and van den Boom, D.C. (2007), 'Child adjustment and parenting in planned lesbian-parent families', *American Journal of Orthopsychiatry*, 77: 38–48.

Brewaeys, A. (2001), 'Review: Parent-child relationships and child development in donor insemination families', *Human Reproduction Update*, 7: 38–46.

Brewaeys, A., Golombok, S., Naaktgeboren, N., de Bruyn, J.K. and van Hall, E.V. (1997a), 'Donor insemination: Dutch parents' opinions about confidentiality and donor anonymity and the emotional adjustment of their children', *Human Reproduction*, 12: 1591–7.

Brewaeys, A., Ponjaert, I., van Hall, E.V. and Golombok, S. (1997b), 'Donor insemination: Child development and family functioning in lesbian mother families', *Human Reproduction*, 12: 1349–59.

Brewaeys, A., Ponjaert-Kristoffersen, I., van Steirteghem, A.C. and Devroey, P. (1993), 'Children from anonymous donors: An inquiry into homosexual and heterosexual parents' attitudes', *Journal of Psychosomatic Obstetrics & Gynaecology*, 14: 23–35.

Chan, R.W., Raboy, B. and Patterson, C.J. (1998a), 'Psychosocial adjustment among children conceived via donor insemination by lesbian and heterosexual mothers', *Child Development*, 69: 443–57.

Chan, R.W., Brooks, R.C., Raboy, B. and Patterson, C.J. (1998b), 'Division of labor among lesbian and heterosexual parents: Associations with children's adjustment', *Journal of Family Psychology*, 12: 402–19.

Clamar, A. (1989), 'Psychological implications of the anonymous pregnancy', in J. Offerman-Zuckerberg (ed.), *Gender in Transition: A New Frontier*, New York: Plenum: 111–120.

Collins, W.A. and Steinberg, L. (2006), 'Adolescent development in interpersonal context', in W. Damon and R.M. Lerner (eds), *Handbook of Child Psychology, Vol. 3. Social, Emotional, and Personality Development* (sixth edition), New York: Wiley, 1003–67.

Cordray, B. (1999/2000), 'A survey of people conceived through donor insemination', *DI Network (now Donor Conception Network) News*, 14: 4–5.

Daniels, K. Gillett, W. and Grace, V. (2009), 'Parental information sharing with donor insemination conceived offspring: A follow-up study', *Human Reproduction*, 24: 1099–1105.

Daniels, K.R., Grace, V.M. and Gillett, W.R. (2011), 'Factors associated with parents' decisions to tell their adult offspring about the offspring's donor conception', *Human Reproduction*, 26: 2783-90.

Daniels, K. and Meadows, L. (2006), 'Sharing information with adults conceived as a result of donor insemination', *Human Fertility*, 9: 93–9.

Ehrensaft, D. (2008), 'Just Molly and me, and donor make three: Lesbian motherhood in the age of assisted reproductive technology', *Journal of Lesbian Studies*, 12: 161–78.

Ethics Committee of the American Society for Reproductive Medicine (2004), 'Informing offspring of their conception by gamete donation', *Fertility and Sterility*, 81: 527–31.

Ethics Committee of the American Society for Reproductive Medicine (2009), 'Access to fertility treatment by gays, lesbians, and unmarried persons', *Fertility and Sterility*, 4: 1190–3.

Flaks, D.K. Ficher, I. Masterpasqua, F. and Joseph, G. (1995), 'Lesbians choosing motherhood: A comparative study of lesbian and heterosexual parents and their children', *Developmental Psychology*, 31: 105–14.

Franz, S.D. and Allen, D. (2001), *The Offspring Speak: First International Conference of Donor Offspring*, Toronto: The Infertility Network.

Fulcher, M. Sutfin, E.L. Chan, R.W. Scheib, J.E. and Patterson, C.J. (2006), 'Lesbian mothers and their children: Findings from the contemporary families study', in A.M. Omoto and H.S. Kurtzman (eds), *Sexual Orientation and Mental Health: Examining Identity and Development in Lesbian, Gay, and Bisexual People*, Washington, DC: American Psychological Association: 281–99.

Gartrell, N., Banks, A., Reed, N., Hamilton, J., Rodas, C. and Deck, A. (2000), 'The National Lesbian Family Study: Interviews with mothers of five-year-olds', *American Journal of Orthopsychiatry*, 70: 542–8.

Gartrell, N., Deck, A., Rodas, C., Peyser, H. and Banks, A. (2005), 'The National Lesbian Family Study: 4. Interviews with the 10-year-old children', *American Journal of Orthopsychiatry*, 75: 518–24.

Gartrell, N., Peyser, H. and Bos, H. (in press), 'Planned lesbian families: A review of the U.S.A. National Longitudinal Lesbian Family Study', in D.M. Brodinsky A. Pertman and D.B. Kunz (eds), *Lesbian and Gay Adoption: A New American Reality*, Oxford: Oxford University Press.

Goldberg, A. (2010), *Lesbian and Gay Parents and Their Children: Research on the Family Life Cycle*, Washington, D.C.: American Psychological Association.

Golombok, S. and Badger, S. (2010), 'Children raised in mother-headed families from infancy: A follow-up of children of lesbian and single heterosexual mothers at early adulthood', *Human Reproduction*, 25:150–7.

Golombok, S., Cook, R., Bish, A. and Murray, C. (1995), 'Families created by the new reproductive technologies: Quality of parenting and social and emotional development of the children', *Child Development*, 66: 285–98.

Golombok, S., MacCallum, F., Goodman, E., and Rutter, M. (2002), 'Families with children conceived by donor insemination: A follow-up at age 12', *Child Development*, 73: 952–68.

Golombok, S., Tasker, F., and Murray, C. (1997), 'Children raised in fatherless families from infancy: Family relationships and the socioemotional development of children of lesbian and single heterosexual mothers', *Journal of Child Psychology and Psychiatry*, 38: 783–92.

Grusec, J.E. and Hastings, P.D. (2007), *Handbook of Socialization: Theory and Research*, New York: Guilford Press.

Hamilton, R. on behalf of 19 donor-conceived adults (2002), 'Donor conceived adults challenge the ethics of anonymity', *Journal of Fertility Counselling*, 9: 33–34.

Hewitt, G. (2002), 'Missing links: Identity issues of donor conceived people', *Journal of Fertility Counselling*, 9: 14–20.

Howe, D. and Feast, J. (2000), *Adoption, Search & Reunion: The Long Term Experience of Adopted Adults*, London: Children's Society.

Hunter, M. Salter-Ling, N. and Glover, L. (2000), 'Donor insemination: Telling children about their origins', *Child Psychology and Psychiatry Review*, 5: 157–63.

Jadva, V., Freeman, T., Kramer, W. and Golombok, S. (2009), 'The experiences of adolescents and adults conceived by sperm donation: Comparisons by age of disclosure and family type', *Human Reproduction*, 24: 1909–19.

Jadva, V., Freeman, T., Kramer, W. and Golombok, S. (2010), 'Offsprings' experiences of searching and contacting their donor siblings and donor', *Reproductive BioMedicine Online*, 20: 523–32.

Kirkman, M. (2003), 'Parents' contributions to the narrative identity of offspring of donor-assisted conception', *Social Science and Medicine*, 57: 2229–2242.

Kirkman, M., Rosenthal, D. and Johnson, L. (2007), 'Families working it out: Adolescents' views on communicating about donor-assisted conception', *Human Reproduction*, 22: 2318–2324.

Landau, R., Weissenberg, R. and Madgar, I. (2008), 'A child of "hers": Older single mothers and their children conceived through IVF with both egg and sperm donation', *Fertility and Sterility*, 90: 576–83.

Landau, R. and Weissenberg, R. (2010), 'Disclosure of donor conception in single-mother families: Views and concerns', *Human Reproduction*, 25: 942–8.

Lindblad, F. Gottlieb, C. and Lalos, O. (2000), 'To tell or not to tell – what parents think about telling their children that they were born following donor insemination', *Journal of Psychosomatic Obstetrics and Gynecology*, 21: 193–203.

Lorbach, C. (2003), *Experiences of Donor Conception: Parents, Offspring and Donors through the Years*, London UK: Jessica Kingsley Publishers.

Lycett, E. Daniels, K. Curson, R. and Golombok, S. (2004), 'Offspring created as a result of donor insemination: A study of family relationships, child adjustment, and disclosure', *Fertility and Sterility*, 82: 172–9.

MacCallum, F. and Golombok, S. (2004), 'Children raised in fatherless families from infancy: A follow-up of children of lesbian and single heterosexual mothers at early adolescence', *Journal of Child Psychology and Psychiatry*, 45: 1407–19.

Mac Dougall, K., Becker, G., Scheib, J.E., and Nachtigall, R.D. (2007), 'Strategies for disclosure: How parents approach telling their children that they were conceived with conceived with donor gametes', *Fertility and Sterility*, 87: 524–33.

Mahlstedt, P.P., LaBounty, K. and Kennedy, W.T. (2010), 'The views of adult offspring of sperm donation: Essential feedback for the development of ethical guidelines within the practice of assisted reproductive technology in the United States', *Fertility and Sterility*, 93: 2236–46.

McCandlish, B. (1987), 'Against all odds: Lesbian mother family dynamics', in F.W. Bozett (eds), *Gay and Lesbian Parents*, New York: Praeger, 23–36.

McGee, G., Brakman, S. and Gurmankin, A. (2001), 'Debate: Disclosure to children conceived with donor gametes', *Human Reproduction*, 16: 2033–6.

McWhinnie, A. (2001), 'Gamete donation and anonymity: Should offspring from donated gametes continue to be denied knowledge of their origins and antecedents?', *Human Reproduction*, 16: 807–17.

Morrissette, M. (2006), *Voices of Donor Conception*, Minnesota: Be-Mondo Publishing.

Murray, C. and Golombok, S. (2005), 'Solo mothers and their donor insemination infants: Follow-up at age 2 years', *Human Reproduction*, 20: 1655–60.

Nachtigall, R.D., Tschann, J.M., Quiroga, S.S., Pitcher, L. and Becker, G. (1997), 'Stigma, disclosure, and family functioning among parents of children conceived through donor insemination', *Fertility and Sterility*, 68: 83–9.

Owen, L. and Golombok, S. (2009), 'Families created by assisted reproduction: Parent-child relationships in late adolescence', *Journal of Adolescence*, 32: 835–48.

Patterson, C.J. (1992), 'Children of lesbian and gay parents', *Child Development*, 63: 1025–42.

Patterson, C.J. (1994), 'Children of the lesbian baby boom: Behavioral adjustment, self-concepts and sex role identity', in B. Greene and G.M. Herek (eds), *Lesbian and Gay Psychology: Theory, Research, and Clinical Applications*, Thousand Oaks, CA: Sage Publications, 156–75.

Patterson, C.J. (1996), 'Lesbian Mothers and Their Children: Findings from the Bay Area Families Study', in J. Laird and R.J. Green (eds), *Lesbians and Gays in Couples and Families: A Handbook for Therapists*, San Francisco: Jossey-Bass, 420–37.

Patterson, C.J. (2005), 'Lesbian and Gay Parents and Their Children: Summary of Research Findings', in *Lesbian and Gay Parenting: A Resource for Psychologists (second edition)*, Washington, D.C.: American Psychological Association.

Patterson, C.J. and Hastings, P.D. (2007), 'Socialization in the context of family diversity', in J.E. Grusec and P.D. Hastings (eds), *Handbook of Socialization: Theory and Research*, New York: Guilford Press, 328–51.

Paul, M.S. and Berger, R. (2007), 'Topic avoidance and family functioning in families conceived with donor insemination', *Human Reproduction*, 22: 2566–71.

Rumball, A. and Adair, V. (1999), 'Telling the story: Parents' scripts for donor offspring', *Human Reproduction*, 14: 1392–9.

Scheib, J.E., Riordan, M. and Rubin, S. (2003), 'Choosing identity-release sperm donors: The parents' perspective 13–18 years later', *Human Reproduction*, 18: 1115–27.

Scheib, J.E., Riordan, M. and Rubin, S. (2005), 'Adolescents with open-identity sperm donors: Reports from 12–17 year olds', *Human Reproduction*, 20: 239–52.

Scheib, J.E., Ruby, A. and Benward, J. (2008), 'Who requests their sperm donor's identity? Analysis of donor-conceived adult requests at an open-identity program', *Fertility & Sterility*, 90: S8–9.

Schover, L.R., Thomas, A.J., Miller, K.F., Falcone, T., Attaran, M. and Goldberg, J. (1996), 'Preferences for intracytoplasmic sperm injection versus donor insemination in severe male factor infertility: a preliminary report', *Human Reproduction*, 11: 2461–4.

Somerville, M. (2010), 'Children's human rights to natural biological origins and family structure', *The Jurisprudence of the family: Foundations and Principles Symposium at Bratislava School of Law May 28–29*: Bratislava, Slovakia.

Spencer, L.W. (2007), *Sperm Donor Offspring: Identity and Other Experiences*, Charleston, S.C.: BookSurge Publishing.

Steckel, A. (1987), 'Psychosocial development of children of lesbian mothers', in F.W. Bozett (eds), *Gay and Lesbian Parents*, New York: Praeger: 75–85.

Tasker, F.L. and Golombok, S. (1995), 'Adults raised as children in lesbian families', *American Journal of Orthopsychiatry*, 65: 203–15.

Tasker, F.L. and Golombok, S. (1997), *Growing Up in a Lesbian Family: Effects on Child Development*, New York: Guilford Press.

Thorn, P. and Wischmann, T. (2009), 'German guidelines for psychosocial counselling in the area of gamete donation', *Human Fertility*, 12: 73–80.

Turner, A.J. and Coyle, A. (2000), 'What does it mean to be a donor offspring? The identity experiences of adults conceived by donor insemination and the implication for counselling and therapy', *Human Reproduction*, 15: 2041–51.

Vanfraussen, K., Ponjaert-Kristoffersen, I. and Brewaeys, A. (2001), 'An attempt to reconstruct children's donor concept: A comparison between children's and lesbian parents' attitudes towards donor anonymity', *Human Reproduction*, 16: 2019–25.

Vanfraussen, K., Ponjaert-Kristoffersen, I. and Brewaeys, A. (2002), 'What does it mean for youngsters to grow up in a lesbian family created by means of donor insemination?', *Journal of Reproductive and Infant Psychology*, 20: 237–52.

Vanfraussen, K., Ponjaert-Kristoffersen, I. and Brewaeys, A. (2003a), 'Why do children want to know more about the donor? The experience of youngsters raised in lesbian families', *Journal of Psychosomatic Obstetrics and Gynaecology*, 24: 31–8.

Vanfraussen, K., Ponjaert-Kristoffersen, I. and Brewaeys, A. (2003b), 'Family functioning in lesbian families created by donor insemination', *American Journal of Orthopsychiatry*, 73: 78–90.

Wechsler, D. (1974), *Manual for the Wechsler Intelligence Scale for Children – Revised*, New York: Psychological Corporation.

Wechsler, D. (1989), *Wechsler Preschool and Primary Scale of Intelligence – Revised: Manual*, New York: Psychological Corporation.

Werner, C. and Westerståhl, A. (2008), 'Donor insemination and parenting: Concerns and strategies of lesbian couples. A review of international studies', *Acta Obstetricia et Gynecologica Scandinavica*, 87: 697–701.

6

Donor-Conception as a 'Dangerous Supplement' to the Nuclear Family

What can we learn from parents' stories?

David Gurnham[1]

Introduction

Parents who conceive using donor sperm or eggs must come to terms with the fact that there is a third party outside of the family to whom their child is genetically related. Although for many such families this is of no consequence at all, there are also parents for whom it seems to cause anxieties that influence their perceptions of themselves in relation to their donor, and their decisions regarding whether, when and how to disclose the genetic facts to their donor-conceived child. In this paper I focus on various empirical studies that have elicited information on the way parents tend to assert a hierarchy between themselves as 'true' parents and the donors as external to the idea of parenthood. I suggest here that our understandings of the sorts of things parents say – and don't say – in this regard can be illuminated by a deconstructive reading. While I accept that there are important positive reasons that explain parents' choice of words, my interest is in deconstructing the empirically observed narratives in order to draw out a less comfortable reading. Some parents do continue to worry that allowing their own status as parents to be supplemented by the fact of gamete donation in some way endangers the security or stability of their family and their relationship with their child. While actual interference by donors in DC families has only ever happened in practice when *known* donors have been used, I want to argue here that the particular deployments of rhetoric in the parents' narratives betray a more far reaching anxiety about status.

'Real' parents and 'dangerous supplements'

According to some commentators, we live in a post-modern age in which the proliferation of reproductive technologies has made possible a hitherto unimaginable 'fragmentation' of parenthood (Sheldon 2005; Boyd 2007;

Parry and Doan 1994). In such conditions, a concern about the 'reality' of parenthood that seeks to exclude exterior elements seems an old-fashioned essentialist preoccupation with the traditional nuclear family model which should not be 'addressed' so much as simply left behind (Boyd 2007: 71). However, recent legal conflicts between, for example, lesbian parents and their sperm donors, make it clear that for some social parents there are still reasons to fall back onto the idea of the nuclear family in order to assert the legitimacy of the family that either cannot or chooses not to reproduce heterosexually (Lind and Hewitt 2009; Polikoff 2001–2; Kelly 2004–5; Kelly 2008–9; Dempsey 2004; Boyd 2007: 402). The new configurations of the relationship of opposition between the nuclear family and what lies outside of it, as well as more traditional examples, open up opportunities for deconstructive critique and this is the concern of this chapter. The chapter focuses on the rhetorical manoeuvres and metaphorical allusions deployed by parents to assert their priority as distinct from 'mere' gamete donors, whether known or unknown, based on this relationship of opposition. In his critiques of canonical western philosophers such as Rousseau, Derrida showed how such rhetoric is vulnerable to being deconstructed due to the difficulties of fully mastering the linguistic hierarchies of 'internal' over 'external'. Thus chapter will show how such critique also points to the difficulties for social parents in maintaining such a clear distinction between themselves as parents and donors as the external, disconnected supplement.

Although it is often denied that deconstruction offers a critical method as such, Derrida's approach of deconstructing the logic of rhetorical assertions of hierarchy can provide a useful perspective for reading claims about the 'reality' of things, or efforts to put a chosen concept *beyond* the usual problems of linguistic ambiguity and doubt. For example, Rousseau valued certain primal modes of expression such as the pure natural voice particularly highly because they seemed to issue directly from the soul, unlike the more 'cultured' artifices such as harmony, writing and painting that all rely on external marks and secondary interpretation. Rousseau complained that writing – external to spontaneous living expression – could only be a 'supplement' to nature because unlike natural expression it was standardized and repeatable in different contexts disconnected from the original speaker. This indeed is the great advantage of writing, but it also brings with it the dangers of written words being misunderstood, misinterpreted, corrupted, etc. Furthermore, Rousseau saw such cultural additions to natural expression as *dangerous* supplements in the sense that, in falsely appearing to recreate the natural (or 'real') itself, people would mistake them for true expression and thus allow themselves to be misled and misinformed. This simultaneous attraction and danger of the supplement is the quality of 'iterability' that Derrida (1997: 141–164, 165–268) in his critique of Rousseau attributes to *all* forms of expression. Irrespective of whether spoken or written, all words derive meaning from the context of their use, and since context cannot be fully determined in advance, neither can the meaning of the words (Derrida 1992: 84). As Critchley (1992: 38–9) puts it: 'In deconstruction, both success and failure of meaning are the effects of the 'iterability' of words: that they are repeatable in, and affected by, contexts that cannot be pre-determined.' This leads to a critical perspective that sees supplementation as a necessary symptom of language-use. Adopting such a view means that assertions of the 'reality' of things are always deconstructable as rhetorical strategies for mastering and dominating context. This is how I propose here to approach the parents' narratives about their status. I want to examine the ways in which this logic of the 'dangerous supplement', escaping from its proper place as the subordinated external addition to nature (in our case a supplement to natural fertility), can illuminate our readings of parents' stories of status and reality.

The place of the genetic in the 'reality' of parenthood

The idea that parents have an ethical duty to tell their children that they were donor-conceived is now the orthodox position in many countries. In the UK this is reflected in law by the removal of donor anonymity by the Human Fertilisation and Embryology Authority (Disclosure of Donor Information) Regulations 2004. In countries such as the United States and Canada, which have tended to operate on a more laissez-faire basis of allowing individual clinics to set their own standards, here too the evidence suggests a move towards open-identity as a norm (Mahlstedt 2010: 2236–7)[2].

Deciding whether to tell or not to tell

Before we examine the ways in which parents tell their DC children about their genetic parenthood, we ought to first consider the prior question of whether to tell in the first place. Since a child of two lesbian women or a single woman will always know that their family set-up is 'different' to that of many of their peers, non-disclosure is generally only an option for heterosexual couples. It is possible that this option not to disclose may continue to cause its own stress and conflict within families, and some studies indicate that men in particular may find the prospect of disclosing particularly difficult (Eisenberg 2008; Applegarth 2010; Mahlstedt 2010: 2243–4). Parents committed to not disclosing the fact of donor conception might feel entitled to argue that, the true meaning of parenthood being fully accounted for in the social bond, it is simply unnecessary to explain the use of donor gametes to the child (Shehab 2008). But parents taking this view must come to terms with the fact that it has become orthodox for both regulatory and advisory bodies to encourage parents to look upon disclosure as an ethical duty, and furthermore that children benefit from being told as early as possible (Montuschi 2006: 2)[3]. The thorny legal and ethical questions surrounding family secrets and what rights (if any) a donor-conceived child has to know who his/her genetic parents are, have generated much critical debate which I do not go into here (Gurnham and Miola 2012; Smart 2007: 127–9; Eekelaar 2006: 74). However, this move towards openness about genetics throws up further questions. For example, if the matter of genetic relatedness between parent and child is insignificant when placed against the quality of social parenting, what would be the harm in disclosing it to the child? There are of course many banal truths which do not need to be told, and there are also important truths which not to tell would incur the same moral approbation as telling a lie. The fact that being 'honest and open' according to currently orthodox ethical attitudes requires parents to acknowledge the supplement, necessarily implies that it means *something* and by implication that social parenting means slightly less than everything even within the most loving and devoted families. A British parent is quoted by the Donor Conception Network (DCN) as saying: 'You are the people in the whole world that they should be able to trust most of all, and to me it would be wrong [not to disclose]. In essence, if you are not telling you are lying.' (Montuschi 2006: 1). Thus the discourse of truth in donor-conception demonstrably exceeds social parenthood, and pressures parents to confront the *irrelevant-yet-essential* fact that their child is genetically related to someone outside of the family. It is an idea of the supplement as external yet disruptive that Derrida draws out of Rousseau's disparaging remarks about writing and other 'artful ruses' and that I want to show can also similarly be found in parents' reported experiences of donor conception.

'Scripts' for telling: Problems and solutions in parents' narratives

There are two themes that can be drawn out from the parents' narratives on themselves as parents and on the donor. The first is the ambiguity caused simply by wielding everyday notions such as the 'real', 'true' or 'natural' in order to distinguish oneself in this context. The second, which I address further below, is the use of rhetoric that may offer an escape from these linguistic ambiguities: emphasizing binary hierarchies between the parent and the donor in the form of natural/artificial, present/absent, internal/external.

The ambiguity of the 'real'

Our first concern then is the ambiguity of the 'real'. Society continues to struggle with the idea of separating sex and reproduction (McCandless and Sheldon 2010), and as a result, parents will often lack a satisfactory vocabulary for describing themselves and the relative position of the donor (Diduck 2007). 'Real' is a clumsy and an ambiguous word that is enlisted to express the relative significance of the two roles, and like Derrida's 'supplement', seldom provides a convincing way to distinguish two ideas, especially when the criteria of judgement is itself in doubt. The Donor Conception Network (DCN) acknowledge this in their advisory literature to parents, warning them not to take too personally or seriously their children's ignorant invocations of the 'real' to refer to the biological/genetic gamete provider (Montuschi 2006; Mac Dougall 2007: 527–8; Kelly 2008–9). And it is not only children who are at risk of confusing themselves in this way. Consider this man speaking at a seminar in Germany:

> If I had a child via DI, of course, I would be the father. But the donor is also the father, he is the biological father. But I don't want my child to grow up not knowing who is the 'real' father. So I need to ask myself: who am I and who is he in relationship to our child? And, how do we differentiate (between us) when we talk to our child about this? (Daniels and Thorn 2001: 1794)

We might suggest that the speaker's confusion could be eliminated by a simple change of terminology, i.e. by choosing a word other than 'father' to describe the sperm donor, which would eliminate the need to speak about the 'real' at all (Montuschi 2006: 6). That he seems unwilling or unable to do so may reflect the tenacity of a genetic idea of parenthood in everyday language, which is also reflected in other empirical studies. For example, Fiona Kelly's research in Canada involving forty-nine lesbian mothers found that 'reality' with regards to parenthood in the lesbian mothers' language was marked by doubt and anxiety over the lexicon of father/donor. It is very clear from Kelly's research that a large part of the problem stems from a frustration at a public cultural-linguistic framework in which the heteronormative genetic idea of parenthood is given priority. The references to pauses and hesitations are presumably included by Kelly to give a sense of the difficulties for her subjects in situating themselves and their family within this framework:

> 'Carey': I'll talk about [my son's] 'dad'. Whereas other time I'll say [my son's] 'donor'. Just [pause], it's [pause], it is [pause], 'cause neither is completely accurate. He's really in between. (Kelly 2008–9: 206)

> 'Jasmine': As far as Chris goes I mean he knows that Bianca and I are his parents. But if Neil [the donor] comes to something like one of his performances or something and he introduces him as 'father', um, they will defer to him. And that kind of stuff. 'Cause we don't have the right words for it. Yes, he's the biological father and yes he may be important in Chris's life, but [sigh] don't defer to him. (Kelly 2008–9: 206)

Kelly's mothers overwhelmingly feared that, despite the fact that they and not the donor/father undertook the chief parenting role, 'the symbolic weight attached to fatherhood would always prevail' (Kelly 2008–9: 203). We should note here that 'Carey' and 'Jasmine' both opted to use known donors, and thus their remarks about the donors/fathers being involved in the child's life are not directly applicable to regulated donor conception in the UK, in which there is no possibility of contact between the child and the donor until the child is eighteen and chooses to access identifying information held by the clinic. However, beyond the prosaic questions of access, the *linguistic* ambivalence in these narratives regarding the family life and the symbolic significance reluctantly and resignedly accorded to genetic 'fatherhood' is telling. If references to the 'real' and other related words are invoked in order to get *beyond* text and to circumvent textual ambiguities then these examples would suggest that this strategy may be very difficult. Both the man's efforts in the first passage and the lesbian mothers' in the second in this regard remain hopelessly mired in the very textual treacle from which they are trying to escape.

Overcoming the ambiguity: Narrating the externality of the donor

In stark contrast to the confusions and ambiguities admitted to above, parents also seem to re-assert their status, both through confident statements about the reality of associating parenthood with parent*ing*, and also through a judicious choice of language when explaining the truth to their children of their genetic origins. For an example of the first strategy we might look once more to Kelly's Canadian study:

> Sylvie: I like to use a term here which, I call myself the front line parent. ... That means that I'm the parent who's there 24 hours. I'm there for the emergencies. I'm there for the heartache and the emotional, whatever. You know, to bear it all. I'm the one who has committed to doing that work and that has little to do with biology. Really little. (Kelly 2008–9: 199)

And what of the language used to explain donor conception to their children? Parents assert the primacy of their own status by stressing the significance of their being physically present to the child and the relative disconnection and distance of the donor. The explanation that the parent gives to the child about the latter's genetic origins asserts and reinforces a linguistic claim: that the *full meaning* of the parent-child relationship is captured in the social relation. Research by Rumball and Adair (1999: 1395) in New Zealand revealed that narratives used by parents to explain to their child his or her genetic origins tended to refer to a 'kind man' that provided 'seeds', or else to a doctor that provided the 'help' needed to complete the family. They emphasize that the baby conceived is the product of the loving relationship between mother and father, with the 'seeds' or 'help' a natural consequence of that relationship, and the gametes provided a component part. Lycett (2005: 816) corroborates this picture, revealing some inventive methods employed by donor conception parents in London for diminishing and drawing attention away from the donor's input. One family emphasized the distance between donor and child by comparing gamete donation to giving blood, similarly anonymous:

> They've seen me giving blood so I said it was like that, like it was giving a blood donation but this was cells for someone else to help them make him [child] born and the same was as I didn't know who my blood had gone to, he would never know who had given him cells.

Mac Dougall (2007: 529–531) reveals that in Northern California, while men are especially drawn to metaphors of mechanical breakdown in their explanations, women more commonly use more personal 'helper'-type stories. Lycett (2005: 816) underlines this: 'We [father and son] were having a bath together and I was saying to him, "Your [testicles] will get bigger than mine... because mine don't work very well..." then we told him that we used somebody's seeds.' There is some evidence that lesbian accounts may tend to combine the 'spare parts' and 'helper' techniques in disclosure narratives that are perhaps slightly more complex but are no less directed to the same goal of diminishing the status and significance of the gamete donor. For example, one lesbian mother wrote on the American Donor Sibling Registry discussion forum: 'We just told him matter-of-factly that he didn't have a dad. He had two mums. ... We told him that there was a man who helped us have a baby because you need a man part and a woman part to make a baby' (Montuschi 2006: 15). The Donor Conception Network offers this advice for telling very young children: '... you can point this out [the clinic or hospital where they were conceived] as you would any other item of interest like a fire engine or a big crane... "and that's where she (and Daddy) *needed some help to have you*"' (Montuschi 2006: 10 emphasis added). The two narratives quoted above combine 'mechanical breakdown' and 'helper' stories to impress upon the child the status of the 'real' (i.e. social) parent, and to underline the relative superficiality of the genetic connection with the gamete donor. The point of the story is that there should arise in the child's imagination a gulf between him/herself and the donor, in contrast to the proximity of the social parent. The story's aim is to convey the exteriority and otherness of the 'supplement', and to show that if there is any resemblance between it and the loving family it once helped, such resemblance is a dim and distant one. In the DCN advice quoted above, the fertility clinic is imagined as a sort of repair garage, and the 'help' that Daddy received there by implication one of the many public amenities of the city, on a level with a school or the fire services, pointed out to the child but barely noticed.

Interpreting the parental narratives

A positive, practical and prosaic reading of the parental narratives

Before offering a deconstructive reading of these narratives, it must first be acknowledged that there are a number of positive and straightforward reasons why parents would want both to assert the full reality of their parenthood status and also to underscore this with 'disclosure scripts' that emphasize the externality of the donor. First and arguably most obviously, parents need to acknowledge a young child's relatively unsophisticated notions of parenthood and also their likely ignorance about sexual reproduction.

Therefore metaphors of 'helpers', 'seeds' and mechanical failure are used to convey what would otherwise be unintelligible biological information. Parents' own narratives will be coloured by many children's simplistic association of the genetic with the social parent. This means that explaining that, for example, their genetic 'father' is someone other than their social father risks implying that they were 'abandoned' by their 'real' father, and this highlights the practicality of metaphors that divert the child from such an impression.

Second, such narratives may be the best way for parents to talk positively about the 'alternative' nature of their family. Dempsey (2004: 81) has argued that the opportunity for women to break away from the traditionally assumed 'compulsory heterosexuality' of reproduction allows for a positive fragmentation of our nuclear concept of family, allowing recognition of a variety of different roles (Rich 1982/2007). In support of such a view, there is evidence that some lesbian couples do use the fact of the donor's genetic relatedness creatively and positively to empower their reproductive choices. Consider this example of the latter type, from an interview with a U.S. lesbian couple whose choice of an anonymous donor seems to have been an imaginative and creative exercise:

> Some people seemed too nerdy, you know they played badminton or didn't drink coffee or something... The donor we finally picked was a doctor, 6 foot 4 inches, played basketball and drank coffee. We felt like if we met him, we could relate to him, and maybe our child would inherit some of his qualities that we liked. (Tober 2001: 139)

Such a good-humoured approach to locating the donor in the reproductive narrative suggests that some parents are comfortable exploring the possibilities of parenthood without attempting to negate the idea of the donor as a person or personality in his own right. Other empirical studies reinforce this impression. For example, Landau (2008: 280) recounts how one donor-conception mother she interviewed said that her child had once called her 'Mother-Father'. We might deconstruct this remark as a claim that she as sole parent herself occupied the full meaning of 'parent' with no room within that concept for any supplement. But we could also read it as meaning that the terms we have traditionally used to refer to parents are not as fixed as we once thought, and that they may be turned to new and different purposes to reflect changing social attitudes to a multiplicity of alternative family forms (McGuinness and Alghrani 2008: 282).

Furthermore, research by Scheib and Ruby (2008) on contact between families who share the same donor has suggested that 'alternative' or 'non-traditional' families (for example those headed by single women) may often perceive a positive role for the genetic contribution to a child's life. Scheib and Ruby found not only that these families they interviewed often voluntarily opted for open-identity donation, but also that they were likely to sign up to networks set up to match children from the same donor. Households headed by a single woman particularly seem to view the genetic relation between their child and the donor positively, often actively seeking out their children's genetic half-siblings in order to extend their own family for the sake of their children (2008: 38). Similarly, interviews conducted in Belgium (operating a system of donor anonymity) by Vanfraussen *et al.* (2001: 2024) with lesbian mothers and their children revealed that the mothers interviewed tended to prefer using the same donor for each of their children, so that despite not having any possibility of a relationship with the donor, the children would show the same physical resemblances as would the children of a traditional heterosexual nuclear family. Again we might read this deconstructively as evidence of an unacknowledged deference to genetic connections as a supplement for social parenthood. However, it is equally possible to read the study as showing a relaxed and confident attitude amongst many lesbian parents towards the possible impact or implication of there being a person outside the family who is genetically related to their child. It suggests that there may well be a place to consider all manner of bases on which to build a family, incorporating biological, social and intentional indicators of what constitutes a parent (Sheldon 2005). These examples show that the broader picture I draw out in below – namely of parents using oppositional rhetoric to draw attention away from the donor as a 'real' person, and thereby to strengthen their own status as parents in their narratives of family – does not necessarily apply to everyone. For families using donor gametes to self-consciously create an 'alternative' family structure it seems that there may be pleasure to be had in bringing the donor 'to life', perhaps even involving the child in this creative process.

Anxiety and confidence together: Deconstructing the narratives

The positive interpretation of the narratives given above is plausible in the context of families that are in fact comfortable with their status as non-genetic (social) parents. However, the strongly oppositional language used by many other parents suggests that further analysis may be warranted. I want to suggest that we can deconstruct the extent to which the metaphors used depersonalize and even dehumanize the donor as provider of spare parts, and that this highlights traditional anxieties amongst parents about a possible loss of status. Mac Dougall (2007) interprets her own research results in this way, pointing out that men are particularly likely to discourage the child even to think of the donor as fully human, encouraging them instead to think of the donor as defined only by their physical contribution. Other studies have also reported a greater level of stress and pessimism about the status of the donor amongst men and heterosexual donor-conception families, than among women (Applegarth 2006; Mahlstedt 2010). It is easy to understand how the widely presumed association between heterosexuality and fertility asserts pressure on infertile heterosexual couples to do what they can either to cover up or explain their failure to create a family in the 'natural way' (Rich 1982). For example, the DCN advice refers to heterosexuals who must initially 'grieve' their incapacity to beget their own child (Montuschi 2006: 5).

The documented impact of such assumptions on heterosexual parents, and infertile men in particular, is arguably underlined by the reported 'added-value' of forging some other kind of biological bond, such as through gestation, giving birth and breast feeding, all of which are unavailable to non-biological social fathers (Murray *et al.* 2006: 617; Shehab 2008; Landau 2008: 582; *contra* Kelly 2008–9). Within this picture of heterosexual impotence, the depersonalizing metaphors used to downplay the status of the donor betray a lack of confidence in the non-genetic parental bond. On this view, the rhetoric of exteriority highlights a fear amongst parents that the donor may usurp the father's parenting status in the child's estimation simply by virtue of the genetic relation and the donor's imagined relative potency (Lycett 2005: 814). However, we should be wary about being too hasty to settle on a gender reading of the studies. After all, other studies have found that lesbian families, while not 'dehumanizing' the donor, also tend to downplay the donor in such a way that arguably betrays anxieties. For example, the forty-five Belgian mothers interviewed by Vanfraussen *et al.* (2001) for the study cited above, all attested to having always been open and honest about the children's genetic identity. However, three quarters of them were opposed to the removal of donor anonymity, citing their worry that their family unit needed to be protected from 'interference' by a third party (i.e. the sperm donor) (2022–3).

My point here is not to determine whether the characteristics of parents' narratives about themselves or their donor can be explained by gender or sexuality etc. Nor is it to establish whether parents who choose donor conception feel comfortable or anxious about their status or their relationship with their donor. These are empirical questions which, whilst very important, are not central to the linguistic and theoretical concerns of this chapter. What I want to suggest here is that, using strategies of deconstructive reading, it is possible to pursue questions about some of the deeper connections between personal narratives and broader established philosophical and linguistic themes. Derrida's contribution to critical theory has been to reveal ways in which these connections can be analysed at the level of language. As I have very briefly outlined here, oppositional rhetoric in which the 'real' or 'authentic' is asserted against the 'artificial' or 'external', can be analysed as attempts to master the ambiguities that arise when common parlance is challenged by new and emerging social arrangements and/or technological possibilities. Parents struggle to express themselves by relying on talk of the 'real' parent, and may also use forcefully oppositional language to reinforce the externality of the donor. Given what we know about the negative feelings that some parents have about the potential impact that the revelation of donor conception might have on their family, we may read this rhetoric as revisiting Rousseau's condemnation of nature's 'dangerous supplement'. By being forced to tell a 'truth-about-the-family' that includes a starring role for the donor, parents' narratives may betray a fear amongst some that the supplement they used to make their family possible will succeed in masquerading as an integral part of that family in the minds of others, at their expense.

Conclusion

Donor-conception families show a marked ambivalence about the significance of the genetic relation that is exterior to the family. Of course there are obvious methodological problems in drawing strong implications directly from empirically-elicited narratives without re-inscribing a claim to truth and the reality of parenthood that I have tried to deconstruct. In this short critique, I have attempted to connect the narratives of parenthood emerging from empirical studies to wider concerns about truth and representation. My use of Derrida's logic of the 'dangerous supplement' – by which concepts escape simple dichotomies of presence and absence, truth and falsity, etc – is not intended to assert a further layer of truth-about-parenthood, and much less a prescriptive account of what parents should or should not say to their child. New reproductive technologies and family arrangements are reshaping both ethical and linguistic contours of society. This reshaping brings with it opportunities for positive questioning of traditional nuclear family values and assumptions, but it also creates new anxieties and ambiguities about status and relationship which must be acknowledged and understood.

Notes

1 I would like to thank Anne Quéma, Kerry Macintosh, Joanna Scheib and Paul Hastings, as well as the editors for their very helpful comments and suggestions on earlier drafts.
2 In force from April 2005.
3 See also the UK's HFE Authority Code of Practice, Eighth Edition (2009) para 20.8.

References

Applegarth, L.D., Riddle, M.P., Amoroso, K., Josephs, L., Grill, E. and Cholst, I. (2006), 'Families created by ovum donation: preliminary data on parents' thought and feelings about the donation experience and disclosure', O-133.
Boyd, S.B. (2007), 'Gendering Legal Parenthood: Bio-genetic ties, intentionality and responsibility', *Windsor Year Book of Access to Justice* 25: 63–94.

Critchley, S. (1992), *The Ethics of Deconstruction*, Oxford and Cambridge, Mass.: Blackwell.

Daniels, K.R. and Thorn, P. (2001), 'Sharing information with donor insemination offspring: a child-conception versus a family-building approach', *Human Reproduction*, 16(9): 1792–1796.

Dempsey, D. (2004), 'Donor, Father or Parent? Conceiving paternity in the Australian Family Court', *International Journal of Law, Policy and the Family*, 18: 76–102.

Derrida, J. (1992), *Act of Literature*, London and New York: Routledge.

Derrida, J. (1997), *Of Grammatology*, trans. Spivak, G.C., Baltimore: The Johns Hopkins University Press.

Diduck, A. (2007), '"If only we can find the appropriate terms to use the issue will be solved": Law, identity and parenthood', *Child and Family Law Quarterly*, 19(4): 458.

Eekelaar, J. (2006), *Family Law and Personal Life*, Oxford: Oxford University Press.

Eisenberg, M.L. (2008), 'The perceptions of donor gametes from male and female members of infertile couples', *P-209*, 90, Supplement 1.

Gurnham, D. and Miola, J. (2012), 'Reproduction, Rights and the Welfare Interests of Children: The Times They Aren't A-Changin', *King's Law Journal*, 23(1): 29-50.

Habermas, J. (2003), *The Future of Human Nature*, Cambridge: Polity.

Jones, C. (2009), 'The identification of "parents" and "siblings": New possibilities under the reformed Human Fertilisation and Embryology Act', in J. Herring, J. Wallbank, and S. Choudhry, (eds), *Rights, Gender and Family Law*, Oxford: Routledge-Cavendish).

Kass, K. (1992), 'The meaning of life – in the laboratory', in K.D. Alpern (ed.) *The Ethics of Reproduction*, Oxford: Oxford University Press: 98–116.

Kelly, F. (2002), 'Redefining Parenthood: Gay and lesbian families in the Family Court – the case of Re Patrick (2002)', *Australian Journal of Family Law*, 16: 204.

Kelly, F. (2004–5), 'Nuclear norms or fluid families? Incorporating lesbian and gay parents and their children into Canadian Family Law', *Canadian Journal of Family Law*, 133.

Kelly, F. (2008–9), '(Re)forming Parenthood: the assignment of legal parentage within planned lesbian families', *Ottawa Law Review*, 40: 185–223.

Landau, R. (2008), 'A child of "hers": older single mothers and their children conceived through IVF with both egg and sperm donation', *Fertility and Sterility*, 90(3): 577–583.

Lind, C. and Hewitt, T. (2009), 'Law and the complexities of parenting: parental status and parental function', *Journal of Social Welfare & Family Law*, 31(4): 391–406.

Lycett, E., Daniels, K., Curson, R. and Golombok, S. (2005), 'School-aged children of donor insemination: a study of parents' disclosure patterns', *Human Reproduction*, 20(3): 810–819.

Mac Dougall, K. (2007), 'Strategies for disclosure: how parents approach telling their children that they were conceived with donor gametes', *Fertility and Sterility*, 87(3): 524–533.

Mahlstedt, P.P. (2010), 'The views of adult offspring of sperm donation: essential feedback for the development of ethical guidelines within the practice of assisted reproductive technology in the United States', *Fertility and Sterility*, 93(7): 2236–2246.

McCandless, J. and Sheldon, S. (2010), 'The Human Fertilisation and Embryology Act (2008) and the Tenacity of the Sexual Family Form', *Modern Law Review*, 73(2): 175–207.

McConvill, J. and Mills, E. (2003), 'Re Patrick and the rights and responsibilities of sperm donor fathers in Australian family law', *Queensland U Tech L & Just*, 3: 298–319.

McGuinness, S. and Alghrani, A. (2008), 'Gender and Parenthood: the case for realignment', *Medical Law Review*, 16, 261–283.

Montuschi, O. (2006), *Telling and Talking about Donor Conception with 0–7 year olds: A Guide for Parents*, London: Donor Conception Network.

Murray, C. MacCallum, F. and Golombok, S. (2006), 'Egg donation parents and their children: follow-up at age 12 years', *Fertility and Sterility*, 85(3): 610–618.

Parry, A. and Doan, R.E. (1994), *Story Re-Visions: Narrative Therapy in the Postmodern World*, New York and London: the Guildford Press.

Plato (1990), *Phaedrus*, R. Hackworth (trans.), Cambridge: Cambridge University Press.

Polikoff, N. (2001–2), 'Breaking the link between biology and parental rights in planned lesbian families: when semen donors are not fathers', *Georgetown Journal of Gender and Law*, 2: 57–90.

Rich, A. (1982/2007), 'Compulsory Heterosexuality and Lesbian Experience', in R. Parker and P. Aggleton (eds), *Culture, Society and Sexuality: A Reader*, London and New York: Routledge.

Rumball, A. and Adair, V. (1999), 'Telling the story: parents' scripts for donor offspring', *Human Reproduction*, 14(5): 1392–1399.

Scheib, J.E. and Ruby, A. (2008), 'Contact among families who share the same sperm donor', *Fertility and Sterility*, 90(1): 33–43.

Shehab, D., Duff, J., Pasch, L.A., Mac Dougall, K., Scheib, J.E. and Nachtigall, R.O. (2008), 'How parents whose children have been conceived with donor gametes make their disclosure decision: contexts, influences and couple dynamics', *Fertility and Sterility*, 89(1): 183.

Sheldon, S. (2005), 'Fragmenting Fatherhood: the regulation of reproductive technologies', *Modern Law Review*, 68(4): 523–553.

Smart, C. (2007), *Personal Life: New Directions in Sociological Thinking*, Cambridge: Polity Press.

Tober, D.M. (2001), 'Semen as Gift, Semen and Goods: Reproductive workers and the market in altruism', *Body and Society*, 7(2–3): 137–160.

Vanfraussen, F., Ponjaert-Kristoffersen, I. and Brewaeys, A. (2001), 'An attempt to reconstruct children's donor concept: a comparison between children's and lesbians parents' attitudes to donor anonymity', *Human Reproduction*, 16(9): 2019–2025.

Legal and Regulatory Sources

Human Fertilisation and Embryology Act 1990, London: HMSO.

Human Fertilisation and Embryology Authority Code of Practice, Eighth Edition (2009).

The Human Fertilisation and Embryology Authority (Disclosure of Donor Information) Regulations 2004. London: HMSO.

Re D (contact and parental responsibility: lesbian mothers and known father) [2006] EWHC 2 (Fam) [England & Wales].

Re Patrick (an application concerning contact) (2002) 28 Fam LR 579 [Aus].

Thomas S. v Robin Y., 599 NYS 2d 377 (Fam Ct 1993) [US].

7

Choosing Single Motherhood?

Single women negotiating the nuclear family ideal

Susanna Graham

In recent years there has been a rise in the number of single women intentionally embarking upon motherhood without a partner. These 'Single Mothers by Choice' (SMCs), predominantly heterosexual women in their thirties and forties who are well educated and financially independent (Murray and Golombok 2005a, 2005b; Hertz 2006), can achieve motherhood via various routes but often do so through attending fertility clinics for treatment with donor sperm (Jadva 2009). As a consequence of the Human Fertilisation and Embryology (2008) Act no longer including the clause in the original (1990) Act requiring clinics to consider the child's need for a father in decisions about whether or not to offer fertility treatment, the number of British women able to embark upon single motherhood through this route is likely to increase (Jadva, 2009). However, the prospect of single women accessing fertility treatments has generated much public and political debate. Conservative MP, Iain Duncan Smith, described the bill as 'the last nail in the coffin for traditional family life' (Gamble 2009) and as another blow for fatherhood: due to its departure from the nuclear family, the ethics of the choice to embark upon motherhood without a partner is questioned.

This chapter will explore the ethical connotations surrounding single heterosexual women becoming parents through the use of assisted reproductive technologies (ARTs), namely donor sperm. It will explore how the phenomenon has been framed as challenging the nuclear family ideal, the role of men as fathers and in doing so potentially jeopardizing the welfare of children. However, by reviewing the current literature on single motherhood by choice, as well as drawing upon new empirical research exploring the motivations, experiences and decision-making of single women in the UK embarking upon motherhood through the use of donor sperm, this chapter will show that in their pursuit of motherhood these women are not outwardly rejecting the nuclear family but instead reworking their ideas about motherhood and relationships in an aim to salvage at least some of the nuclear ideal they had imagined for themselves. Finally, by examining research detailing the wellbeing of children raised by SMCs, and the experiences of women pursuing this choice, this chapter will suggest that although single motherhood by choice may not be seen as the ideal by those who embark upon it, their children are very much planned, loved and wanted and appear to be functioning well. It is perhaps the planned nature of their parenthood, their creative and flexible approach to achieving it, as well as their class and financial privilege, that allows the successful reworking of the nuclear family into what appears to be a thriving emerging family form.

Single mothers by choice: Rejecting the nuclear family ideal

Much of the concern surrounding women actively pursuing single motherhood pertains to norms and ideals about what a family *should* be like (Graham and Braverman, in press). Consequently single motherhood by choice is compared to the 'gold standard' family: the traditional nuclear family with its married mother and father and genetically related children. The choice to create a family that diverges from this norm is criticized; the nuclear family is deemed 'natural' and 'good' whilst families that diverge from it, including the single mother by choice, or circumstance[1], are depicted as 'unnatural' and 'bad' (Correia and Broderick 2009; Fineman 2009).

Of course this traditional imagery has already been challenged and redefined through social changes such as voluntary childlessness, out of wedlock births and high divorce rates leading to single parent or 'blended' families. Likewise the genetic basis of parenthood in the nuclear family has been challenged through the practice of adoption as well as infertile heterosexual couples utilizing third-party assisted conception. Nevertheless, in this context ARTs have generally been used to replicate the image, if not the reality, of the nuclear family. Donor sperm can be seen as a 'treatment' for infertility, chosen to match the physical characteristics of the infertile male partner who will assume all rights and responsibilities of the resultant child: they will be able to 'pass' as the genetically related nuclear family. However, the role of ARTs in creating single parent families can be seen to *purposely* undermine the nuclear family ideal. Single motherhood is no longer the result of circumstance, the breakdown of the nuclear family, but actively created from the outset. Through the incorporation of a medicalized route to conception, the concept of this choice and men's absence from it become more visible in the public realm. As such, the reduction of men's contribution to procreation and family life to that of a distant sperm provider has been described as 'the feminist dream come true' (Davies 2009). Moreover, in contrast to the ideology of traditional procreation, single women using donor sperm to conceive draws connotations of consumerism, 'buying a baby' (Soiseth 2008: 104), picking a 'father' from a catalogue of sperm donors. Single motherhood by choice can therefore be seen to depart not only from the physicality of the nuclear family ideal consisting of a mother and father and their genetically related children, but also the ideology behind it.

Mother and father as best

Why is the nuclear family held as the ideal and the decision to become an SMC deemed 'unnatural' and 'bad'? Much of the concern regarding single parent families arises from the poor child outcomes thought to be associated with this family form. Research has consistently shown that children raised in single parent families are more likely to experience a variety of cognitive, emotional, and behavioural problems than children living with married parents (Amato 2005; Coleman and Glenn 2009; Dunn et al. 1998; Pryor and Rodgers 2001).

However, the processes affecting single parent families, and subsequent child outcomes, may vary considerably (McLanahan and Sandefur 1994). For example, children of divorced parents tend to experience more disruption, parental conflict and 'father loss' whilst unmarried, lone mothers may experience more stress and economic insecurity (McLanahan and Sandefur 1994; Coleman and Glenn 2009). It could be assumed that SMCs will not experience such difficulties. They are typically older, financially secure professional women (Murray and Golombok 2005a,b; Hertz 2006; Jadva et al. 2009). Nor will their children experience the conflict and 'father loss' associated with the separation or divorce of their biological parents. Moreover, SMCs can be differentiated from all single mothers by circumstance through having chosen to be single mothers from the outset. Children from SMC families may therefore not experience these poor outcomes.

The importance of fathers

Despite *choosing* to enter single motherhood, the practical difficulties of parenting without a partner remain. Moreover, central to the ideal of the nuclear family is the belief that a child should have a (genetically related) mother and father. Based on stereotypes of what mothering and fathering entail, it has been presumed that children need both a mother and father for appropriate psychological and sex-role development. Studies have shown that mothers spend more time interacting with children in a nurturing and care-giving role whilst fathering involves more breadwinning, stereotypically masculine tasks and play with children (Yeung 2001; Hawkins et al. 2006; Lamb 2010). Thus the 'essential father' theory has evolved: boys need fathers to inhibit antisocial behaviour and develop appropriate masculine identities and girls need fathers to help deter promiscuity, teen pregnancy and substance abuse (Blankenhorn 1995; Popenoe 1996). However, a recent review exploring how parental gender influences child development did not identify any gender-exclusive parenting styles (Biblarz and Stacey 2010); mothers and fathers may differ in their parenting roles within the traditional division of labour but this does not mean that women can't, or won't, take on traditionally masculine parenting styles.

Men may not be required for adequate parenting but does this mean that a child does not need a *father*? The majority of children from divorced families still have contact with their fathers and will be influenced by them. Likewise, children born to lone mothers are likely to know who their father is even if they have minimal contact with him. However, when single women pursue motherhood through an unknown donor not only is there an absent physical and legal father but also no intimate knowledge of him. Proponents such as Velleman (2005) claim that such knowledge is necessary to inform a person's identity and as a consequence deem gamete donation morally wrong. Even when an open-identity[2] donor is used, offspring will not have the opportunity to obtain identifying information about their genetic father until the age of eighteen, perhaps too late to be incorporated into identity formation. The ethics of single motherhood by choice is therefore questioned not only due to its departure from the structure of the nuclear family but also by undermining the perceived importance of knowing one's genetic origins.

Single mothers by choice: Reworking the nuclear family ideal

How do SMCs feel about forming families outside the nuclear ideal? How do they perceive the choice they are making and what are their thoughts regarding the importance of fathers? By drawing upon the current literature regarding single motherhood by choice as well as in-depth interviews carried out with twenty-three single women in the UK embarking upon motherhood through the use of donor sperm[3], this section will explore how these single women conceive of their departure from the nuclear family ideal and how they rework their plans for motherhood by forming a family they hope will not be to the detriment of their future child.

'Single mothers' by choice?

In contrast to the view that SMCs purposely embark upon a parenthood that deprives their child of a father, research suggests that these women did not necessarily *choose* single motherhood. Studies have shown that the decision to pursue solo motherhood has only been taken when faced with limited prospects of finding a partner with whom to have a child in the time frame that their increasing age and decreasing fertility will allow: many SMCs would have rather become mothers in the context of a relationship (Mannis 1999; Bock 2000; Hertz 2006; Jadva *et al.* 2009; Murray and Golombok: 2005a).

My own research further elucidates the ambivalence many feel in pursuing this 'choice'. The majority of the participants experienced grief in giving up the prospect of a nuclear family, both for themselves and their future child. Single motherhood by choice was never the plan but an option that had to be incorporated into their life trajectory if they were to pursue motherhood:

> Maybe there are single women out there who are completely happy being single and never want to be in a relationship but I think underneath it this is always either Plan B or C, or even Plan Z for most people. For me this is definitely Plan Z. (Melissa[4], age thirty-six)

The majority of participants were in their late thirties or early forties when finally deciding to embark upon motherhood through the use of donor sperm, many only really starting to seriously consider it as an option when they realized that 'even if [they] met someone tomorrow it would be too late'. Even at this point, embarking upon motherhood alone was not something embraced wholeheartedly. All had put much effort into dating, many 'ferociously Internet dating', joining clubs and societies and embracing all social situations with the hope of meeting a suitable partner. As one participant, Rachel, disclosed, even when preparing for her IVF cycle she was hoping that 'any minute something [would] happen and [she] wouldn't have to go down this route'. At the heart of this ambivalence lay grief at departing from the ideal of having children with a loving partner. Abby described how she repeatedly rejected her friends' suggestions to use a sperm donor:

> It felt like, as much as it was a positive suggestion from them, it felt like they were saying you don't have to have the husband and the family unit. Why don't you just do the one bit of it on your own? And I just thought no I want what you've got. I want the whole package. My drive to have children was never, 'I want to have children at all costs and I'll do it on my own'. It was 'I want to have a family'. Me and the bloke and the children we have created together. That's what I wanted. I didn't want to go down this route.

Despite the sadness at being unable to have the family they had imagined for themselves, being single and experiencing an 'overwhelming drive' for motherhood meant these women had to overcome their grief and think about pursuing motherhood without a partner:

> It took a very long time thinking about whether it was right to do it. Because in a way I really believe that children are made from two people that love each other and want to create a family. But if that is not an option you just have to draw a way around really. Because if you are running out of time you just have to see what option you have to have a child. And then have a father. (Anna, age forty)

The nuclear family ideal is reworked: finding a partner is temporarily put on hold whilst motherhood through donor sperm is pursued.

Donors as fathers

It was not just their desire for motherhood within the context of a relationship that caused these women uneasiness about departing from the nuclear family ideal but also what their decision would mean for their future child:

> Throughout the whole thing my main concern has been whether I am being selfish and whether a child, a teenager, an adult is at some point going to turn round to me and ask 'Why did you do that? You've denied me knowing my father'. (Sally, pursuing motherhood with an open-identity donor at a UK clinic)

None of the participants mentioned poor child outcomes in single mother families as a concern about embarking upon single motherhood. However, they did feel that men and women parented in different ways and that a balance of male and female influence would be beneficial to children. As such, and in line with the existing SMC literature (see Hertz and Ferguson 1997; Hertz 2002, 2006; Jadva *et al.* 2009) all participants had thought about men in their lives who could act as male role models for their children. However, their concern regarding the absence of a father extended beyond the practical importance of a masculine influence to a more symbolic importance that included *knowing* one's father. Similar to Velleman's claim that gamete donation 'purposely severs a connection of the sort that normally informs a person's identity' (2005: 363) these women feared that using a sperm donor would be detrimental to their child's sense of identity. As Ruth who was particularly interested in her own family history stated,

> I just thought I can't bring a child into the world where it doesn't have that; it will only have half the knowledge not the whole of it. I felt it would be difficult for the child not to be able to know half of itself.

The desire for their child to 'know' themselves through 'knowing' their father initially led many participants to seek known donors who would play some role in the child's life. In doing so they were decoupling having a child from the context of a relationship but holding on to the idea of their child having a physically present father. However, finding the 'right' known donor proved difficult. Some potential known donors didn't feel comfortable taking on a 'part-time father' role whilst others were rejected because they didn't take the role seriously enough. A sperm donor was seen as preferable to a man who could, but didn't, take on an active father role; they wanted to spare their child from feelings of 'father loss'.

Normalizing the incorporation of an unknown sperm donor into their trajectory for motherhood proved difficult for most participants. One woman, when initially researching options for motherhood, was unable to even type the words 'sperm donor' into Google. Several described how they had joked with friends about resorting to donor sperm if single at a certain age but none had ever really thought they would be 'a woman who used a sperm donor'. Jessica shared her uneasiness with the situation:

> You imagine the person who you'll have a child with and they have all these things. They come with a history and friends. They come with stories and bad habits and they come with physical characteristics and favourite jumpers and the bazillion things that make up a person. And then I can strip everything away and I have some genetic fluid in a vial and that's it.

Conceiving a child with an unknown donor was far removed from the imagined conception between 'two people who love each other and want to create a family'. The absence of a physical father for their child, and the knowledge about him as a person, was a stumbling block for many: they wanted their child to have a father, not some 'genetic fluid in a vial'.

There was much complexity and ambivalence regarding the meaning of the sperm donor and his role in enabling this family form (see also Gurnham, this volume, for a more detailed discussion of the ambiguous role sperm donors play in family formation). However, the donor was a visible actor (albeit symbolically) in the majority of participants' pursuit of motherhood:

> Some people think it should be anonymous completely and so it's just you – you are the parent and there is nothing else, just a blank. And I'm saying that there is never just a blank because you come from one other person too. You can't be a blank. (Anna, importing open-identity sperm into the UK)

Kirkman (2004) has proposed that in the absence of another man claiming the role of father (as is the case where donor sperm is used by heterosexual couples), the sperm donor is more likely to be publicly represented as the child's father. Indeed, for the eleven women in the present study who had imported sperm from abroad, they had done so in order to seek information that could fill the 'blank' left by the absent partner and father: they wanted to be able to tell their child as much as possible about their 'father' and felt limited by the amount of information available about UK donors. In contrast to the fear that single women accessing donor sperm is a 'blow to fatherhood' and 'the feminist dream come true', it appears that even when single women use 'genetic fluid in a vial' to conceive, this fluid is personified in an attempt to recreate an image of a father. From long medical and family histories to baby pictures and audio-tapes of the donor talking about himself, the European and American sperm banks give single women an opportunity to *choose* a particular donor. However, despite the eugenic fears that this choice may ignite (see Hanson 2001; Pennings 2000) and the consumerist connotations of 'buying' 'designer babies', the most commonly cited reason for choosing a particular donor was that he sounded 'nice' and 'friendly'. Scheib *et al.* (2000) also found that factors such as whether the donor sounded like someone she or her child would like to get to know and whether he sounded like a good, well-rounded person, were important criteria in choosing open-identity donors. The single women in this study were found to be more likely to care about such matters than partnered women (whether in a heterosexual or lesbian relationship) when choosing their donor. Perhaps knowledge about the donor as a person is more important for women where there will not be a second parent present in the resulting child's day-to-day life. For the participants in the current study, the extra information the imported sperm provided was certainly reassuring to the women themselves but more importantly was vital information for their child, both for self knowledge and identity formation, and telling others about their 'father':

> I know a lot about his dad, his donor. Of course, it's not the same as having their dad there day to day but it's more than it could have been. Also it's easier for the child now. They can say, 'My dad is a teacher and lives in America' rather than, 'I don't know what he does. I don't know how tall he is'. (Anita, importing open-identity sperm into the UK)

Along with the male role models who will be physically present, these women hope that the stories and images they can provide about their child's donor during their childhood will mean they have adequately reworked the fatherhood expectation of the nuclear family into their own family form.

Whereas some women felt it was important to have chosen a particular donor and often likened this to choosing a partner, others felt comfortable being assigned a donor and knowing little about him as they felt this reflected the 'randomness' of falling in love:

> It almost introduces that random element of the random man that you meet. You wouldn't line up ten men and decide which to marry. (Natasha, using a UK clinic's open-identity donor selected for her by staff)

Whether reifying or downplaying the significance of choosing a donor, these women were trying to recreate aspects of conventional procreation in their own plans for motherhood. Moreover, even when the significance attached to donors was reduced, the importance of fatherhood remained prominent; instead of reifying the donor as a father figure, fatherhood was perceived as a purely social role. Claire described how her ambivalence towards donors enabled her to shift from using an open-identity donor when seeking treatment abroad to subsequently using a cheaper, truly anonymous donor:

> I don't think it's a father. Whilst I listen here with British opinion being able to meet the donor, I think what are you going to find out about that person in eighteen years' time? They're never going to be a father. They're still just going to be a sperm donor and what benefit does that bring? You might find out they are in prison or they've died or they are this or that. I'm just not 100 per cent convinced there is a particular benefit to that. I can see it from a genetic, family history point of view, but, no, to me a donor is a donor and that's the end of it. And I think you've got to think about it like that otherwise you are just kidding yourself and someone else.

For Claire reworking a sperm donor into a family narrative is a step too far; a sperm donor will never be a father; fatherhood is not purely genetic in origin and nor should a sperm donor be personified.

Temporary single motherhood

Whatever their thoughts about donors, all participants in the current study hoped for a partner in the future. Indeed, the importance these women placed on relationships actually led them to see single motherhood by choice as a positive step towards a lasting partnership. Focusing on motherhood at the same time as trying to find the 'right' relationship was deemed incompatible. Such a mindset meant they were judging potential men as fathers rather than partners, forcing a discussion about children very early in the relationship. With their perceived dating life longer than their reproductive life, pursing motherhood alone was seen to 'buy time' so that in the future they would once again be able to concentrate on finding a partner:

> It would be nice to meet someone in a relaxed way, without that pressure and not sort of panic and get together with someone purely for that purpose but be with someone because you love them and know them and don't want anything from them. (Rachel, 38)

Many expected that the single nature of their motherhood would only be temporary. Moreover, by pursuing motherhood through sperm donation, rather than having a child in a short-term relationship, they felt they would not only spare themselves and their children the pain and conflict of a break up, but also make it easier to form a relationship in the future without the presence of a 'messy ex'. Given the current high divorce rates (see Coleman and Glenn 2009) these women saw their own family building option as preferable to a temporary nuclear family. Furthermore, many of these women hoped a future partner would adopt their donor-conceived child who lacked a legal and present father. The idea of becoming a mother through sperm donation and then finding a partner allows them to come as close as possible to the image of the nuclear family ideal they had imagined for themselves.

Single motherhood by choice: A legitimate family form

Even if single women creating families using donor sperm do not purposely reject *the* nuclear family, nor the position of men within it, they still create families that diverge from the form believed optimal for children's welfare. Is the welfare of children in this family form jeopardized?

A long-term follow up of a small sample of single-parent families in the UK where the child had been raised since the first year of life without a father, or father-figure, in a financially stable family home, were found to be similar to traditional families in a range of measures assessing quality of parenting and child psychological adjustment at age six (Golombok *et al.* 1997), twelve (MacCallum and Golombok 2004) and eighteen (Golombok and Badger 2010). In early adulthood those from solo mother households showed lower levels of anxiety, depression, hostility and problematic alcohol use than their counterparts from traditional families and the same levels as those raised in lesbian couple families, indicating that this family form may actually be 'better' for children than the nuclear family held as ideal.

Initial studies specifically assessing the psychological wellbeing of children conceived to single women using donor sperm have shown they are functioning well. Murray and Golombok (2005a,b) found these children showed fewer emotional and behavioural problems than a matched comparison of DI children in a heterosexual two-parent family at the age of one, and again at two. Likewise, donor-conceived children to single women in the US (Chan *et al.* 1998) were found to be functioning well at age seven and Weissenberg *et al.* (2007) reported the socio-emotional development of children born to Israeli SMCs to be within normal limits. In addition, research from families headed by lesbian parents has challenged the heteronormative assumptions underlying theories about what children need from their families, leading to the perspective that child wellbeing depends more on family processes and parenting abilities than structure (Patterson 2009; Stacey and Biblarz 2010). Given that SMCs have been found to express positive parenting skills (Murray and Golombok 2005a,b), in fact showing greater joy and pleasure in their child and lower levels of anger than their married counterparts, as well as not suffering from the financial instability deemed to be the most significant factor influencing the poor child outcomes in single parent families (McLanahan and Sandefur 1994), the evidence so far suggests that the SMC family can provide a positive environment for child wellbeing.

Despite being the sole parent, SMCs have described themselves as well supported (Hertz and Ferguson 1997; Jadva *et al.* 2009). Furthermore, a few of the participants in my own study actually anticipated that the absence of a second parent might be an advantage of single motherhood by choice. Rather than depending upon the self-contained, nuclear family, they would be forced to create a robust social network and as a result their child would be exposed to many different people and personalities.

In addition, all participants were keen to stress the planned nature of their motherhood. Although Anna felt a lot of grief about becoming an SMC, she could also see how her choice could impact positively upon any future child:

> I also know that these kids are going to have so much better parents than so many. They are really lucky, they're going to have a really mature mother who has really thought this through and has thought of every angle, really wants it and is going to put everything in. They've got a better start than lots of kids.

Age, emotional maturity and financial stability, characteristics of this population, are marshalled to legitimize this path to motherhood. Bock (2000), described how SMCs in a support group in California used such characteristics, as well as the term 'single mother by *choice*', to distinguish themselves from other single mothers. Although ambivalent about whether they had actually *chosen* this family form, the participants in the current study were keen that others should know that they had considered all the implications, especially for the child, of their route to motherhood. The intentional and planned manner of their pursuit of parenthood, the support of others, as well as the love and time they felt they could give a child became incorporated into their ideals for family life. As one participant, Sally, disclosed, she stopped asking herself whether embarking upon single motherhood by choice was right when she realized it wasn't about families being 'black and white, right and wrong' but whether it was an 'OK' decision for the child. She hoped it was.

Regardless of whether the departure from the nuclear family is chosen or not, single motherhood by choice is clearly a planned route to parenthood where the potential child seems to be at the forefront of decision-making. There are increasing numbers of self help books and online forums promoting it as a family building option, as well as prominent media coverage including films and soap operas incorporating single motherhood through sperm donation into their storylines. Perhaps as this and other emerging family forms, both by choice and circumstance, gain prominence in the public imagination, such family forms will no longer need to be justified against the nuclear family. Whereas becoming a SMC currently seems to be a last resort for older women finding themselves without a partner but desiring motherhood, as this and other emerging family forms become more known and accepted within society, perhaps women will be able to pursue single motherhood with less trepidation and regret at its departure from the nuclear family.

Notes

1 The term single mother by circumstance is used here to describe mothers who have become single through separation, divorce or death of a partner, or through an unplanned pregnancy where the genetic father is not involved. In contrast, Jane Mattes, founder of the US national organization 'Single Mothers by Choice', defines the concept as 'a woman who decided to have or adopt a child, knowing she would be her child's sole parent, at least at the outset' (Mattes 2011). In this chapter only single motherhood by choice as pursued through ARTs will be discussed.

2 An open-identity donor, also known as an identity-release donor, agrees to have his identity released to offspring if the offspring request it after the age of eighteen.

3 This data has been gathered as part of PhD research exploring the decision-making and experiences of single women embarking upon motherhood through the use of donor sperm. These women all identified as heterosexual and were between

the ages of thirty-three and forty-six. All were pursuing motherhood by accessing fertility clinics for treatment with sperm from unknown donors.

4   Pseudonyms have been used throughout this chapter. Any identifying information has been removed or altered to protect the identity of participants and maintain confidentiality.

References

Amato, P. (2005), 'The impact of family formation on the cognitive, social and emotional well-being of the next generation', *Future of Children*, 15: 75–96.

Biblarz, T. and Stacey, J. (2010), 'How does the gender of parents matter?', *Journal of Marriage and Family*, 72: 3–22.

Blankenhorn, D. (1995), *Fatherless America: Confronting our most urgent social problem*. New York: Basic Books.

Bock, J. (2000), 'Doing the right thing? Single Mothers by Choice and the struggle for legitimacy', *Gender and Society*, 14: 62–86.

Chan, R.W., Raboy, B. and Patterson, C.J. (1998), 'Psychosocial adjustment among children conceived via donor insemination by lesbian and heterosexual mothers', *Child Development*, 69: 443–457.

Coleman, L. and Glenn, F. (2009), *When couples part: Understanding the consequences for adults and children*, London: One Plus One.

Correia, H. and Broderick, P. (2009), 'Access to reproductive technologies by single women and lesbians: Social representations and public debate', *Journal of Community & Applied Social Psychology*, 19: 241–256.

Davies, B., 'Daddies be Damned! Who are the British women who think fathers are irrelevant?', Daily Mail, 31 October 2009.

Dunn, J., Deater-Deckard, K., Pickering, K., O'Connor, T.G. and Golding, J. (1998), 'Children's adjustment and prosocial behaviour in step-, single-parent, and non-stepfamily settings: Findings from a community study', *Journal of Child Psychology and Psychiatry*, 39:1083–1095.

Fineman, M. (2009), 'The sexual family', in M.A. Fineman, J.E. Jackson and A.P. Romero (eds), *Feminist and queer legal theory: Intimate encounters, uncomfortable conversations*, London: Ashgate.

Gamble, N. (2009), 'Considering the need for a father: the role of clinicians in safeguarding family values in UK fertility treatment', *Reproductive Biomedicine Online*. 19: 15–18.

Golombok, S. and Badger, S. (2010), 'Children raised in mother-headed families from infancy: a follow-up of children of lesbian and single heterosexual mothers at early adulthood', *Human reproduction*, 25: 150–7.

Golombok, S., Tasker, F. and Murray, C. (1997), 'Children raised in fatherless families from infancy: Family relationships and the socio-emotional development of children of lesbian, single and heterosexual mothers', *Journal of child psychology and psychiatry*, 38: 783–791.

Graham, S. and Braverman, A. (In Press), 'Solo and selective: Men and women choosing to become Single Parents by Choice', in P.M Richards, J. Appleby and G. Pennings (eds), *Reproductive Donation: Policy, Practice and Bioethics*, Cambridge: Cambridge University Press.

Hanson, F. (2001), 'Donor insemination: Eugenic and feminist implications', *Medical Anthropology Quarterly*, 15: 287–311.

Hawkins, D., Amato, P. and King, V. (2006), 'Parent-adolescent involvement: The relative influence of parent gender and residence', *Journal of Marriage and Family*, 68: 125–136.

Hertz, R. (2002), 'The father as an idea: A challenge to kinship boundaries by single mothers', *Symbolic Interaction*, 25: 1–31.

Hertz, R. (2006), *Single by chance, mothers by choice. How women are choosing parenthood without marriage and creating the new American family*, New York: Oxford University Press.

Hertz, R. and Ferguson, F. (1997), 'Kinship strategies and self-sufficiency among single mothers by choice: Post modern family ties', *Qualitative Sociology*, 20: 187–209.

Jadva, V., Badger, S., Morrissette, M. and Golombok, S. (2009), '"Mom by choice, single by life's circumstance..." Findings from a large-scale survey of the experiences of single mothers by choice', *Human fertility*, 12: 175–84.

Kirkman, M. (2004), 'Saviours and satyrs: Ambivalence in narrative meanings of sperm provision', *Culture, Health and Sexuality*, 6: 319–335.

Lamb, M.E. (2010), 'How do fathers influence children's development? Let me count the ways', in M.E. Lamb (ed.), *The Role of the Father in Child Development*, Hoboken, New Jersey: John Wiley & Sons.

MacCallum, F. and Golombok, S. (2004), 'Children raised in fatherless families from infancy: a follow-up of children of lesbian and single heterosexual mothers at early adolescence', *Journal of Child Psychology and Psychiatry*, 45: 1407–1419.

Mannis, V. S. (1999), 'Single Mothers by Choice', *Family Relations*, 48: 121–128

Mattes, J. (2011), Single Mothers by Choice, http://www.singlemothersbychoice.com/about (accessed April 2011).

McLanahan, S. and Sandefur, G. (1994), *Growing up with a single parent: What hurts, what helps*, Cambridge, Massachusetts: Harvard University Press.

Murray, C. and Golombok, G. (2005a), 'Going it alone: Solo mothers and their infants conceived by donor insemination', *American Journal of Orthopsychiatry*, 2: 242–253.

Murray, C. and Golombok, S. (2005b), 'Solo mothers and their donor insemination infants: follow-up at age 2 years', *Human Reproduction*, 20: 1655–60.

Patterson, C. (2009), 'Children of Lesbian and Gay Parents: Psychology, Law, and Policy', *American Psychologist*, 64: 727–736.

Pennings, G. (2000), 'The right to choose your donor: a step towards commercialization or a step towards empowering the patient?', *Human Reproduction*, 15: 508–514.

Popenoe, D. (1996), *Life without father: Compelling new evidence that fatherhood and marriage are indispensible for the good of children and society*, New York: Free Press.

Pryor, J. and Rodgers, B. (2001), *Children in Changing Families: Life after Parental Separation*, Oxford: Blackwell Publishing.

Scheib, J., Riordan, M. and Shaver, P. (2000), 'Choosing between anonymous and identity-release sperm donors: Recipient and donor characteristics', *Reproductive Technologies*, 10: 50–58.

Soiseth, A. (2008), *Choosing you: Deciding to have a baby on my own*, Berkley: Seal Press.

Velleman, D. (2005), 'Family History', *Philosophical Papers*, 34: 357–378.

Weissenberg, R., Landau, R. and Madgar, I. (2007), 'Older single mothers assisted by sperm donation and their children', *Human Reproduction*, 22: 2784–91.

Yeung, W.J., Sandberg, J.F., Davis-Kean, P.E. and Hofferth, S.L. (2001), 'Children's time with fathers in intact families', *Journal of Marriage and Family*, 63: 136–154.

8

Surrogacy

Reinscribing or pluralizing understandings of *family*?

Mary Lyndon Shanley and Sujatha Jesudason

Introduction

Surrogacy – the practice whereby a woman agrees to bear a child that she will relinquish at birth to the intended parent(s) who commissioned her pregnancy – may seem either to reinforce the norm of the genetically based nuclear family or radically to reshape dominant understandings of 'family'. In the relatively short span of twenty-five years since surrogacy entered the world of infertility treatment, it has gone from being regarded as a vehicle for heterosexual married couples to form a family that resembles as closely as possible the one that would have been formed through sexual relations between the parents, to being a potential means for expanding the array of families and family-like relationships.

Given the depth and rapidity of these changes, it is not surprising that the ways people understand the place of surrogacy in family formation is by no means uncomplicated or uncontested. These anxieties and concerns extend across the political spectrum and confound the usual divisions of 'left' and 'right', 'progressive' and 'conservative'. Some social conservatives who seek to maintain the family as a lifelong union between a man and a woman and their biological or adopted children see the use of surrogates by married couples as a way to bring a 'priceless child' into a family. And some feminists and queer theorists who are happy to break down what they see as the exclusionary and repressive structures of the heterosexual nuclear family reject surrogacy on one or more of the grounds that it oppresses women, commodifies what should not be for sale, overvalues the genetic tie, reinforces class and racial privilege, and ignores children's wellbeing.

The apprehensions about surrogacy, on both the right and the left, signal uncertainty about the norms and boundaries society places on definitions of family and family formation practices, and we should pay close attention to the disquiet they invoke. What people think affects what they – and society – do, and what people do affects how they – and society – think. We agree with

Valerie Hartouni that 'the issue with respect to the panoply of new reproductive practices and processes is not whether these new practices are good or bad; [but] rather, how we should think them and how they will think us' (Hartouni 1997: 132, quoting Marilyn Strathern). Whether surrogacy leads to a re-inscription or expansion of the traditional nuclear family will depend on the practices and regulations that stem from our collective understanding.

In shaping that understanding it is crucial that theorists, practitioners, and policy-makers listen carefully to those directly engaged in surrogacy: the intended parents, the surrogates, the egg and sperm (gamete) donors, and offspring. Until more of their accounts and reflections on their experience are available, our thoughts are provisional, but there is enough material on surrogacy to indicate directions in which exploration is needed. Our examination of surrogacy here is rooted in the American context; while urgent and important attention needs to be paid to cross border surrogacy practices and arrangements, that analysis requires attention to globalization, power disparities, gender relations and cultural clashes in more ways than we can undertake here.

We contend that society should regard surrogacy as akin to other practices like adoption, step parenting, parenting in blended families, co-parenting in same-sex families, and foster parenting; all of these create parent-child relationships other than through sexual coitus, and reconfigure to some extent the traditional nuclear family. By contrast, when surrogacy is used to imitate the traditional family it moves into troubling territory. There is a risk of undervaluing the gestational labour and caregiving relationship between the surrogate and fetus. Whole new sets of relationship are being created through surrogacy that we are just beginning to understand: relationships between surrogates and intended parents, between the surrogate and the fetus, between the gamete donors and future child, and between the surrogate's family and the intended parents and future child.

To be forthright about our own position, we do not think that surrogacy is inevitably or inherently unethical, but find that current ways of conceptualizing and understanding what surrogacy 'is about' run grave risks of contributing to the exploitation of individual surrogates and the oppression of women as a group, and are often inadequate, misleading and harmful representations of the human relationships and responsibilities entailed in this kind of family formation. We begin our discussion by noting the consequences of the fact that much of the discourse about surrogacy is shaped by the medical context that focuses attention on the medical treatment of infertility rather than on the social issue of family formation. This framework also influences legal discourse that examines the ethics and logistics of assigning legal parenthood in surrogate arrangements. Medical and legal discourses encourage a view of surrogacy as a contractual agreement between individuals or as a 'gift of life'. Both these conceptualizations focus on adult individuals and fail to capture the complexity of the relationships among intentional parents, surrogate (and her family), and the person who will come into being as a result of their joint actions. We argue that a different framework is needed, one that draws attention to the profound interconnectedness, relationship and dependency that surrogacy involves; focuses on the wellbeing of the child; and publicly affirms a pluralism of family forms.

Traditional frameworks: Contract and gift

Heterosexual couples turn to surrogacy in the course of medical treatment for biological infertility either because the woman lacks a womb or has suffered repeated miscarriages, and gay couples or single men turn to surrogacy to deal with what has become known as 'social infertility', their inability to have a biologically related child without a gestational surrogate and in some cases gamete donor(s). Likening it to 'The Inferno', Melanie Thernstrom described her struggle with infertility as finding herself in a 'dark woods, the right road lost' (Thernstrom 2010, 30). For people like her, surrogacy is usually the 'last resort' to bring a child into a family.

People either find a surrogate themselves (sometimes a friend or relative) or work through an agency that screens applicants and creates dossiers from which intended parents select a candidate. The intended parents often meet the selected surrogate (and perhaps her husband and children) in person. They settle on a fee (typically $30,00–$60,000), and draw up a contract. The contract may state expectations concerning 'lifestyle' issues like diet, smoking, exercise, and travel, and more serious matters such as whether the couple or surrogate may request (or demand) termination of a pregnancy. The surrogate then enters the medical realm for the testing, hormone injections, embryo transfer, and post-transfer monitoring.

Doctors whose practice includes in vitro fertilisation (IVF) and surrogacy understand themselves to be bound by the norms of medical ethics. Psychological evaluation and counselling for all parties seem warranted in order to insure fully informed consent. The American College of Obstetricians and Gynecologists argues that it is imperative that both the commissioning parents and the surrogate have separate legal counsel, since 'unless independent legal representation and mental health counselling are mandated, women serving as surrogate mothers may be particularly vulnerable to being exploited' (ACOG 2008, 3). Some people suggest that the surrogate have her own doctor monitor the pregnancy, since the intended parents' doctor, in an effort to achieve a birth, might tolerate risks that the surrogate's physician might not accept.

It is important to note that the focus of all these proposals is on forging a mutually acceptable agreement among adults. The biomedical solution to the unfulfilled longing to raise a child makes 'patients' of both intended parents and surrogate (and gamete providers, if any) (Mamo 2007), and the role of ethicists and oversight bodies (medical associations, bar associations, the state) is to insure that the participants be protected from harm and that their consent be fully informed and not subject to any kind of coercion. The background picture or understanding of what is going on is the coming together of rational and self-interested parties to agree on the terms of their cooperation and future action. Medical regulation of assisted reproductive technologies (ARTs), Naomi Cahn remarks, are 'focused on gamete safety or truth in advertising, [and] cater only to the parents as patients, not to the families they are creating' (Cahn 2012: 49). Because egg extraction, IVF, and introduction of the embryo into another woman's womb are medical procedures, it is easy to overlook the fact that the *goal* of treatment is not medical (these procedures do not after all, 'cure' infertility), but rather social – the establishment of a parent-child relationship.

In addition to articulating expectations, anticipating disagreement, and avoiding discord, the surrogacy contract is intended to make it clear that the surrogate is not assuming the role of a 'mother', and to establish the new family on firm ground. This is a significant departure from both cultural and legal traditions that regarded the woman who gave birth as the child's mother. By contrast, the surrogacy contract specifies that the intended parents will be the child's legal parents and the contract is the instrument by which motherhood is transferred from the woman who has borne, to the woman who will raise, the child.

In the early days of surrogacy, married heterosexual couples turned to alternative insemination to have the surrogate conceive using the husband's sperm; the surrogate therefore had both a genetic and gestational tie to the fetus. (Some critics argued that a surrogate should not be called a 'surrogate mother' but rather a 'surrogate wife'.) In the 'Baby M' case, the New Jersey Supreme Court ruled that the surrogate mother, Mary Beth Whitehead, and the intended father, William Stern, were the legal parents of the child, citing the fact that Whitehead was the genetic as well as the gestational mother. The judge granted custody to Stern and his wife Elizabeth, and visitation rights to Whitehead, based on his perception of the best interests of the child. But as gestational surrogacy has eliminated the genetic tie between surrogate and fetus, the surrogate's claim to be recognised as a legal parent has diminished; gestation is characterized as a kind of labour and the surrogacy contract as an employment contract.

Concerns about the ethics of surrogacy have grappled with the assignment of parental rights through contract from the outset. Barbara Katz Rothman condemns contract pregnancy as a manifestation of 'liberal philosophy [that] is an articulation of the values of technological society, [reflecting] the vision of everything, including our very selves, as resources' (Rothman 1989: 63). Selling reproductive labour risks turning a woman into simply a vessel or carrier, distorting or denying the bonds (physical, psychological, and emotional) between mother and fetus (Anderson 1990: 81). Even without a genetic link between surrogate and fetus, argues Carole Pateman, the 'logic of contract as exhibited in surrogate motherhood' is to 'sweep away any intrinsic relation between the female owner, her body and reproductive capacities', an extreme instance of the alienation of the self entailed in wage labour (Pateman 1988: 216). Against this position, other feminists like Debra Satz argue that people who 'conceptualize the problem with pregnancy contracts in terms of the degradation of the mother-fetus relations' often read into the social practice of pregnancy a 'maternal instinct, a sacrosanct bonding that takes place between a mother and her child-to-be' (Satz 2010: 22). Satz insists that this essentializes both women and mothers; not all women want to become mothers, and not all mothers feel an indissoluble or sacred bond to their fetuses or children. Rather, both having and raising children are not simply 'natural' functions for women, but should be the result of conscious and informed decisions that effect not only their bodily experience, but also of their life's trajectory.

The role of liberal ideology and 'contract' in legitimating contracts for procreation, and in creating and sustaining the distinction between gestational surrogate and 'mother', is striking. The surrogacy contract relies on individual choice, consent and market mechanisms to create a framework that makes assigning legal parenthood predictable and unambiguous. Charis Thompson captures the way in which liberal premises make the transmission of parenthood from gestational surrogate to intended parents possible in her account of the surrogacy agreement between intended parents, Ute and her husband, and the gestational surrogate, Vanessa. Ute and her husband took Vanessa out for meals and bought her fancy clothes during her pregnancy; Vanessa spoke of how exhilarating the intimacy with the couple was during the pregnancy. But after birth Ute and her husband gradually cut off their relationship with Vanessa. Thompson comments that they regarded their relationship to Vanessa as a labour contract regulated by the norms of capitalism: they paid Vanessa and appropriated the product of her reproductive labour, the baby. '[O]nce the baby was born, Vanessa was in many ways just like any other instrumental intermediary that had been involved in establishing the pregnancy, such as the embryologist or even the petri dish. ... Because she had been commercially contracted, the logic of disconnection was the same' (Thompson 2005: 165). In her study of surrogacy, anthropologist Hélena Ragoné speculated that the primacy of the 'hegemonic biogenetic model of kinship' (the 'blood tie') in US ideologies of kinship made intended parents more solicitous of and likely to maintain contact with traditional surrogates than with gestational surrogates (Ragoné 1999: 74–76). The trend to gestational surrogacy could therefore promote the notion that once the contract is fulfilled a 'clean break' between surrogate and the intentional parents' family is appropriate.

Arms-length liberal market transactions do not always remain arms-length, however, and create highly complex human relationships. Despite the crucial role of the surrogacy contract, both surrogates and intended parents use the language of 'gift' to describe the nature of the surrogate's contribution. One intended mother wrote that she 'kept having this random baby fantasy that M is pregnant during Christmas time and I wake up Christmas morning to a phone call from her in which she plays our baby's heartbeat for us. There is nothing greater that could be under the Christmas tree' (Sara 10/13/09 http://mumbaimaybe.blogspot.com/). Surrogates also use the language of gift because 'it reinforces the idea that having a child for someone is an act that cannot be compensated' (Ragoné 1999: 71). Ragoné speculates that surrogates speak of their gift to the intended parents because 'gift' suggests that the relationship survives despite the monetary exchange. 'Even though surrogates are discouraged from thinking of their relationship to the couple as a permanent one, surrogates recognise that they are creating a state of enduring solidarity between themselves and their couples' (Ragoné 1999: 71). And in acknowledging that the surrogate is giving them the 'gift' of a child, the intended parents seem to 'accept a permanent state of indebtedness to their surrogate' (Ragoné 1999: 72).

It is crucial to recognise that neither the language of 'choice' – central to our society's understanding of contract – nor the language of 'gift' does away with the enormous disparity in economic status between most surrogates and intended parents. Women who become surrogates in the US are not desperately poor (because intentional parents want women who are in good health and with whom they feel comfortable, and class is relevant to both these considerations). But a payment of $30,000 is a significant enticement to a potential surrogate. Because surrogacy is not covered by medical insurance, the out-of-pocket cost of at least $100,000 to the intentional parents means that it is a practice only the rich can afford. Money translates into political and social resources and power, and the disparity of wealth means that the intentional parents have many more resources to enforce their will than does the surrogate. (Economic disparity is far greater and so more worrisome in most inter-country surrogacy.) Additionally, in traditional surrogacy, intentional parents sought surrogates of their race; with gestational surrogacy a woman of any race will do since the physical characteristics of the surrogate will not be passed on to the child. Clearly the demands of social justice require that surrogacy be regulated in order to limit the vulnerability of surrogates and of the persons who come into being as a result of surrogacy (ACRJ 2005). To conceptualize surrogacy adequately more is needed than choosing between the competing images of surrogacy that portray it as a free market transaction or a priceless gift (understood by different commentators as either contributing to women's autonomy or their oppression). Fortunately, new understandings that attend to the complex relationships formed by surrogacy, to the wellbeing of the future person, and to the new family form that surrogacy creates are emerging, in large part from participants themselves.

Emergent frameworks: Collaboration and care

Thinking about surrogacy not as just a strategy for 'solving' infertility and creating a legal parent-child relationship for the intended parents brings into focus often overlooked dimensions of the practice. Both intended parents and surrogates regard the surrogate's 'job' as protecting and nurturing a developing life before separating from it at birth. Bringing someone into being through IVF and gestational surrogacy is an act both of production using raw materials (gametes), technology and incubation, and also of caregiving. To provide that care requires the cooperation and collaboration of intended parents and surrogate akin to that in other non-traditional, non-nuclear families, and suggests the need for both specific medical and legal regulations regarding the formation of families by surrogacy.

The distancing that takes place through the medicalization of surrogacy and the contracting of the surrogate's body and labour is complicated by the fact that the 'product' of the labour is a human being who develops not simply within but as part of the surrogate's body. Our everyday language reflects the distinctness of mother and fetus when it says that pregnant women are 'expecting' the babies that doctors 'deliver' to them (Rothman 1989: 100; Young 1990: 167). Pregnant woman and fetus, however, are not yet, or are not in every way, distinct entities; nor are they the same. Adrienne Rich describes the fluidity of the boundary between self and other during pregnancy: 'In early pregnancy, the stirring of the foetus felt like ghostly tremors of my own body, later like the movements of a being imprisoned within me; but both sensations were my sensations, contributing to my own sense of physical and psychic space' (Rich 1976: 47). Iris Young points out that the pregnant woman 'experiences herself as a source and participant in a creative process. Though she does not plan and direct it, neither does it merely wash over her; rather, she is this process, this change' (Young 1990: 167). Mother and fetus are connected through placental tissue and a constant exchange of blood and body fluids. They are at one and the same time distinct and interrelated entities, and during the period of gestation the woman's wellbeing and that of the fetus are inextricably related. In order to take care of their child, the intended parents must promote the wellbeing of the surrogate.

We don't yet have the language to describe the many new relationships that form during surrogacy between gamete donors, parents, children and surrogates. For example, Melanie Thernstrom calls her egg donor 'Fairy Goddonor' and suggests labelling the relationship between the surrogates' children and her children born through surrogacy 'gestational siblings', 'they don't share a mother, father or genes, but they were carried in the same body and they learned its fathomless chemical language' (Thernstrom 2011: 33).

The closest many surrogates come to describing the relationship between themselves and the child born is that of an aunt with her nephew or niece, or a friend's child. Surrogate Mom writes in her blog, 'Do I love the first little boy I gave birth to? Absolutely! But like an aunt loves her nephew. I'll spoil him when I see him and on birthdays and holidays... but beyond that I'm not worried about him' (Surrogate Mom 01/29/10 http://surrolife.blogspot. com/). TXSurromom uses a similar image: 'I respect any IPs [intended parents] that need their privacy afterwards (although I'm secretly thrilled that E&J want me to be sort of aunt-like figure!) but it warms my heart to know that I'll get to see their baby hit his/her milestones!' (TXSurromom 06/29/10 http://www.txsurromom.blogspot.com/). Of course, although these surrogates hope to be an 'aunt-like figure' in the child's life, they have no control over what the relationship will be in the future, and might find themselves being treated as an 'instrumental intermediary' once the baby is born.

Jennifer Parks suggests that caregiving activity should include both of the intended parents (not simply the intended mother) spending time with the pregnant woman during the course of the pregnancy. While Parks is writing about intercountry surrogacy, her observations are relevant to domestic arrangements as well:

> On one account, the couple forms a contract with the relevant parties, makes payment, and returns to their home country until the point of birth, at which time they go back to pick up the 'product' of their contract. On another account, the couple develop a relationship with the surrogate, providing not just monetary, but other forms of support; they are physically present for periods of the pregnancy. The attitude of care and concern for their surrogate and their child is instantiated in their physical presence, and establishes (for emotional, relational, as well as legal purposes) the fact of their intention to parent. Such actions recognise that the story that will be told to their child one day could significantly impact his or her identity: a couple cannot simply claim 'we wanted you and welcomed you', but have to express that moral attitude in action. Being present and available for the pregnant surrogate long before the point of birth establishes the child-to-be as a particular other to whom the commissioning couple have an obligation of care and concern. (Parks 2010, 337–38)

The reasons to care for the surrogate during pregnancy have to do with both her (and therefore the fetus's) physical wellbeing, and with the psychological and emotional wellbeing of all parties engaged in this collaboration to create a new family.

Parks' consideration of the 'narrative difference' the commissioning couple's physical presence during pregnancy makes for those who are born from a surrogacy arrangement brings those persons – who are far too often ignored in discussions – into sharp focus. In thinking about their possible concerns and interests, it is important to keep in mind that they are not simply 'children', but persons who will become adults for whom personal and social identity are of life-long importance.

Two interests of these offspring cry out for recognition and regulations: they have a right to full information about those who contributed to their conception and birth, and to parent(s) who are unquestionably legally responsible for them. Adult adoptees have performed valuable service in making the public aware of the importance of open records; recently, a lawsuit in British Columbia declared that donor conceived offspring have equal rights with adoptees to know their genetic forebears (*Pratten v. British Columbia* 2011). In 2011, Washington became the first US state to ban anonymous sperm and egg donation. When offspring conceived from Washington sperm and egg donation banks or agencies reach age eighteen they can access their donors' medical histories and their full names, unless a donor has specifically refused to have his or her name released. While secrecy or deception about whether a surrogate bore the child is unlikely (the fact that the child's mother was not pregnant is obvious), offspring should have a right to learn not only the fact that they were carried by a surrogate, but also the identity of the surrogate and of any gamete provider. As Parks argues, the child born of surrogacy deserves 'the same opportunity to be enveloped in a family history and narrative as their naturally conceived counterparts', a narrative that begins not at birth but well before. It is not simply medical information that is at stake, but a full sense of social location (Blythe and Firth 2009; Ravitsky 2010). Melanie Thernstrom points out that the family narrative can be important to the parents as well: 'When I tried to think about why I don't want to have donor-and-surrogacy amnesia, it isn't that it seems unfair to them (although it is), but that it erases our own experience of how our children came to be' (Thernstrom 2011: 43).

Persons born through surrogacy also have a right to legally recognised parents. In many jurisdictions legal parentage is clear, but some states do not have statutes that assign legal parentage in surrogacy. It is crucial to have the intentional parents be unequivocally responsible for the person from the moment of birth; cases continue to arise in which intended parents refuse to take custody because of a change of mind or marital status, or because of a disability in the child. (And in Michigan, a surrogate challenged the parental rights of an intended mother months after birth because she learned the mother suffered from mental illness.) One of us argued twenty years ago that surrogacy contracts should be unenforceable if the surrogate changed her mind during pregnancy or immediately after giving birth due to intense bonding with the child (Shanley 1995). This may still be desirable as a way to insist on the significance of the embodied relationship during pregnancy, but both of us now prefer trying to devise other ways to recognise the surrogate's labour, her dignity, and her relationship to the fetus/child/adult.

Numerous accounts from participants in surrogacy suggest that clarity about the rights and responsibilities of intended parents can occur along with a positive relationship between intentional parents and surrogate. Many surrogates and intentional parents regard themselves as involved in a new process of *family formation*. Their 'extended family' relationship can begin at the time of conception or at the initial contact between commissioning parents and surrogate. Alexandra Kuczynski was present at the embryo transfer and accompanied Cathy, the surrogate, to doctor's appointments throughout the pregnancy. Cathy, for her part, invited Alex to feel the baby move in her uterus and consistently referred to her as the 'Mama' during pregnancy (Kuczynski 2008: 64). Kuczynski comments, 'I searched the literature for a way to understand our relationship, one that is unprecedented in the history of human association ... When Cathy told me that she considered the couple for whom she gave birth a year earlier as close as extended family, I wondered: Do we all have to have Thanksgiving together? If so, for how many years? And which husband carves the turkey?' (Kuczynski 2008: 74).

The new kinds of relationships intended parents and surrogates are forging bear some resemblance to those between adoptive parents and birth mothers in open adoption. The movement for open adoption that began in the 1970s insisted on opening records and facilitating contact between relinquishing parent(s) and child. Open adoption focuses attention on the child's interest in a full narrative of his or her origin. The language and imagery of 'gift' has been central in open adoption, portraying the birth mother as an agent capable of making responsible and informed decisions concerning her offspring (Modell 1999; Yngvesson 1997, 2002; Cahn 2012). Judith Modell observes that 'the adopted child in an open arrangement is alienated neither from his blood parent nor from his legal parent' (Modell 1999: 40). Open adoption entails not a one-time transfer of the child from one 'owner' to another, but rather makes possible ongoing relationships of 'reciprocity, gratitude, responsibility, and compulsory solidarity' (Modell 1999: 57). Surrogacy arrangements that recognise the collaborative basis of the process of family formation join adoptive families in advancing the acceptance of diverse family forms, and insisting that the moral imperative of both these practices is not to supply a child to needy adults but rather to provide legal parents and stable homes to all children.

Foster parenting does not transfer the status of legal parent to the foster parents but is a powerful reminder both of society's obligation to provide care for children and of adults' capacity to act cooperatively on behalf of children. Despite the fact that foster families are most frequently in the public eye when they are the site of abuse or neglect, many foster homes provide children with the physical and emotional care they need to thrive (Wozniak 1999). Blended families, step-families, and multi-generational households all show that more than two adults can be in significant relationships with a child. Some scholars call for some kind of legal status (not parental rights and responsibilities, but perhaps visitation rights) for significant 'other' adults in a child's life: 'Legally recognising a plurality of parental relationships may go a long way towards valuing and validating a variety of relationships valued by both adults and children and may move us away from viewing children as entities over whom adults should be driven to seek exclusive possession' (Narayan 1999: 86). Whether or how the law might acknowledge adults-child relationships other than those of the custodial parents is beyond the purview of this chatper, but our discussion shows that cabining 'the family' generated by surrogacy into a model of the two-parent nuclear family fails to capture the nature of the complex relationships that surrogacy entails and to recognise that many other families chafe against this normative framework as well.

Conclusion

Surrogacy is a still new, and complicated, arrangement for family formation. Instead of the traditional man and woman engaging in heterosexual intercourse to produce a child, bringing a child into the world through surrogacy minimally involves intended parents, a surrogate, gamete donor(s), and the surrogate's family, in addition to surrogacy agencies, lawyers, nurses and fertility doctors. Negotiating and managing these relationships require breaking new ground and creating new practices and understanding, which is impossible when people cling to the notion that surrogacy is simply a variation on traditional family formation. As Melanie Thernstrom notes,

> If you consider third-party reproduction to be simply a production detail in the creation of a conventional nuclear family – a service performed and forgotten – then acknowledging the importance of outsiders could make it all seem like a house of cards. But if you conceive of the experience as creating a kind of extended family, in which you have chosen to be related to these people through your children, it feels very rich. (Thernstrom 2011: 44–45)

To account satisfactorily for the intricacies and needs of this experience, we must first abandon the goal of making all families conform as closely as possible to the nuclear heterosexual family. It is only then that we acknowledge the extraordinary interdependency, caregiving, and ongoing connection that surrogacy requires. The discourse and practice of surrogacy will probably always vacillate between oppressive and free labour, biological and social ties, contract and gift, and autonomy and interdependence. Participants, medical and legal professionals, ethicists, and activists and theorists must continually engage the tensions generated by this method of forming families, creating and recreating new meaning and practices. But if we maintain a focus on the social relationships of all those involved – gamete donors, surrogates, intended parents and future children – we can more accurately recognise these emerging and diverse family formation relationships.

References

Allen, A.L. (2005), 'Open Adoption Is Not for Everyone', in S. Haslanger and
    C. Witt (eds), *Adoption Matters*, Ithaca, NY.: Cornell University Press, 47–67.
American College of Obstetricians and Gynecologists (2008), Committee Opinion
    No. 397. February 2008: 1–6.

Anderson, E.S. (1990), 'Is Women's Labor a Commodity?', *Philosophy and Public Affairs*, 19: 71–92.

Asian Communities for Reproductive Justice (ACRJ) (2005), *A New Vision for Advancing our Movement for Reproductive Health, Reproductive Rights, and Reproductive Justice*. Oakland, CA.

Bellafante, G. (2005), 'Surrogate Mothers New Niche: Bearing Babies for Gay Couples', *New York Times*, May 27.

Blythe, E. and Firth, L. (2009), 'Donor-Conceived People's Access to Genetic and Biographical History: An Analysis of Provisions in Different Jurisdictions Permitting Disclosure of Donor Identity', *International Journal of Law, Policy, & Family*, 23: 174 passim.

Cahn, N.R. (2009) *Test Tube Families: Why the Fertility Market Needs Legal Regulation*, New York: New York University Press.

Cahn, N.R. (2012), 'The New Kinship', *Georgetown Law Journal*, 100: 2–74 (prepublication pagination).

Dolgin, J.L. (2008), 'Biological Evaluation: Blood Genes, and Family', *Akron Law Review*, 41.

Hartouni, V. (1997), Cultural Conceptions: On Reproductive Technologies and the Remaking of Life. (University of Minnesota Press).

In the Matter of Baby M, 537 A.2d 1227 (N.J. 1988).

Kuczynski, A. (2008), 'Her Body, My Baby', *New York Times Magazine*, November 30.

Mamo, L. (2007), 'Negotiating Conception: Lesbians' Hybrid-Technological Practices', *Science, Technology & Human Values*, 32: 369–93.

Modell, J.S. (1999), 'Open Adoption and the Rhetoric of the Gift', in L.L. Layne (ed.), *Transformative Motherhood: On Giving and Getting in a Consumer Culture*, New York; New York University Press.

Narayan, U. (1999), 'Rethinking Parental Claims in the Light of Surrogacy and Custody', in U. Narayan and J.J. Bartkowiak (eds), *Having and Raising Children: Unconventional Families, Hard Choices, and the Social Good*, University Park: Penn State University Press.

Parks, J.A. (2009), 'Rethinking Radical Politics in the Context of Assisted Reproductive Technology', *Bioethics*, 23(1): 20–27.

Parks, J.A. (2010), 'Care Ethics and the Global Practice of Commercial Surrogacy', *Bioethics*, 24(7): 333–340.

Pateman, C. (1988), *The Sexual Contract*, Stanford, CA: Stanford University Press.

Pratten v. British Columbia (Attorney General), 2011 BCSC 656 (decided 19 May 2011).

Qadeer, I. and John M.E. (2009), 'The Business and Ethics of Surrogacy', *Economic and Political Weekly* (Delhi), January 10: 10–12.

Ragoné, H. (1999), The Gift of Life: Surrogate Motherhood, Gamete Donation, and Constructions of Altruism. In Transformative Motherhood: On Giving and Getting in a Consumer Culture. Linda L. Layne, ed. New York: New York University Press. Pp. 65–88.

Ravitsky, V. (2010), '"Knowing Where You Come From": The Rights of Donor-Conceived Individuals and the Meaning of Genetic Relatedness', *Minnesota Journal of Law, Science & Technology*, 11(2): 655–84.

Rich, A. (1986), *Of Woman Born: Motherhood as Experience and Institution*, New York: W.W. Norton.

Roberts, D. (1995), 'The Genetic Tie', *University of Chicago Law Review*, 62(1): 209–73.

Robertson, J. (1994), *Children of Choice: Freedom and the New Reproductive Technologies*, Princeton: Princeton University Press.

Rothman, B.K. (1989), *Recreating Motherhood*, New York: W.W. Norton.

Satz, D. (2010), *Why Some Things Should Not Be for Sale: The Moral Limits of Markets*, New York: Oxford University Press.

Shanley, M.L. (1995), '"Surrogate Mothering" and Women's Freedom: A Critique of Contracts for Human Reproduction', *Signs*, 18(3).

Shanley, M.L. (2004), *Making Babies, Making Families*, Boston: Beacon Press.

Solinger, R. (2001), *Beggars and Choosers: How the Politics of Choice Shapes Adoption, Abortion, and Welfare in the United States*, New York: Hill and Wang.

Spar, D.L. (2006), *The Baby Business: How Money, Science, and Politics Drive the Commerce of Conception*, Cambridge, MA: Harvard Business School Press.

Strathern, M. (1992), *Reproducing the future: Essays on anthropology, kinship and the new reproductive technologies*, Manchester: Manchester University Press.

'Surrogate mothers fulfilling gay men's parenthood dreams' (2008), Agence France-Presse (AFP), May 5.

Thernstrom, M. (2011), 'My Futuristic Insta-Family', *New York Times Magazine*. January 2.

Thompson, C. (2005), *Making Parents: The ontological choreography of reproductive technologies*, Cambridge, MA: MIT Press.

Wozniak, D.F. (1999), 'Gifts and Burdens: The Social and Familial Contexts of Foster Care', in L.L. Layne (ed.), *Transformative Motherhood: On Giving and Getting in a Consumer Culture*, New York: New York University Press.

Yngvesson, B. (1997), 'Negotiating Motherhood: Identity and Difference in "Open" Adoptions', *Law & Society Review*, 31(1): 31–80.

Yngvesson, B. (2002), 'Placing the "Gift Child" in Transnational Adoption', *Law & Society Review*, 36(2) (Special Issue on Nonbiological Parenting): 227–256.

Young, I.M. (1990), 'Pregnant Embodiment: Subjectivity and Alienation', in *Throwing Like a Girl*, Bloomington: Indiana University Press.

9

Licensing Parents

Regulating assisted reproduction[1]

Adrienne Asch

Introduction

In 1980, Hugh LaFollette published a compelling argument for the licensing of all parents. Recognizing the significance and responsibilities of parent-child relationships, he contended that a decent society should pay as much attention to protecting children from those who were manifestly unfit parents as it did to protecting patrons of barbershops from incompetent barbers. As LaFollette himself acknowledged, any parental licensing scheme would encounter both practical hurdles and fierce ideological opposition. He also conceded that any interference with creating and sustaining parent-child relationships would need to avoid enshrining a narrow set of cultural values and biases. It also had to recognize the limitations of the data on what makes for 'good-enough' parenting, and to honour the fact that children can survive and thrive in circumstances that outsiders might think difficult and distressing. Nevertheless, LaFollette made a powerful case for rethinking the connection between biological procreation and social parenthood.

Such rethinking takes on new significance in light of developments in assisted reproduction technology (ART) over the past thirty years that have effected a practical separation of procreation and parenthood. In the context of assisted reproduction, I will claim that whether or not an individual or couple has a right to parent the child they create biologically, they have no right to the assistance of third parties in creating a child for them to parent. Further, although it may be appropriate for the state or private clinics to set fitness conditions for providing reproductive assistance, such standards have often been mistakenly conditioned on factors with no relevance to effective parenting, such as marital status and sexual orientation. Instead, reproductive assistance should be conditioned on a kind of parental fitness specific to collaborative reproduction: a willingness to modify the ideal of the self-contained nuclear family to accommodate the more complex relationships created by third-party involvement. In particular, reproductive assistance should be conditioned on the willingness of prospective parents to disclose to the child the manner of his creation, and to enable the child to learn about and establish contact with the people who contributed to his existence. This is a weaker claim than LaFollette's, since it calls for the imposition of conditions on a positive right to reproductive assistance, not a negative right to 'keep' the child one has produced.

I will also consider another important aspect of parental fitness for assisted parenthood – an openness about the traits of the child to be created; a willingness to accept a wide variety of children as one's own. As well as urging that clinics modulate, if not eliminate, their own selectivity, I will conclude that openness and flexibility on the part of prospective parents is best achieved by sensitive counselling and education.

Licensing parents and assisted reproduction

In 2007, Richard Storrow extended LaFollette's ideas to the ART context, reviewing practices in the United States and laws and practices in several other countries that have developed systematic approaches to determining which persons should and should not receive ART services. Storrow opposed denials of ART services unless there was reason to believe that the prospective parent or parents would cause significant harm to children or would be determined unfit using standards analogous to those used in cases of termination of parental rights. In the decades between LaFollette's proposal for reproduction in general and Storrow's formulation for assisted reproduction, scholars, standard-setting bodies, and law commissions in many countries have taken different approaches to oversight of ART services. Those that view assisted reproduction as analogous to unassisted reproduction generally oppose any legal or professional gate-keeping. By contrast, those who compare family-building through assisted reproduction with child placement in adoption tend to support or accept more review.

Supporters of professional or legal gate-keeping generally contend that although society cannot institute parental licenses and protect children from physical, psychological, or social harms if they are born through sexual reproduction, that same society should protect as-yet-unconceived children from foreseeable adverse consequences by refusing to aid the adults who might be responsible for negative outcomes. Cohen (1996) and Coleman (2002) argue that providers of ART services should not aid in the births of children likely to experience serious impairments. Nations with a protectionist view towards psychological and social harms include the Czech Republic, Taiwan, Korea, and Japan, which restrict services to married heterosexual couples (reviewed in Jones and Cohen 2001)[2].

Prospective parents are rejected in both the un-regulated and the regulated nations of the world. Exclusions may be both categorical (no single people, same-sex couples, people over fifty years old, with histories of substance abuse or psychiatric diagnosis) (Gurmankin *et al.* 2005); or they may follow an individualized determination of unsuitability (too narcissistic, depressed, or controlling) (Center for Surrogate Parenting 2003). As Jones and Cohen (2001) and Storrow (2007) discuss in their reviews of the worldwide ART situation, some countries are more permissive than others in accepting reproductive services without regard to marital status or sexual orientation. Ease of travel and the popularity of what some refer to as 'reproductive tourism' enable people who don't like the laws in their home country to go elsewhere for help. Although laws in many nations restrict ARTs to heterosexual couples, Belgium, South Africa, Spain, most Australian states, and the Netherlands have no such limitation (Jones and Cohen 2001). Prospective parents from Sweden who don't want adult children to have contact with the providers of eggs or sperm need only obtain gametes from Denmark, where providers are permitted to remain anonymous.

In the United States, no state or federal laws govern access to ARTs save to prohibit discrimination against groups protected under state and federal civil rights statutes[3]. Decisions about eligibility rest with private fertility clinics and individual practitioners. As the American Society for Reproductive Medicine explains in statements discussing requests for service by people who are HIV-positive (2002), postmenopausal (2004b), of uncertain child-rearing ability (2004c), or gay, lesbian, or single (2006), practitioners typically balance respect for the procreative liberty of adults with concern for the wellbeing of future children, and with sensitivity to differing views of professional integrity and responsibility. Practitioners report that they would use their professional judgment in assessing whether particular ART candidates should receive services (Stern *et al.* 2001; Gurmankin *et al.* 2005).

Yet despite findings from the aforementioned surveys that clinic directors felt they had the right and responsibility to reject would-be parents for medical, psychological, or social reasons, most centres operated without written policies about whom to treat; program directors who reported that they would be extremely likely to turn away people based on certain characteristics did not always collect information about those characteristics. For example, 11 per cent of directors claimed they would be slightly, and 71 per cent said they would be very, likely to refuse a couple if the man had been abusive to his existing children, but not all programs actually inquired about relationships with existing children or about the children's physical or mental wellbeing (Gurmankin *et al.* 2005). Whether or not programs are learning about sexual orientation, marital status, substance abuse, or financial stability of those who seek them out, respondents to the most recent survey of US practitioners reported that only 4 per cent of all applicants were denied services in the year preceding the survey (Gurmankin *et al.* 2005). Only 1 per cent of denials were for what the clinic directors or the researchers called 'social' reasons[4].

By contrast to instances where practitioners rejected ART applicants for social factors that they believed would influence the children negatively, there are documented instances in which non-conforming adults who received ART services caused dismay in the media, the public, and the scholarly community. A transgender man with a functioning uterus reported that after many practitioners refused to treat him and his wife, he became pregnant with a baby created from his wife's egg and anonymous sperm (Beatie 2008). Claudia Martinez received artificial insemination notwithstanding being a single, unemployed woman with developmental disabilities (McClain 2001). After learning of the services to Martinez, bioethicist Arthur Caplan commented 'as this case proves, there are no guidelines, no rules or regulations governing who becomes pregnant with this technology, and there should be... No one has to make sure the woman is capable of caring for a child. No one has to consider if she will be a fit parent' (McClain 2001: A1). The practitioner who treated Ms. Martinez counters that it is not his business to decide who will be a fit parent but instead to provide medical services and treat health problems like diabetes and hypertension that prevented Martinez from maintaining her first pregnancy. Robertson (2009) noted that similar calls for increased oversight and regulation occurred after a woman who already had six children using assisted reproduction then gave birth to eight more. But he also quotes practitioners who insist that if people using coital reproduction can decide to have large families, so can people using ARTs.

Responding to requests for services from individuals and couples who don't fit the original profile of the heterosexual married couple seeking IVF after unsuccessful attempts to have their own genetic child, the Ethics Committee of the US ASRM developed guidelines on treating postmenopausal women, same-sex couples and single people, and those whom some suspected would be poor parents (Ethics Committee of the ASRM 2004b, 2006, 2004c respectively). These guidelines make room for practitioner diversity: they condone those who deny services based on concerns about how children will fare, and also support practitioners who refuse to deny services based on such concerns when the vast majority of the population can become parents without review of their child-rearing potential. Steinbock (2005) cogently defends this pluralist stance that tolerates practitioners whose principles compel them to decline some applicants, as well as practitioners prepared to treat those who make other professionals and segments of the general public decidedly uneasy. (A distinct issue is presented by practitioners morally committed to a different policy than those of the organizations for whom they work.)

Procreative liberty vs. the right to parent

The principal arguments against any form of gate-keeping flow from beliefs about the procreative liberty of adults (Robertson 1986, 1994, 2004), and convictions that outside monitoring of families-in-making or families once-created undermines the intimacy and privacy that distinguish familial relationships from all others (Brighouse and Swift 2006). I will contend that the first argument is of only limited relevance to those seeking reproductive assistance: it defends the liberty of individuals seeking to provide assistance to make their products or services available, but not the liberty of recipients to use those products or services in creating a child over whom they will have parental authority. The second argument makes the unwarranted assumption that screening prospective parents for eligibility will interfere with the intimacy or privacy of the family relationships established by those found eligible.

Robertson's defence of procreative liberty, for people refraining from and engaging in coital or assisted reproduction, rests on his commitment to adults' freedom to make decisions about their own bodies and lives. That defence bears more on the freedom of gamete providers and gestators to use their reproductive capacities and materials than on the reproductive opportunities of the recipient prospective parents. Procreative liberty cannot be invoked in opposition to professional or legal scrutiny and limit-setting for recipients. Couched in the language of 'passing on one's genes' or 'deciding how to use one's body', Robertson's arguments help gamete providers and gestators; they do not help the people typically understood as the ART patients (or perhaps consumers) – those who want to become social, rearing parents. If procreative rights are grounded in control over one's own body, the privacy of sexual relationships between consenting adults and, per Robertson, the desire to ensure one's genetic continuity, those values do not entitle people to assume the grave responsibility of raising a child. If providers have a right to give or sell their reproductive products and services, then prospective parents may have a right to receive or purchase those services. But that would not give them the right to become the social parent of any child resulting from the transaction.

The second argument, about intimacy, rests on a concern that access restrictions on ART will interfere with the family relationships of those granted as well as those denied access (Robertson 1994; Steinbock 2005). The claim is that the intimacy that should characterize parent-child relationships cannot flourish if outsiders control the terms of that relationship. But this claim seems unwarranted, or at least unsupported. As long as the parents deemed eligible to receive reproductive assistance enjoy the same parental rights as those who reproduce without such assistance, there is no reason to believe that the initial screening will cramp or chill the relationships they establish with their children.

More broadly, it is difficult to argue for a right to become a parent, as opposed to a right to be free from interference or coercion in matters of reproduction. The right of biological parents to parent any child they produce, though called into question by LaFollette (1997, 2010), arguably can be seen as a right of the latter sort – a negative right to be free from having one's biological child taken away. Prospective parents who require reproductive assistance, in contrast, would have to claim a positive right to that assistance – a harder claim to establish.

Moreover, whether or not individuals have a right to state support in acquiring a child to parent, it is not clear why they would have a right to parent a child with whom they have some kind of biological connection. Even if the desire for a biological connection is reasonable and defensible, it need not be given the same weight as the more general desire to parent a child or form a family.

People may believe that prospective parents are likely to be more loving, devoted, or generally fit if they had some biological connection to the child rather than none. It is here that LaFollette's arguments against a presumption of fitness apply *a fortiori*: if we cannot presume parental fitness on the basis of full or standard biological connections, we can hardly do so on the basis of the partial ones made possible by ARTs. The ability to use one's genetic material and reproductive capacities to bring a child into being has nothing to do with the skills needed to protect, support, value, guide, socialize, love, respect, and respond to the individuality of children once they are born. Scholars and societies have rarely had to justify the presumption that biological relationships would create the desire and capacity to rear (but see Gheaus 2011 for such an attempt); instead, they have relied on this presumption and made it hard to overcome. Perhaps the assumption springs from the conviction that genetic connectedness, the notion that a child was 'flesh of my flesh', would create the psychological and social identification with children Bartlett (1988) described as an essential part of parental responsibility (see Richards 2010). But there is no research to support that conviction, and much to support the view that parents can be equally effective when the child they raise has no biological connection to them (Golombok 2000). The strength of the link between biological capacity and parental fitness is certainly called into question by the number of children who are abused or neglected by their biological parents, as well as by the psychological, social, and academic difficulties of children unwanted by the biological parents who raised them (David *et al.* 1988). Genetic relatedness by itself cannot yield the prerequisites for adequate parenting.

It is certainly understandable that many prospective parents seek such a connection. No matter how much they recognize that most of parenting is social and consists in the many daily acts that support, teach, and inculcate values and interests in a child after its birth, many people look forward to seeing themselves, their partner, and other relatives in the new child. Families have seemingly endless conversations about whom the child resembles. Many women and their partners often view a wanted pregnancy as the beginning of their parental experience. Low- and high-tech means of giving the infertile couple a genetically-related child that the woman carries to term are often costly in dollars, time, and psychological resources. Undoubtedly the researchers and clinicians who pioneered the means for infertile heterosexual couples to achieve biological parenthood have both responded to and strengthened the desire for these expected biological ties to children. But the desire for a parental role and a meaningful relationship with a biologically connected child cannot be seen as a social or political right[5]. The person who cannot or does not wish to engage in sexual intercourse that could lead to reproduction may well have the qualities of responsiveness, empathy, and demandingness to help a child become an exemplary family member, worker, and citizen, but she is not entitled to acquire gametes with which to make an embryo she can then gestate.

Parental responsibility and assisted reproduction

The previous section suggested that it is better to approach access to reproductive assistance in terms of the responsibilities of parenting, and the welfare of the future child, than to invoke an indefensible right to become a parent. In this section, I will argue that such a focus on parental responsibility and child welfare may favour more open access to ARTs, based on the willingness and capacity of prospective parents to take on a demanding, difficult, but intensely rewarding task.

Scholars, practitioners, and policy-makers who maintain a primarily rights-based, adult-centred view of parenthood understandably fear proposals that would limit access to family-creation services. Elsewhere I and others have contended that procreative liberty may not be the best banner under which to raise claims to the goods of parenting (Bartlett 1988; Asch 1995; Murray 1996; Ryan 2001; O'Neill 2002; Cutas and Bortolotti 2010). Onora O'Neill (2002: 66) wryly points out that 'limiting childbearing may promote individual autonomy, but having children generally curtails it'. If we moved from an adult autonomy, rights-based to a relationship- and responsibility-based view of parenthood, we might better serve the welfare of future children. I believe that professionals and prospective parents should embark upon a family-building enterprise focused on the needs of the children they seek to raise. Paramount among those needs is the potential for a secure, reliable, tie to someone who will combine acceptance of a child's individuality with the expectation of cooperation in joining the community of a family and the larger society (Darling 2007). As Katharine Bartlett writes, 'responsibility describes a certain type of connection that persons may experience in their relationships with one another. That connection is one of identification. Identification ... must be positive and affirming; it seeks what is good for the other person' (1988: 299). Bartlett's description of what it means to be a responsible person captures something at the heart of the parental project, a project that ideally should motivate those seeking to become parents:

> Responsibility ... is a self-enlarging, open-ended commitment on behalf of another ... We want a society in which parent-child relationships are strong, secure, and nurturing... [O]ur ... concern is how the interests of both parent and child link together in relationships. Responsibility is a critical dimension of these relationships. Parents being responsible for children ... fits the best picture we have of ourselves. (Bartlett 1988: 299–300)

Accepting this responsibility- and relationship-based understanding of parenting should lead professionals not so much to refuse access to ARTs or to adoption but rather to challenge the adults who seek their aid to ask themselves hard questions about whether they are up to the task of identifying with and responding to the needs of the child they are bringing into their lives.

This concern with parental responsibility and child welfare, however, is not reflected in prevailing educational and medical social practices. If US society wished to ensure minimal welfare of all its future children, it might make learning about parenthood part of its public education; develop safe and effective male and female reversible vaccines to prevent unintended procreation (Battin 1996); and develop methods of assessing the capacities of adults to be responsive and demanding. People who understand what their society expects of them, and want the responsibilities and relationship that come with parenting, have at least the knowledge and motivation to care for and about their children.

Without a serious commitment to child welfare, US society accepts biological connection as the appropriate prelude to social parenthood. This assumption influences thinking about how children should be raised when biology does not lead to parental destiny. Fearing that adults without a genetic identification with children might not fulfil parental responsibilities, adoption professionals have instituted a form of licensure by the complex screening process that evaluates prospective adoptive parents through in-depth interviews, reference checks, and a home study. Yet despite the ubiquitousness of such assessments, standards of acceptance vary widely from agency to agency and have reflected many of the cultural biases discussed above in the world of ARTs. Moreover, according to conversation with adoption professionals at a major centre for adoption research and policy, the standards used to assess prospective adopters have never been correlated with child outcomes (Georgia Deoudes 2000, personal communication); I have found no subsequent research on the efficacy of the adoption assessment process.

In the case of parents who employ ART, there has been some outcome research. That research has found that the experience raising genetically connected children is similar to but *more* positive than that of raising genetically related children conceived without assistance (Brewaeys *et al.* 1997; Golombok *et al.* 2002). The similarities between the IVF or ICSI-created parent-child constellation and the families created without assistance should make us especially wary of practitioners who want to act as gate-keepers for the people seeking their assistance to create biologically related offspring from their own gametes.

To urge that child rearing be seen in terms of responsibility and relationships is not to endorse standard psychosocial screening criteria. Clinicians who would deny a woman the opportunity to parent based on her being postmenopausal, or being single, in a lesbian relationship, or having a cancer history, must demonstrate why she does not have the requisites for child-rearing.

The extensive research conducted by and reviewed by Golombok (2000) indicates that typical demographic characteristics such as parental age, marital status, sexual orientation, and genetic relatedness to a child are not the factors that predict effective parenting. Rather, the factors that do predict success are the capacities to foster a child's secure attachment and to respond to the needs of the individual child.

Given the cultural biases and questionable assessment methods that have plagued adoption, there is good reason not to incorporate its version of parental screening into the process of assisted reproduction. At the same time, however, the roles of third parties in some forms of ART create additional responsibilities for the prospective parents who employ their services. They must consider what relationship, if any, these people will have with the family they have helped create.

Clinicians who started out by providing ARTs for the heterosexual infertile couple increasingly find that they are being asked to create children who won't be raised by some or any of the people to whom the children owe their biological existence. When same-sex couples, single people, or heterosexual couples seek to create children using others' gametes or gestational services, they have moved away from the parenthood through biological assistance to a family that blends biologic and adoptive parenting. Unlike the two parents in ordinary reproduction and in most IVF- and ICSI-reproduction, collaborative arrangements can give a child three biologic contributors and additional social parents. Genetic and gestational contributors may be known by or unknown to the intended rearing parents, but in many cases the commissioning parent or parents don't plan to tell the child how she was created, or that certain gametes were requested in hopes of giving her particular physical, cognitive, or personality attributes.

Examples abound:

- A heterosexual married couple in their thirties selects sperm from a sperm bank's profiles and plan to keep the method of conception a secret from their families and their child.

- A twenty-something couple finds out that the woman's uterus can't hold a baby and creates an embryo to be gestated by an anonymous woman who will not meet them and whose role will never be known to the child.

- Less common, but not a hypothetical case, is that of a postmenopausal woman who wants to carry and raise a child created from her daughter's egg fertilized with the sperm of the mother's current husband, the daughter's stepfather.

- Single women request help in forming families using sperm of known or unknown others.

- In order for both members of a lesbian couple to share a biological connection to a child, one woman will provide the egg to be fertilized with the sperm of her partner's brother, and then the embryo will be implanted in and gestated by the first woman's partner.

- An infertile Pakistani couple asks for an embryo made up of gametes from Caucasians so that the child they bear and raise will escape the ethnic prejudice that has plagued their lives in Great Britain (Van Dijck 1994).

These situations illustrate some of the complexities of third-party or collaborative reproduction. There are different numbers of contributors and widely varying relationships between them and the parents who relied on their assistance. Gamete provision and gestational services may indeed produce children with a genetic connection to someone who will raise them. But the children will also be affected throughout their lives, though to an unknown extent, by their genetic or gestational connection to someone outside of their parent or parents. The professionals are creating children who could not have come about without these technologies and social arrangements. These complexities create special responsibilities for parents, and one goal of education and screening for third-party ART services must be to ensure that prospective parents understand these responsibilities and are willing and able to fulfil them.

Selectivity, secrecy, and the parent-child relationship

I conclude by articulating my vision of how parents and practitioners can best discharge their responsibilities to the children they create and raise. The circumstances of parental selectivity in gamete providers and in gestators, along with the fact of having created a child with discontinuities in his biologic and social parentage (whether or not the child knows these facts), give rearing parents unique responsibilities and give clinicians a significant counselling and gate-keeping role. First, parents who employ ART should limit their selectivity among possible providers and display a willingness to accept a wide variety of kinds of children. Second, those parents must be willing to disclose their child's origin to her in age appropriate ways, and to give her any information they have about the identity and medical history of the (other) biological contributors to her existence. Their parenting responsibilities will include helping the child understand his origins, a responsibility that distinguishes the job of the ART parent from the job of biological parents raising a child. Gate-keeping should focus on ensuring that prospective parents are ready for that responsibility.

Choosing collaborators

As soon as ARTs involve genetic material and gestational services outside of the intended rearing parent or parents, the people who will raise the child must choose the others to participate in the child's creation. Sometimes the intended parents choose a gamete provider or gestator based on a previous friendship or familial connection and look forward to involving the person in their child's life. More commonly the commissioning parent or parents do not select the reproductive collaborators based on past or future relationship but on information they glean from photographs, essays, sometimes an in-person or telephone interview, and the knowledge that professionals approved them for their role. People often base their selections on the hope that some or all of the attractive physical and personality characteristics will be transmitted to the child genetically or will assure a safe intrauterine environment. Gamete providers and gestators are not selected for anything but the particular attributes recipient parents seek. Unlike mate selection, with which this version of reproduction is erroneously compared, people do not select a partner for a child-rearing project knowing that everyone will have both desirable and less attractive qualities. Moreover, the typical collaborator has had and will have no other relationship, role, or responsibility in the life of the adult; when partners decide to become parents together with or without assistance, the parenting is only one important part of a multi-faceted relationship. To the extent that people select partners based on what they think the partner will be like as a parent, they are selecting for many reasons; for a complex relationship, and for a partner in parenting; they are not selecting someone to raise a child with, and make a life with, solely based on height, complexion, or intelligence.

As I've argued, it is hard to claim that access to ART services and the resulting parent-child relationship is any kind of right, since no one has a right to anyone else's genetic material or reproductive services, and no one has a right to a child with particular genetically-transmitted characteristics. In other work, I've also argued against parental selectivity, whether they were screening for or against particular traits (Asch and Wasserman 2005). Using third-party collaborators raises concerns similar to and different from those I've described previously. Intense efforts at genetic and gestational selectivity expose a tension within ART that should trouble practitioners and challenge prevailing practices. ART is promoted as a means of permitting individuals and couples to come as close to unassisted reproduction as their biological or social circumstances permit. Practitioners treating an infertile heterosexual couple using their own gametes and gestation are helping to replicate the randomness of ordinary reproduction. The couple's genetic endowment is taken as a given; the partners have not selected each other primarily on the basis of the traits they hope to pass on to their offspring (extreme claims about assortative mating notwithstanding). In contrast, practitioners helping anyone select particular gametes and gestators are working to minimize the chance qualities of reproduction and trying to give prospective parents greater control over their future child than they would have exercised had they been able to procreate without assistance.

The Pakistani couple described previously (Van Dijck 1994) are seeking to create a child whose phenotypic characteristics deliberately differ from their own. They are being selective in trying to create a child with particular attributes that they themselves could not replicate with biologic reproduction. The practitioner is not merely helping an infertile couple create a child, but a very particular kind of child, with features they could not have obtained from their own genes. In doing so, the practitioner and parents come closer to making a child to order. It is particularly problematic in a case like this, where their selectivity is, in Margaret Little's (1998: 163) phrase, complicit with 'suspect norms of appearance' concerning skin colour and ethnicity that help to perpetuate racism.

Practitioners who do not wish to become involved in these forms of selection could refuse services to everyone who wanted to select eggs, sperm, embryos, or gestators. In order to avoid unjustified and unjustifiable discrimination based on marital or partner status, age, or sexual orientation, these practitioners would have to refuse to serve both the heterosexual and homosexual couple and single women or men who needed outside biological contributions. These practitioners could still help people who needed gametes or gestational services if the prospective parent or parents brought in collaborators with whom they had relationships.

My own opposition to selectivity is more comprehensive; it stems from my conviction that responsive and responsible parenting entails the capacity for welcoming exactly the mystery that new human beings have always been and will continue to be, regardless of attempts to shape and control them before and after birth. I'm aware that I'm offering a norm for ideal parenting that many will not share and for which I may fail to make a compelling argument. But this norm receives support from studies of parenting styles for children born with and without reproductive assistance, which find that among the most important correlates of positive child outcomes are the qualities of the parent-child relationship, in particular, parental responsiveness to the child's individuality (Golombok 2000; Ehrensaft 2005; Darling 2007).

The willingness to accept a wide variety of children as one's own reflects an attractive ideal of parenthood. It is, however, more difficult and less appropriate to require of prospective parents than a willingness to disclose the child's origins. It is more difficult to require because selectivity pervades the culture and practice of contemporary reproductive medicine. It is less appropriate to require because fertility clinics themselves aggressively promote selectivity and screen donors for various inherited conditions.

Clinics do not have to reject selectivity altogether to modulate it both in their own practices and in their clients' decision-making. The current emphasis on selectivity fuels the false beliefs in the power of genetics and fails to prepare parents for the child who defies what the gametes might have predicted. Practitioners could place less emphasis on the 'quality' of the genetic material they provided and offer clients less information about the 'credentials' of their providers, and they could encourage their clients to broaden their range of acceptable gamete providers and gestators.

Let me be very clear that I'm not interested in preventing those who need gametes or gestation from reproducing. I'm arguing that fertility specialists should be wary of helping people meet very particular standards for who is an acceptable collaborator or child. Prospective parents do not have the right to demand biological contributors with as long a list of paper qualifications as an elite college may use in selecting its entering class. But it may be difficult for clinics to discourage parents from being too finicky when they do so much to promote selectivity, from screening providers on the basis of family history to advertising their elite providers.

More needs to be said about how a society generally prepared to accept 'designer families' should guide or regulate their creation. I favour a policy that discourages screening out but that emphasizes the promotion of flexibility and openness in the people who will become parents with third-party assistance. At the same time, I recognize that people who are searching for help from a stranger for this intimate activity of creating a new human being want to establish a sense of confidence in and appreciation for any collaborator participating in this project. But clinic staff willing to meet these demands should be reminding everyone who seeks eggs from a woman who played chess and the cello that the genetic son of the chess-playing cellist may have no aptitude for or interest in either pastime.

Learning about collaborators

The parental selectivity issues for practitioners, parents, and ultimately the children, are rivalled in complexity by issues of the child's knowledge of and relationship with collaborators. Any counselling of service recipients should incorporate discussion of dreams, hopes, expectations, and fears about family life after the long-sought child goes home. The conversation should include the much-debated topic of whether and how to tell children about where they came from. My proposals extend the US Ethics Committee ASRM (2004a) guidelines on disclosure to offspring about their conception; they go further than the ASRM in calling for practitioners to acknowledge the problems but support greater parental openness. In doing so, I draw on insights from the limited social science data available on families formed through collaborative reproduction (consonant with Scheib and Hastings' discussion in this volume). But I am also advancing my own normative views about parenthood. Explaining to a child that the people raising her took these steps to become parents can support the secure attachment all children are thought to need (Golombok 2000).

By contrast, secrecy about how the child came to exist can perpetuate the fundamental tension or ambivalence about biological origins inherent in the use of third-party ART. When Nachtigall *et al.* (1998) report that non-disclosing parents consider the information confidential within the couple and not necessary for the child, the parents are denying the very concerns that led them to choose this method of family creation (see Scheib and Hastings, this volume). Why don't these parents consider that their concerns could matter to the child? In a world ever more convinced of the power of genes and gestation to exert lifelong influence, non-disclosing parents are telling themselves that the child won't care about these biological facts. Exactly how can the parents hold such a view at the same time that they worked to obtain help from others who had particular desired characteristics?

Although non-disclosing parents may have additional reasons for secrecy I'll discuss shortly, the claim of irrelevance is one practitioners should challenge. Genes and gestation don't predict everything about any future person, but they certainly influence appearance, health, and perhaps facets of cognitive and behavioural functioning. It is hard to make sense of the claim that only rearing counts, and that biology isn't important, in the face of parental efforts at giving the child a certain biology. If ART users didn't believe that genetics was significant for their child's future, and if genetic origins would have relatively little effect on their experience of parenthood, these users might first try to adopt an existing child from their own country or abroad. I am not suggesting that adoption is morally preferable to the use of ART, but rather trying to underscore the claim that because the child's biologic origins matter to the people who ultimately raise it, the parent or parents shouldn't suppose these origins will not matter to the child.

So far, the data available on family lives created through collaborative reproduction don't provide decisive conclusions about the effects of disclosure versus openness or collaborator anonymity versus known collaborators. Single parents and same-sex couples cannot keep secret the fact that others played a genetic or gestational role in the child's creation; instructive for majority heterosexual families and ART practitioners is the evidence that even if these children do not know who their genetic fathers are, they appear comfortable and able to function well both within their rearing families and with peers and adults at school and in the larger community. In one study of ten-year-olds in lesbian homes in the US, Gartrell *et al.* (2005) report that children who knew their genetic fathers generally enjoyed relationships with them, but the ones whose fathers remained anonymous did not evidence much concern about this state of affairs. Extensive research on children created by artificial insemination and raised by single women or lesbian couples consistently indicates that children fare at least as well on measures of social and academic development and on relations with their families as those living in heterosexual families (Golombok 2000; Perrin 2002; Gartrell *et al.* 2005; Paige 2005; Scheib and Hastings, this volume).

Writing about lesbian social, non-biological mothers in a 1997 report on European artificial insemination families, Brewaeys *et al.* articulate the apprehensions that many heterosexual, as well as gay and lesbian parents, have about their role when there is a reproductive collaborator: 'the social mothers, the biological mothers' partners, opted significantly more often for an anonymous donor than the biological mothers. These results suggest that the parent who lacks a genetic relationship with the child may experience the donor as more threatening to his/her position in the family than does the biological parent, regardless of the parent's gender' (1997: 1595). The parents in heterosexual couples who opt for secrecy about their use of a collaborator could fear that if the child learns that the person she thinks of as her mother or father has not contributed the typical genes or gestation, the child may discount or reject the non-biological parent. For these parents, secrecy about how their family differs from typical families appears to safeguard family stability and the child's attachment to both parents (Cook *et al.* 1995; Nachtigall *et al.* 1998; Golombok *et al.* 2002).

Families of egg provision and gestational collaboration are being studied, but most available research focuses on two-parent heterosexual ART families who have used artificial insemination. Fearful that secrecy in ART would lead to the negative consequences attributed to the 'lethal secrets' described by Baran and Pannor in their (1989) study of the children of donor insemination in the US, and aware that adopted children benefited from learning about their birth parents, some in the ART world insist on both openness and the availability of identity information (Donor Conception Support Group 1997; Daniels 2004). Others who focus on the dissimilarities between ART and adoption argue that the stance for disclosure or identity information is misguided, contrary to the strong preferences for secrecy in large numbers of ART parents surveyed in many countries, and premature in the absence of data on problematic outcomes (Cook *et al.* 1995; Brewaeys *et al.* 1997; Nachtigall *et al.* 1998; Golombok *et al.* 2002). Research from many studies in the US, Europe, and Australia cited in the Ethics Committee of the US ASRM's (2004a) disclosure guidelines, suggests no indications that planned disclosure before a child's adolescence is harmful; by contrast, accidental disclosure in adolescence or adulthood appears to produce negative consequences.

I have found no reports in any studies of planned parental disclosure suggesting adverse effects for parents or children, and conversely, some indications of parental relief and apparently positive effects on children's relations with genetic and non-genetic parents (Scheib *et al.* 2003; Lycett *et al.* 2005; Lalos *et al.* 2007). The ART families with school-aged and early-adolescent children didn't differ from one another in parent-child relationships or children's outcomes based on whether or not parents had explained the child's biologic origins (Golombok *et al.* 2002), and all families appeared to be faring as well as or better than children of unassisted reproduction, adoption, or IVF without collaboration (Brewaeys *et al.* 1997; Golombok *et al.* 2002). Being raised in families with both biological and non-biological parents, whether or not children know about the arrangements that brought them about, does not appear to have any adverse effects on children. As previously cited work has shown, what goes on between parent and child, not the number of parents, their genetic relatedness, or their sexual orientation, best predicts children's development (Golombok 2000; Ehrensaft 2005).

That most ART families are doing well does not argue that secrecy is morally preferable; the data merely indicate that most families are good enough. Findings that families with secrets are doing all right up to the child's adolescence don't invalidate the reports that adolescent and adult children of ARTs (mainly donor insemination) have been distressed to learn of their origins when these revelations were accidental or occurred in moments of family disruption by death or divorce. The available data on these late-adolescent and adult discoveries of donor insemination origins don't permit sorting out whether the distress resulted from the content of what was revealed, the fact that a secret had been kept, or the manner and circumstances of revelation. Nonetheless, psychologists who have studied family secrets in many contexts observe that 'secrecy about one's beginnings is particularly difficult to justify, as it places a lie at the center of the most basic of relationships – the one between parent and child' (Schaffer and Diamond 1993). I appreciate those clinicians and bioethicists who caution against replacing the previous adamancy for secrecy and anonymity with an uncritical demand for openness and available identity-information (Klock 1997; Shenfield and Steele 1997; Ehrensaft 2005). Nonetheless, I am persuaded by practical, psychological, and moral arguments for at least openness about the fact of third-party assistance, and preferably the possibilities for identity-release and contact with, all the people who played a role in a child's biological existence.

Furthermore, I believe that professionals who counsel collaborators and rearing parents towards openness can underscore the value and priority of the non-biological components of parent-child relationships and family life. A parent quoted by researchers studying collaborative reproduction in Sweden puts my point well: 'The staff should be rooting for the child. They should be aware that what they are doing is more than giving medical treatment. It is about creating a life for someone who will grow up to be an individual with rights and possibilities' (Lalos *et al.* 2007).

As a practical matter, the child may want or need medical information that can best be provided through genetic analysis. With increasingly common and useful DNA testing, rearing parents may find it impossible to withhold the facts from their children for fear that their children will be deprived of health-promoting or life-saving information. But medical information is hardly the only reason children may want knowledge of or contact with the people who contributed to their existence. Long before a child or young adult needs to learn that his unknown genetic mother's family has a history of adult-onset diabetes, he needs to know that he can rely upon and trust what his parents tell him about themselves, about himself, and about the world.

As a psychological matter, the child's life with the people who care for and about him is what counts. It is hard to understand why that sense of 'mother' and 'father' will not survive a simple, matter-of-fact explanation that he doesn't look like his mother because she didn't contribute her genes. She has been contributing to his life ever since she was pregnant with him or began nurturing him. The rearing parents who fear that they will lose a child's love if the child finds out that she grew in someone else's belly forget all the other things that have gone on in their interactions with their child. They can teach an immensely valuable life lesson to their child by explaining that although her father couldn't give her his genes, he gives her time and attention. No parent can do everything for a child that they might like or that a child might want; but children can live with an honest explanation of what couldn't happen and can value what they receive.

The practitioners who link commissioning parents with collaborators should help parents imagine how they can explain a child's conception and birth in ways that do not minimize the biological significance of origins, the planning that gave rise to the collaboration, and the shared life they now lead. There is every reason for parents to be at least comfortable with, if not proud of what they have done to fulfil their goal of child-rearing. Although they may think they can avoid helping a child deal with any sense of shame or embarrassment by keeping origins secret, they are expending immense energy in guarding a simple biological fact that is of material significance to the child. The literature about others who try to conceal what they think of as stigma, and who try to pass as something they are not, suggests that concealment and pretence drain psychic resources from living life (Goffman 1963).

When a child created with ART starts asking about her birth, as all children seem to do, her parents should introduce the idea that they wanted her, and got help from someone who provided the egg, sperm, or womb they needed to bring her into the world. As the child gets older, but probably before adolescence, they can explain how the 'someone' was selected and can tell the child something about that person. If parents don't explain about collaborators, they're actually beginning a chain of falsehoods.

Often discussions about disclosure versus secrecy are tied to debates about the pros and cons of collaborator anonymity, but the topics can be considered separately. In order for parents to possess relevant medical history, practitioners must obtain and provide at least non-identifying information of the sort the parents examined when they selected collaborators initially. Ideally, collaborators would consent to having their identities made available to the children when they became legal adults, so that those children could establish contact if they, like their parents, regarded biological origins as important. Practitioners should encourage parents to disclose the fact that there was a collaborator regardless of how much information they can give the child about who the person is.

The ART professionals should recognize that they are providing more than medical treatment and should include serious conversation and counselling in their expected work with people who seek them out. They should be developing parent-to-parent networks, offering parents material they can use to explain the facts to the children, and working to change the parents' language from 'disclosure' and 'secret' to explaining one fact of a child's and family's life. Professionals should enable all those who contribute to a child's life to acknowledge their part in that life. They should present parents with clear information about why they think the secrecy can damage the child psychologically, and how it can be detrimental to their child's relationship with them. Practitioners can explain why they think candour will ultimately be better and much less stressful for everyone involved. They can also provide parents with resources to guide them and tools they can use with their child. If practitioners believe that would-be parents cannot envision telling a child that they selected someone to help create her, perhaps practitioners should advise them to rethink the enterprise. They should hesitate to start a parental project feeling that it would be damaged or compromised unless its origins remain secret from the person it helped create.

Practitioners and future ART parents could learn a lot about creating their families from the gay and lesbian families successfully raising children who know about, and often know personally, the people who helped their parents create them (Gartrell 2005; Mundy 2007). Research shows that children can clearly distinguish rearing parents from biological collaborators, even when they know about the existence of those collaborators, and even when the collaborators go on to participate in the child's life. The facts are likely to be much easier to deal with than they fear, and they can distinguish themselves as parents from biological contributors, just as they distinguish themselves from uncles, grandparents, neighbours, baby-sitters, and family friends who participate in their child's life.

Conclusion

In my own personal utopia, prospective parents wouldn't be so enthusiastic about where their child's genes came from, and if two people couldn't provide the genes or gestation, they might randomly pick gametes or might adopt a child who needed a family. Whether or not they selected gestators or gamete providers from relatives, friends, or profiles, they would tell their child what happened and make room for the child to put them into her life if she wished. Absent anything like my ideal, I'm urging clinicians not to license, but to counsel and converse, to give new entrants into the ART world the benefits of their experience with thousands of others already raising children. Elsewhere I have given qualified endorsement of conscience exceptions for professionals who would decline to provide other medical services (Asch 2006), and I thus must acknowledge that some clinicians may wish to avoid creating children for parents they expect will be ill-equipped to care for them. Clinicians who refuse to treat infertile couples for any reason should refer them to practitioners who might have different standards. And ART practitioners should team up with researchers to follow children and parents through childhood and into adulthood to learn whether their practices foster the kind of responsive parenting everyone thinks children need and deserve.

Acknowledgements

I'm greatly indebted to Renee Witlen and Sara Mrsny for research and discussion on this topic, when I began this project several years ago. Rebecca Marmor and Stephanie Nilles provided extensive research, excellent critiques and moral support. The editors of this volume, and Simon May, gave valuable suggestions for improving an earlier draft. David Wasserman and Dorit Barlevy assisted in implementing those suggestions and clarifying my arguments. These various contributions should not be taken as support for the analysis and conclusions presented here.

Notes

1 This is a revised version of my paper given at the Ethics of Procreation and Parenthood Conference in Cape Town, South Africa in May 2008.

2 Having previously written on the subject of pre-implantation and prenatal diagnosis (Fine and Asch 1982; Asch 1989, 1999, 2000), I will restrict my comments in this essay to other psychological and social harms. In this paper I focus on two of the harms Robertson sees as specific to ARTs: deficient 'child-rearing ability' and 'novel family forms' (2004).

3 There is too little US case law to make many conclusions about how courts will respond to exercises of practitioner discretion. Guadalupe Benitez, denied based on sexual orientation, won her case (Benitez v. North Coast Women's Medical Care Group 2003). In another case, the clinic convinced the jury that factors other than the patient's blindness prompted them to deny service to Tuana Chambers. Three years after Chambers' denial, she obtained insemination services through another clinic and gave birth to a daughter (Hershey 2003).

4   Denials based on clinic opposition to treating people with genetic conditions, or denials stemming from concerns about child-rearing ability of people with disabilities, might have been classified as medical reasons.

5   I agree with Pennings (1999) that children do not have a 'right' to parents of a particular age. But I disagree with Boivin and Pennings' (2005) claim that parenthood as such is a right.

References

Asch, A. (1989), 'Reproductive technology and disability', in S. Cohen and N. Taub (eds), *Reproductive Laws for the 1990s*, Clifton, NJ: Humana Press, 69–124.

Asch, A. (1995), 'Parenthood and embodiment: Reflections on biology, intentionality, and autonomy', *Graven Images, A Journal of Culture, Law, and the Sacred*, 2: 229–236.

Asch, A. (1999), 'Prenatal diagnosis and selective abortion: A challenge to practice and policy', *American Journal of Public Health*, 89(11): 1649–1657.

Asch, A. (2000), 'Why I haven't changed my mind about prenatal diagnosis: Reflections and refinements', in E. Parens and A. Asch (eds), *Prenatal Testing and Disability Rights*, Washington, DC: Georgetown University Press, 234–258.

Asch, A. (2006), 'Two cheers for conscience exceptions', *Hastings Center Report*, 36(6): 11–12.

Asch, A. and Wasserman, D. (2005), 'Where is the sin in synecdoche: Prenatal testing and the parent-child relationship', in D. Wasserman, R. Wachbroit, R. Wachbroit and J. Bickenbach (eds), *Quality of Life and Human Difference: Genetic Testing, Health Care, and Disability*, New York: Cambridge University Press, 172–216.

Baran, A. and Pannor, R. (1989), *Lethal Secrets: The Shocking Consequences and Unsolved Problems of Artificial Insemination*, New York: Warner Books.

Bartlett, K.T. (1988), 'Re-expressing Parenthood', *The Yale Law Journal*, 98(2): 293–340.

Battin, P. (1996), 'Teen Pregnancy: Prevention by education, legislation and immunization' [paper presented at Wellesley College, Wellesley, MA, April 27].

Beatie, T. (2008), 'Labor of Love: Is Society Ready for this Pregnant Husband?', *The Advocate*, 14 February.

Benitez v. North Coast Women's Medical Care Group. (2003), 131 Cal.Rptr.2d 364, 367.

Berg, B.J. (1995), 'Listening to the Voices of the Infertile', in J.C. Callahan (ed.), *Reproduction, Ethics and the Law: Feminist Perspectives*, Indianapolis: Indiana University Press, 80–108.

Boivin, J. and Pennings, G. (2005), 'Parenthood Should be Regarded as a Right', *Archives of Disease in Childhood*, 90: 784–785.

Brewaeys, A., Golombok S., Naaktgeboren N., de Bruyn J.K. and van Hall, E.V. (1997), 'Donor insemination: Dutch parents' opinions about confidentiality and donor anonymity and the emotional adjustment of their children', *Human Reproduction*, 12(7): 1591–1597.

Brighouse, H. and Swift, A. (2006), 'Parents' Rights and the Value of the Family', *Ethics*, 117: 80–108.

Center for Surrogate Parenting (2003), http://www.creatingfamilies.com [accessed October 2011].

Chambers v. University Hospital and M.H. Melmed, M.D. P.C. (2000), Civ. Act. No. 00- N-1794 (CBS) (D.C. Colo. 2000).

Cohen, C. (1996), 'Give me children or I shall die! New reproductive technologies and harm to children', *Hastings Center Report*, 26(2): 19–27.

Coleman, C.H. (2002), 'Conceiving Harm: Disability Discrimination in Assisted Reproductive Technologies', *UCLA Law Review*, 50(1): 17–68.

Cook, R., Golombok S., Bish A. and Murray C. (1995), 'Disclosure of Donor Insemination: Parental Attitudes', *American Journal of Orthopsychiatry*, 65(4): 549–559.

Cutas, D.E. and Bortolotti, L. (2010), 'Natural versus assisted reproduction: in search of fairness', *Studies in Ethics, Law, and Technology*, 4(1): 1–18.

Daniels, K. (2004), *Building a Family with the Assistance of Donor Insemination*, Palmerstone North, NZ: Dunmore Press.

Darling, N. (2007), 'Parenting Style and Its Correlates', http://www.athealth.com/Practitioner/ceduc/parentingstyles.html [accessed October 2011].

David, H.P., Dytrych, Z., Matejcek, Z. and Schuller, V. (eds) (1988), *Born Unwanted: Developmental Effects of Denied Abortion*, New York: Springer Publishing Company.

Deoudes, G. (March 2000) (personal communication).

Donor Conception Support Group (1997), *Let the Offspring Speak: Discussion on Donor Conception*, C. Lorbach (ed.), New South Wales, AU: Donor Conception Support Group of Australia.

Ehrensaft, D. (2005), *Mommies, Daddies, Donors and Surrogates: Answering Tough Questions and Building Strong Families*, New York: The Guilford Press.

The Ethics Committee of the American Society for Reproductive Medicine (2002), 'Human Immunodeficiency Virus and Infertility Treatment', *Fertility and Sterility*, 77(2): 218–222.

The Ethics Committee of the American Society for Reproductive Medicine (2004a), 'Informing Offspring of their Conception by Gamete Donation', *Fertility and Sterility*, 81(3): 527–531.

The Ethics Committee of the American Society for Reproductive Medicine (2004b), 'Oocyte Donation to Postmenopausal Women', *Fertility and Sterility*, 82(1): S254–S255.

The Ethics Committee of the American Society for Reproductive Medicine (2004c), 'Child-Rearing Ability and the Provision of Fertility Services', *Fertility and Sterility*, 82(3): 564–567.

The Ethics Committee of the American Society for Reproductive Medicine (2006), 'Access to Fertility Treatment by Gays, Lesbians and Unmarried Persons', *Fertility and Sterility*, 86(5): 1333–1335.

Fine, M., and Asch, A. (1982), 'The question of disability: No easy answers for the women's movement', *Reproductive Rights National Newsletter*, 4(3): 19–20.

Gartrell, N., Deck, A., Rodas, C., Peyser, H., and Banks, A. (2005), 'National Lesbian Family Study: 4. Interviews With the 10-Year-Old Children', *American Journal of Orthopsychiatry*, 75(4): 518–524.

Gheaus, A. (2011), 'The Right to Parent One's Biological Baby', *Journal of Political Philosophy*, doi: 10.1111/j.1467-9760.2011.00402.x.

Goffman, E. (1963), *Stigma: Notes on the Management of Spoiled Identity*, New York: Simon & Schuster.

Golombok, S. (2000), *Parenting: What Really Counts?*, Philadelphia: Taylor and Francis.

Golombok, S., Brewaeys, A., Giavazzi, M.T. *et al.* (2002), 'The European study of assisted reproduction families: the transition to adolescence', *Human Reproduction*, 17(3): 830–840.

Gurmankin, A.D., Caplan, A.L. and Braverman, A.M. (2005), 'Screening practices and beliefs of assisted reproductive technology programs', *Fertility and Sterility*, 83(1): 61–67.

Hershey, L. (2003), 'Disabled woman's lawsuit exposes prejudices', http://www. raggededgemagazine.com/extra/hersheychamberstrial.html [accessed October 2011].

Jones, H.W. and Cohen, J. (2001), 'IFFS surveillance 01', *Fertility and Sterility*, 76(5): S5–S36.

Klock, S.C. (1997), 'The Controversy Surrounding Privacy or Disclosure Among Donor Gamete Recipients', *Journal of Assisted Reproduction and Genetics*, 14(7): 378–380.

LaFollette, H. (1980), 'Licensing parents', *Philosophy and Public Affairs*, 9(2): 182–197.

LaFollette, H. (2010), 'Licensing parents revisited', *Journal of Applied Philosophy*, 27(4): 327–343.

Lalos, A., Gottlieb, C. and Lalos, O. (2007), "Legislated right for donor-insemination children to know their genetic origin: a study of parental thinking", *Human Reproduction*, 22 (6): 1759–1768.

Little, M.O. (1998), 'Cosmetic Surgery, Suspect Norms and the Ethics of Complicity', in E. Parens (ed.), *Do Means Matter? Enhancing Human Traits: Ethical and Social Implications*, Washington, D.C.: Georgetown University Press: 162–176.

Lycett, E., Daniels, K., Curson, R., and Golombok, S. (2005), 'School-Aged Children of Donor Insemination: A Study of Parents' Disclosure Patterns', *Human Reproduction*, 20(3): 810–818.

McClain, C. (2001), 'Who's "Fit" to Become a Mother?', *The Arizona Star*, February 14: A1.

Mundy, L. (2007), *Everything Conceivable: How Assisted Reproduction is Changing Men, Women and the World*, New York: Alfred A. Knopf.

Murray, T.H. (1996), *The Worth of a Child*, Los Angeles: University of California Press.

Nachtigall, R.D., Becker, G., Quiroga, S.S., and Tschann, J.M. (1998), 'The disclosure decision: Concerns and issues of parents of children conceived through donor insemination', *American Journal of Obstetrics and Gynecology*, 178(6): 1165–1170.

O'Neill, O. (2002), *Autonomy and Trust in Bioethics*, Cambridge: Cambridge University Press.

Paige, R.U. (2005), 'Proceedings of the American Psychological Association, Incorporated, for the legislative year 2004', http://www.apa.org/governance/ [accessed February 2008].

Pennings, G. (1999), 'Measuring the welfare of the child: in search of the appropriate evaluation principle', *Human Reproduction*, 14(5): 1146–1150.

Perrin, E.C. (2002), 'Technical Report: Coparent or Second-Parent Adoption by Same-Sex Parents', *Pediatrics*, 109: 341–344.

Richards, N. (2010), *The Ethics of Parenthood*, New York: Oxford University Press.

Robertson, J.A. (1986), 'Embryos, Families and Procreative Liberty: The Legal Structure of the New Reproduction', *Southern California Law Review*, 59: 501–602.

Robertson, J.A. (1994), *Children of Choice: Freedom and the New Reproductive Technologies*, Princeton: Princeton University Press.

Robertson, J.A. (2004), 'Procreative liberty and harm to offspring in assisted reproduction', *American Journal of Law and Medicine*, 30: 7–40.

Robertson, J.A. (2009), 'The octoplet case – why more regulation is not likely', *Hastings Center Report*, 39(3): 26–28.

Ryan, M.A. (2001), *Ethics and Economics of Assisted Reproduction: the Cost of Longing*, Washington, D.C.: Georgetown University Press.

Schaffer, J.A. and Diamond, R. (1993), 'Infertility: Private pain and secret stigma', in E. Imber-Black (ed.), *Secrets in Families and Family Therapy*, New York: W.W. Norton and Company.

Scheib, J.E., Riordan, M. and Rubin, S. (2003), 'Choosing identity-release sperm donors: The parents' perspective 13-18 years later', *Human Reproduction*, 18: 1115–1127.

Shenfield, F. and Steele, S.J. (1997), 'What are the effects of anonymity and secrecy on the welfare of the child in gamete donation?', *Human Reproduction*, 12(2): 392–395.

Steinbock, B. (2005), 'Do variations in assisted reproductive technology programs' screening practices indicate a need for national guidelines? Another perspective', *Fertility and Sterility*, 84(5): 1551–1552.

Stern, J.E., Cramer, C.P., Garrod A. and Green R.M., (2001), 'Access to services at assisted reproductive technology clinics: A survey of policies and practices', *American Journal of Obstetrics and Gynecology*, 184(4): 592–597.

Storrow, R. (2007), 'The Bioethics of Prospective Parenthood: In Pursuit of the Proper Standard for Gatekeeping in Infertility Clinics', *Cardozo Law Review*, 28(5): 2283–2320.

Van Dijck, J. (1994), *Manufacturing Babies and Public Consent: Debating the New Reproductive Technologies*, New York: New York University Press.

10

Liberal Feminism and the Ethics of Polygamy

Simon Căbulea May

My aim in this chapter is to use the example of polygamous marriage to distinguish two different senses in which a cultural practice could be thought inherently or essentially objectionable. I argue that polygamy is not inherently *vicious*, where this concerns the impact it has on people. However, there is good reason to think that it is inherently *bankrupt*, where this turns on the normative presuppositions of the polygamous ideal. Since the bankruptcy of a practice is an important dimension of moral evaluation, there is a sense in which liberal feminist social criticism should target polygamous traditions as such, and not just their various contingent defects.

I set aside whether the state should restrict the institution of civil marriage to monogamy or whether there ought to be any such public institution at all. Instead, my concern is with the appropriate critical attitudes to adopt towards a society's diverse range of domestic practices once the supposed universality of the nuclear family ideal is rejected; an enthusiastic acceptance of pluralism should not foster indifference towards the persistence of gender inequality under the guise of cultural diversity. Identifying the sense in which a cultural tradition is inherently objectionable can be useful for liberal feminist social ethics, even if no immediate political or legal implications are drawn.

In section I, I define monogamy and polygamy as cultural practices and discuss why some liberal feminists have argued that polygamy as such is no worse than monogamy. In section II, I reject the argument that polygamy is inherently vicious because asymmetric marriages are inevitably inegalitarian in practice. In section III, I defend the conjecture that polygamous traditions are inherently bankrupt insofar as an ideal of asymmetric marriage presupposes stereotypical gender roles. Since monogamy does not share these presuppositions, it is not subject to the same criticism. In section IV, I conclude by discussing the relationship between the bankruptcy of polygamy and its impact.

I

The monogamous marital form is *symmetric*: two people are married to each other and no one else. In contrast, the polygamous marital form is *asymmetric*: one spouse alone has more than one partner and is therefore in some sense the central partner in the overall marriage. There are more complex marital forms, such as symmetric group marriages between three or more people, where each spouse is married to every other spouse, and overlapping structures of polygyny and polyandry (Zeitzen 2008). In addition, polygamy is distinct from polyamory, which I take to involve informal clusters of (primarily non-marital) relationships, especially those characterized by strong opposition to norms of sexual and romantic exclusivity (see Strassberg in this volume). Although these other kinds of relationships present interesting alternatives to the nuclear family, my focus in this chapter is on the critical evaluation of polygamous traditions as just one element in a broader range of domestic arrangements.

Considered as cultural practices, monogamy and polygamy both involve more than several instantiations of their symmetric and asymmetric forms. People inhabit a social world shaped by an array of legal, political, and ethical norms. Social practices include not only patterns of similar behaviour, but conformity to rules and ideals. These norms might be constitutive of the relationship itself – part of what it means to be married – or background values that specify how it is to be desired, promoted, and respected. No critical assessment of monogamy and polygamy can focus exclusively on their abstract structures, since this would ignore how these relationships reflect morally significant social expectations. Thus, very little about whether the cultural practice of polygamy is inherently objectionable can be learned from some imaginative example of countercultural hipsters who enter an asymmetric marriage as an ironic gesture or a playful exemplification of the contradictions of post-modernity. Such examples say little more about the ethics of polygamy as a cultural tradition than masked balls say about the ethics of veiling.

A polygamous culture, then, differs from a social environment in which some people happen to enter asymmetric marriages for reasons peculiar to their individual circumstances. The culture does not simply tolerate polygamy as the idiosyncratic preference of a few eccentrics or as an ad hoc response to shortages in the number of men or women, as may occur after a war or on some sparsely-populated frontier. Instead, polygamous marriage as such is presented as an ideal, either on par with monogamy or as a higher kind of union. Parents typically regard polygamy as a respectable prospect for their children, and the relationship between sister-wives or brother-husbands may be celebrated as a distinctly valuable kind of friendship. Moreover, many members of the tradition may regard the practice as constitutive of their collective identity – a part of who they are or what defines the unity of their group – even if most marriages in the culture happen to be monogamous. When individuals enter polygamous marriages, they see themselves as participating in a historical tradition and as continuing its way of life. A polygamous culture therefore differs from a monogamous culture in terms of the asymmetric nature of its marital ideal, but the two practices cannot simply be reduced to the several instantiations of their respective abstract forms.

Many familiar liberal feminist criticisms of polygamy make sense only once it is characterized as a norm-governed cultural tradition. For instance, traditional expectations about male authority and female subservience can be enforced through a variety of coercive social sanctions. Women who resist or desert polygamous marriages can often be shunned or otherwise penalized for their deviance or self-assertion. Nevertheless, these threats to autonomy are not unique to the practice; polygamy is no more essentially involuntary than monogamy. Since individuals can value aspects of a cultural tradition just because it defines their sense of collective identity, they can freely choose to participate in practices that outsiders might regard as repressive. Cultural norms do not simply push people around against their will or manipulate their preferences like marionettes (Levey 2005). Instead, they are to some extent presupposed in any rational process of reflection about plans of life; individuals can only understand their goals against some background of normal social aspirations, even if they choose to strike out on their own path. Thus, the cultural nature of polygamy is something of a double-edged sword: it helps explain why the practice can be voluntary, just as it explains why it is very often coercive.

If polygamy can be compatible with women's autonomy, then it is reasonable to conjecture that it can be reformed in other respects too. This suggests that it is unwise to object to polygamy as such. If the purely contingent faults of the practice could be removed, then all that would remain fixed about polygamy is its asymmetric form. But treating one particular marital structure as inherently objectionable seems to be a kind of arbitrary form-fetishism. There is good reason to endorse pluralism about domestic relationships; the nuclear family model is not a script built into human nature and marriage itself is only one form of the good life. Alongside these commitments, the complete rejection of asymmetric marriage in particular seems a peculiar fixation, one that may simply betray a residual prejudice against purportedly backward traditions outside the mainstream of contemporary Western society[1]. A number of feminist scholars have accordingly advocated a qualified acceptance of polygamy, arguing that gender inequality is a purely contingent feature of the practice, just as it is a purely contingent feature of monogamy (Brake 2012: 197–200; Calhoun 2005: 1039; Emens 2004: 77; Nussbaum 2000: 229, and 2008: 197; Song 2007: 160).

> The quick dismissal of polygamy on grounds that it, unlike monogamy, is distinctively gender-inegalitarian is the result of smuggling in a set of unstated assumptions about the background social conditions for women, the social practice of polygamy, and its likely legal form that would render it inegalitarian, but that are implausible about plural marriage in a liberal egalitarian democracy. (Calhoun 2005: 1040)

Recent philosophical literature on polygamy has primarily concerned its appropriate legal status. The claim that the state has no good reason to exclude polygamy from the public institution of civil marriage does not imply that the practice is morally unobjectionable in itself; not every illiberal or inegalitarian cultural practice should be prohibited in a liberal egalitarian democracy (Brettschneider 2007: 93; Deveaux 2006: 209; March 2011). Nevertheless, the form-fetishism challenge can be raised within social ethics: why should liberal feminists have any moral objection to polygamy as such, when they oppose moral objections to other unusual cultural practices? No appeal to the constraints of liberal state neutrality is relevant within an ethical conception of valuable social and cultural diversity. Either polygamy is not inherently sexist or liberal feminists must advance some reason why it should not be accepted on par with other kinds of domestic relationships.

We can approach the form-fetishism challenge by assessing the relative merits of opposite-sex monogamy and polygamy between heterosexuals. Neither form of marriage necessarily involves only opposite-sex relationships – just as same-sex marriage is now recognized as a possibility, a polygamist could in principle have any combination of wives and husbands. Nevertheless, it is useful to focus on marriages comprising only direct marital ties between people of different sexes. If the two kinds of marriage are, in essence, morally equivalent, then there should be no morally significant difference between their predominant opposite-sex forms. Thus, we can bracket aside consideration of same-sex marriage between gays and lesbians, and other kinds of family life. If an argument against opposite-sex polygamy is successful, then its extension to same-sex and mixed cases could be considered separately[2].

II

What does it mean to claim that a social practice is inherently or essentially objectionable? It can't simply mean that there are deontological, principled, or non-instrumental moral reasons to reject certain aspects of the practice, since then almost any human activity could be inherently objectionable. Instead, any such claim must pick out some essential feature of the practice and explain why the practice should be criticized in virtue of this particular feature. The objection to the practice should track at least one of its intrinsic characteristics. I have claimed, however, that a tradition of polygamy has at least two essential features: several instances of asymmetric domestic relationships, and a normative element comprising various expectations and aspirations regarding those relationships. In this section, I discuss an argument that polygamy is inherently objectionable in virtue of the first feature. In the next section, I set out an argument grounded in the second feature.

We can say that a social practice is *vicious* to the extent that actual instances of that practice involve some morally objectionable harm or iniquity, either in themselves or through their consequences. The viciousness of a practice is determined by its impact on the interests or status of the people who participate in it or who are otherwise affected by it. An activity is vicious in virtue of the actual difference it makes in the world – what it does to or for people. A social form is inherently vicious if it is inevitably harmful or iniquitous when realized in actual practice. In this case, there will be a moral objection that tracks an intrinsic characteristic of the form. For instance, a morally repugnant relationship of domination is an essential feature of slavery. Similarly, the practice of foot-binding inevitably inflicts great pain and a crippling disfigurement on young girls. Other inherently vicious practices may be more tolerable if the harms they involve are less egregious. There can also be overriding moral reason to engage in an inherently vicious activity: war can be justifiable despite its inescapable moral costs. In contrast, a practice is only contingently vicious if some morally innocuous instances are realistically possible, keeping the general facts about human beings and societies more or less fixed. Alcohol consumption and drug use can cause great harm but do not always do so. Moral objections to these activities track extrinsic characteristics, such as incapacitation and addiction. To say that an activity is inherently vicious is to make a very general claim about the negative moral difference it makes in practice, but this does not imply that it is worse than contingently vicious activities.

Suppose, then, that a cultural practice of polygamy in a liberal society were reformed as much as realistically possible. In any just system recognizing polygamous relationships, husbands and wives would have reciprocal rights and responsibilities, and both polygyny and polyandry would be permitted (Calhoun 2005: 1039–40). Social conditions would preclude the coercive imposition of polygamy and provide effective opportunities for exit. No social norm would imply that men have the right to be obeyed by their wives or that women should be demure and submissive to their husbands. If there were still polygamous marriages in these felicitous circumstances, could liberal feminists identify any ineliminable harm or iniquity?

According to one argument, inequality is built into the asymmetric structure of polygamous marriage (Barry 2001: 369–70; Brooks 2009). On this view, although the worst forms of subordination might be eradicated, the asymmetric structure of the marriage in itself creates inequality. For instance, since the husband in a polygynous family is married to all his wives, and they are married only to him, he has the right to divorce each wife whereas they only have the right to divorce him:

> Even if each wife had a right to divorce on the same terms as the husband, there would still be a structural asymmetry because no wife could 'divorce' another wife if she found that this other wife made the marriage intolerable ... The whole idea of egalitarian polygamy is manifest nonsense. (Barry 2001: 369)

This point can be generalized across the various rights of marriage. Thus, each individual relationship between husband and wife may involve equal rights considered in itself, but the husband seems to have a disproportionate share of rights in a polygynous marriage as a whole: half the rights are held by him whereas the other half are shared between the wives, and only he can exercise rights within each of the family's constitutive marital relationships.

A somewhat different version of the structural inequality argument concerns how the form of the marriage creates a disparity in the spouses' respective capabilities. Inequality may be built into polygynous marriage insofar as the husband's central position provides him with a strategic advantage over his wives (Eskridge 2002: 131–32). For instance, if he can choose which wife to benefit, they may be locked into a competition for his favours. This relative advantage could give him the ability to exploit his wives. Even if he were scrupulously fair, the mere fact that he occupies a uniquely privileged position is itself a morally objectionable violation of equality. Relationships of hierarchy and domination can be superficially benign, especially if they are enveloped in the pleasant sentiments of affectionate intimacy. On this view, polygyny is inherently vicious because it inevitably empowers the husband and in effect grants him a status it denies to his wives. Since the same reasoning applies to the wife in a polyandrous relationship, the conclusion holds for polygamy as such.

In my view, the asymmetric form of a relationship can undermine women's status and wellbeing, but it is not inevitably inegalitarian. First, consider the right to divorce. We can assume that a just liberal society grants a legal right to no-fault divorce that each spouse can exercise unilaterally. This right comprises a cluster of Hohfeldian incidents (Hohfeld 1913). A spouse is at *liberty* to decide whether she wishes to remain married, and she has a *claim* against others that they not prevent her exit from the marriage. At its core, however, the right to divorce is a legal *power*: by exercising her discretion in the appropriate way, she can modify her rights and duties and the corresponding rights and duties of her husband. This means that in divorcing her husband, a woman changes his legal position. Since he also has the right to divorce, he has the corresponding legal power. If he has more than one wife, he has power over each spouse's legal position, whereas his several wives do not. So there is a clear sense in which asymmetric marriage involves some sort of difference in rights. However, this difference does not entail any inequality in rights on the whole. A spouse also holds a legal *immunity* within or alongside her right to divorce, where to have an immunity is to be protected from having one's legal position changed by another. No one but she and her husband can end their marital relationship. This means that each wife in a polygynous marriage possesses an immunity from having her marital status changed by any of the other wives. Consider the example of the wife who cannot divorce another wife she finds intolerable (Barry 2001: 369). Her lack of power just is an immunity held by her counterpart, and this immunity can be a very valuable thing for a spouse to have. For instance, a woman's immunity from having her live-in in-laws unilaterally terminate her marriage protects her from having to curry favour with them. She may find them intolerable, but could be far more concerned that the sentiment is reciprocated. Having a power over other people can be important for one's self-determination, but it can often be more important to have an immunity from them instead, especially if one values the status quo.

In contrast, the husband does not have a similarly extensive set of immunities. His marital status as a whole is vulnerable to the unilaterally-exercised power of each of his wives. If the legal rights and responsibilities of marriage are fully reciprocal, whenever the husband acquires a power by marrying another wife, he simultaneously loses an immunity to having his legal position changed by her. Thus, the disparity cuts both ways: the husband may have more powers than any of his wives, but they retain immunities against each other that he does not have. This does not mean that the asymmetric structure of polygamy cannot involve or exacerbate an inequality in rights. Instead, it means that one cannot simply infer inequality from asymmetry. The question whether the husband is relatively privileged by having legal powers his wives lack, or whether they are relatively privileged by having legal immunities he lacks, cannot be answered in the abstract. The answer depends on how the society's system of family and property law arranges the various legal incidents of marriage and how this arrangement is responsive to underlying social facts.

For instance, one might simply assume that if a husband marries a second wife, he can unilaterally decide that she will move into the household he shares with his existing wife. But this need not be the case at all. If a man ought to have no more authority than a woman over who is to live in their shared residence, then he will need to get her approval before someone else moves in. Similarly, one might suppose that if a husband and one of his wives divorce, she would be obliged to leave the family household and he would remain with his other wives. But one may as well imagine that the husband would be obliged to leave if any of his wives decided to divorce him. In a just society, the laws governing the distribution of property and parental rights upon the dissolution of a marriage can be designed to counteract the unfair advantage that one or other spouse might otherwise have. This means that one cannot tell who is advantaged by the asymmetric distribution of legal incidents in a polygamous marriage without knowing their specific content and the implications they have for each spouse. Since the central spouse might be disadvantaged just as easily as advantaged by these legal arrangements, asymmetric marriage is not inevitably inegalitarian one way rather than another or, indeed, in any way at all.

The same point holds for the informal capabilities of the partners. One of the core insights of feminism is its scepticism about the sufficiency of formally equal legal rights for properly egalitarian social relationships between men and women. An abstract balance of legal powers and immunities does not guarantee gender equality, since it may be impossible for the law to be fully responsive to the underlying social disparities in status and capability. The distribution of social power in a relationship may be quite different from the distribution of legal rights, so legally egalitarian polygamous marriages may still be thoroughly hierarchical. Nevertheless, it is not always a strategic advantage to be the central party in an asymmetric relationship. For instance, although the wife in a polyandrous marriage might be a powerful matriarch who exercises authority over her husbands, this is by no means inevitable (Zeitzen 2008: 138–44). In a society that traditionally subordinates women, it may be a cultural practice for two men to share a wife, much as they might share a housekeeper or a prostitute. Far from being in a position to exploit them, she would instead be a servant to two masters. Here, the asymmetric marital relationship only serves to compound her subordination. But this very realistic possibility undermines the structural inequality argument: if both polygyny and polyandry can oppress *women*, then neither form is inevitably beneficial to the *central spouse* in the relationship. Whether that spouse's capabilities are promoted by the asymmetry depends on how it reflects the division of power between men and women within that culture and society.

In very different circumstances, instances of both forms of polygamy might oppress the male spouses. This means that there is a continuum of realistically possible social environments in which polygyny is strategically advantageous to the husband at one end and strategically advantageous to the wives at the other. The actual world is, of course, far closer to the former than the latter. Nevertheless, in some possible environments near to the middle of the continuum, there is a balance of power between the spouses. There is no obvious reason why these social worlds could not be ones in which men and women more generally enjoyed the kind of egalitarian social relationships that liberal feminists value. I conclude that the hierarchical characteristics of actual polygamous marriages depend on the underlying distribution of power between men and women, and are not intrinsic to the asymmetric form itself; polygamy is not inherently vicious in virtue of an inevitably inegalitarian structure. This means that there is, as yet, no essential moral difference between polygamy and monogamy.

III

In this section, I turn to a quite different way in which a social practice might be inherently objectionable. Even if polygamy is only contingently vicious, it can still be appropriate to reject the asymmetric marital ideal as such. This is because the impact of a practice on the interests and status of individuals is not the only dimension along which it can be evaluated. In addition, a practice has a *social meaning*, where this is a function of how its various norms should be understood to fit together in a more or less coherent way. For instance, Ralph Wedgwood (1999: 229) claims that, in Western societies at least, marriage has an essential social meaning that includes various expectations about domestic cooperation and sexual intimacy. Spouses would not be properly married if they had no contact or cooperation with each other – their marriage would simply be a sham or in a state of collapse. Since the coherence of a normative system depends on how its elements can be justified, the social meaning of a practice includes anything that its norms presuppose. For instance, some people believe that what justifies the institution of marriage is a commitment to having and raising children and that the meaning of marriage is therefore exclusively heterosexual. On this view, what marriage is 'all about' is a man and a woman building a family together. This interpretation can obviously be contested, since it seems strange to think that domestic and sexual intimacy needs to be justified by procreative goals. If there is no such need, there is no reason to think marriage itself presupposes that spouses ought to have children.

Although the meaning of a social practice may be contested or partially indeterminate, some interpretations are still better than others. The possibility of implausible or disingenuous interpretations of a practice does not imply that social meaning is illusory. However nebulous it may seem, we rely on the idea when we explain our cultural practices to outsiders or try to understand their practices. Different traditions of marriage may have rich variations in social meaning, but they cannot be entirely different if we are to make sense of them as analogous practices. Moreover, we often presuppose facts about social meaning when we assess social institutions – consider whether it is plausible to interpret historical examples of racial segregation without assuming an implicit commitment to racial supremacy (Black 1960: 427).

The impact and meaning of a social practice are interdependent in complex ways, but to see how social meaning can be a conceptually distinct dimension of evaluation, consider two examples. First, the practice of female genital mutilation is inherently vicious, inter alia, because it deprives women of the ability to experience sexual pleasure (Nussbaum 1999: 118–29). Moreover, this effect seems to be its fundamental aim. If so, the best way to interpret traditional clitoridectomy is to see it as expressing a hostile attitude towards female sexuality and a conception of women's subservient role in life (Okin 1999: 14–15, 124–25). So both the impact and meaning of the practice are morally objectionable. Suppose, however, that the practitioners of clitoridectomy become increasingly concerned about its various health risks, preferring that a small symbolic incision be made instead. In this case, the impact of the tradition is substantially altered; what it does is now significantly less dreadful. But the meaning of the tradition remains relatively stable. The symbolic incision arguably presupposes much the same conception of female sexuality as before. If this is the right interpretation, then the tradition is now quite different in one morally important respect – what it *does* to women – but disturbingly similar in another – what it *says* about them.

Second, consider cultural practices premised on an ideology of caste or feudal hierarchy. Such ideologies usually involve harmful effects or iniquitous relationships in some form or another, but this is not essential to them. For instance, suppose the tradition directs high-caste individuals to conduct private cleansing rituals after contact with members of certain lower castes. This practice may go largely unnoticed in the broader society if it is followed by only a few traditionalists, who might themselves accept the propriety of democratic egalitarian norms for public interactions. Thus, the tradition need not be vicious in any obvious way. Nevertheless, it remains morally objectionable insofar as it incorporates a conception of some human beings as essentially unclean or degraded, where this conception is inconsistent with any plausible notion of human dignity. We can say that a practice is inherently *bankrupt*, then, if its essential social meaning includes morally objectionable normative presuppositions. Female circumcision and caste rituals are inherently bankrupt whether or not they are invariably harmful or iniquitous in practice.

I have claimed that polygamous traditions include a general ideal of asymmetric marriage, perhaps alongside a co-equal ideal of monogamous marriage. Polygamy is not simply an ad hoc response to special circumstances or the idiosyncratic preference of a few individuals. Instead, the culture presents polygamy as an appropriate marital form in general; the asymmetric structure is one of the features of marriage that the cultural norm specifically picks out as valuable. The important question to ask about the social meaning of polygamy is not: what impact does this form inevitably have on people? Instead, the question concerns how an asymmetric marital ideal could be rationalized: why should there be a different number of men and women in a marriage? One of the normative presuppositions of opposite-sex polygamy is that there is some basic and enduring difference between men and women such that asymmetric marriage makes good sense as a way of life. Accounting for this difference is the key step in determining whether polygamy is inherently bankrupt. This turns the charge of form-fetishism on its head. The onus is not on liberal feminists to explain why criticism of polygamy is not mere cultural bias. Instead, the onus is on proponents of polygamy to explain why their marital ideal is something more than an arbitrary and senseless prescription.

No boot-strapping appeal to the value of tradition for individuals can explicate its social meaning. The particular intentions of individuals who participate in a cultural practice do not determine what its constitutive norms presuppose, nor do these presuppositions necessarily determine the implicit commitments of individual participants. The simple desire to follow one's tradition may explain why individual members of the practice choose to enter polygamous marriages, but it does not justify why a culture should have that practice in the first place, why it should be constitutive of the group's identity, or why it should continue as a tradition. Thus, one cannot determine the social meaning of polygamy simply by asking why individuals participate in the practice or what their marriages mean to them.

The most plausible interpretation of the gender asymmetry in polygamy is that a cultural ideal of asymmetric marriage implicitly assumes some or other stereotype about men and women's fundamentally different social roles. Some proponents of polygyny argue that it liberates women from domestic drudgery, since it allows the multiple wives to balance careers with their family responsibilities (Emens 2004: 77). But if the ability of small groups of adults to pool their labour and resources were the issue, then the norm should simply advocate communal family forms, with no particular need for an asymmetry between the number of men and women. The polygyny-as-liberation argument implicitly assumes that it is women who should bear primary responsibility for domestic work and child-rearing, since it sees no need for the husband to strike a similar balance. A different justification of polygyny grounds the asymmetry in biological differences between the sexual desires and reproductive capacities of men and women. But this approach relies on some quite dubious background assumptions about the fundamental significance of sex and reproduction in governing human life. There is good reason to object to social practices that define women in terms of a reproductive function or as a means for male sexual gratification.

Different traditions of polygyny and polyandry contain different rationalizations of their marital ideal. The specific assumptions about men and women that make best sense of these norms will accordingly differ from context to context. It is therefore impossible to offer a conclusive argument that all polygamous traditions are inherently bankrupt. Nevertheless, the conjecture may be well-founded. The impossibility of a conclusive argument does not demonstrate that there can be nothing more to the essential social meaning of polygamy than its asymmetric marital ideal. If familiar justifications of polygamy invariably presuppose basic gender stereotypes, then there is good reason to believe that this social meaning tracks the polygamous marital ideal itself. If so, then polygamy is inextricably tied to a sexist conception of men and women, and is to that extent inherently objectionable.

The same argument does not work against monogamous marriage. Although cultural practices of opposite-sex monogamy are often steeped in sexism, this is not intrinsic to them. Since monogamy does not advocate a different number of men and women in marriage, it does not have to posit any basic and enduring gender difference to justify an asymmetry. Instead, the monogamous ideal asserts that there is something distinctively valuable about two people committing to live their lives together. There is no presupposition here that, in the case of heterosexuals, a husband and wife have two quite different roles to play in the marriage. A cultural ideal of monogamy is therefore compatible, as far as it goes, with a vision of a society without ascriptive gender roles:

> In its social structures and practices, one's sex would have no more relevance than one's eye color or the length of one's toes. No assumptions would be made about 'male' or 'female' roles; childbearing would be so conceptually separated from child rearing and other family responsibilities that it would be a cause for surprise, and no little concern, if men and women were not equally responsible for domestic life or if children were to spend much more time with one parent than the other. (Okin 1989: 171)

My goal here is not to defend this conception of a genderless society, nor to argue that any morally acceptable marital ideal must be compatible with it. Instead, my point is simply to illustrate that the essential meaning of monogamy does not include the presupposition that it is plausible to ascribe to polygamy. This means that there is some morally significant intrinsic difference between the two kinds of marriage. Objecting to polygamy in particular is therefore not an arbitrary form-fetishism.

IV

Some sceptics may be entirely untroubled by the examples of symbolic genital incision and private caste rituals: the impact of a social practice on the interests and status of individuals is clearly of moral concern, but why should it also matter whether a cultural tradition is inherently bankrupt or not? One answer to this question is that the social meaning of a practice can affect its impact. There are at least two ways in which this could in principle occur. First, as legal expressivists argue, citizens' political status is constitutively dependent on the social meaning of the law (Anderson and Pildes 2000: 1527–31). To be demeaned by the state is a kind of expressive harm in itself. The same point could hold for cultural norms. If so, the inherent bankruptcy of polygamy might make an immediate difference to the status and interests of the spouses. This is not an implausible suggestion, but there is reason to be cautious. Cultural practices are not entirely analogous to laws. Citizens are governed by the law whether they like it or not, but cultural practices usually include some measure of voluntary choice. Individual participants can have the power to define the terms of their relationships in ways that are at odds with the tradition's normative presuppositions. In particular, there is no obvious reason to think that polygamous spouses could not genuinely accept and abide by norms of gender equality alongside the cultural ideal of asymmetric marriage. If my argument is right, then there would be considerable tension between these two commitments. But this tension does not demonstrate that the wives are unwittingly demeaned by their marriage. Thus, the normative bankruptcy of polygamy does not obviously imply that it is inherently vicious.

Second, a contingently vicious practice can be vicious, when it is, precisely because it is inherently bankrupt. Social meanings often have powerful causal consequences insofar as people adapt their behaviour to their interpretations of cultural norms. If a practice presupposes objectionable gender stereotypes, then this can serve to reinforce sexist attitudes. Other things being equal, it is harder to relinquish beliefs that are needed to make sense of one's surrounding culture and existing commitments. Moreover, an inherently bankrupt practice can have vicious consequences for those who do not participate in it and who may reject its constitutive norms. Thus, participants in a monogamous culture may reject their neighbours' polygamy as a deviation from divine law, but incidentally regard its structure as a better affirmation of gender stereotypes than their own marital form. In this society, polygamous marriages could be significantly more egalitarian than their monogamous counterparts and yet a key source of gender inequality more broadly[3]. Whether these causal relations hold is a contingent matter and so insufficient to warrant any further objection to polygamy as such. Nevertheless, their plausibility is sufficient to demonstrate that an investigation of the inherent bankruptcy of polygamy is not itself a peculiarly rarefied fixation.

Acknowledgments

I am grateful to Elizabeth Brake, Thom Brooks, Sarah Chan, Daniela Cutas, David Gurnham, Thomas Hartvigsson, Mihaela Miroiu, Peter Stone, and Maura Strassberg for their comments on earlier formulations of the ideas expressed here. The chapter was written during my tenure as a fellow at Tulane University's Center for Ethics and Public Affairs.

Notes

1 Justice Waite's infamous denunciation of Mormon polygamy in *Reynolds* is the paradigmatic statement of this prejudice.

2 Since any such extension would depend on how same-sex relationships are valued within the broader culture, I cannot consider it here. My sense, though, is that any cultural ideal of asymmetric same-sex marriage for gays and lesbians – should there ever be such a thing – would simply replicate the same masculine and feminine stereotypes presupposed in the culture's ideal of opposite-sex polygamy for heterosexuals. The mere possibility of same-sex polygamy does not imply that polygamous cultural traditions are free of sexist presuppositions.

3 See Song (2007) for an extended discussion of the interconnections between minority and majority cultures.

References

Anderson, E.S. and Pildes, R.H. (2000), 'Expressive Theories of Law: A General Restatement', *University of Pennsylvania Law Review*, 148: 1503–75.

Barry, B. (2001), *Culture and Equality: An Egalitarian Critique of Multiculturalism*, Cambridge, Mass.: Harvard University Press.

Black, C.L. (1960), 'The Lawfulness of the Segregation Decisions', *Yale Law Journal*, 69: 421–30.

Brake, E. (2012), *Minimizing Marriage: Marriage, Morality, and the Law*, Oxford: Oxford University Press.

Brettschneider, C. (2007), *Democratic Rights: The Substance of Self-Government*, Princeton: Princeton University Press.

Brooks, T. (2009), 'The Problem with Polygamy', *Philosophical Topics*, 37: 109–22.

Calhoun, C. (2005), 'Who's Afraid of Polygamous Marriage? Lessons for Same-Sex Marriage Advocacy from the History of Polygamy', *San Diego Law Review*, 42: 1023–42.

Deveaux, M. (2006), *Gender and Justice in Multicultural Liberal States*, Oxford: Oxford University Press.

Emens, E.F. (2004), 'Just Monogamy?', in M.L. Shanley, *Just Marriage*, New York: Oxford University Press.

Eskridge, W.N. (2002), *Equality Practice: Civil Unions and the Future of Gay Rights*, New York: Routledge.

Hohfeld, W.N. (1913), 'Some Fundamental Legal Conceptions as Applied in Judicial Reasoning', *Yale Law Journal*, 23: 16–59.

Levey, A. (2005), 'Liberalism, Adaptive Preferences, and Gender Equality', *Hypatia*, 20: 127–43.

March, A. (2011), 'Is There a Right to Polygamy? Marriage, Equality and Subsidizing Families in Liberal Public Justification', *Journal of Moral Philosophy*, 8: 246–72.

Nussbaum, M.C. (1999), *Sex and Social Justice*, New York: Oxford University Press.

Nussbaum, M.C. (2000), *Women and Human Development: The Capabilities Approach*, Cambridge: Cambridge University Press.

Nussbaum, M.C. (2008), *Liberty of Conscience: In Defense of America's Tradition of Religious Equality*, New York: Basic Books.

Okin, S.M. (1989), *Justice, Gender, and the Family*, New York: Basic Books.

Okin, S.M. (1999), *Is Multiculturalism Bad for Women?*, Princeton: Princeton University Press.

Reynolds v. U.S. [1879] 98 U.S. 145.

Song, S. (2007), *Justice, Gender, and the Politics of Multiculturalism*, Cambridge: Cambridge University Press.

Wedgwood, R. (1999), 'The Fundamental Argument for Same-Sex Marriage', *Journal of Political Philosophy*, 3: 225–42.

Zeitzen, M.K. (2008), *Polygamy: A Cross-Cultural Analysis*, Oxford: Berg.

11

Distinguishing Polygamy and Polyamory Under the Criminal Law

Maura Irene Strassberg

In North America, criminal polygamy laws date back to the mid- to late-nineteenth century, when polygynist Mormons began to gain political power and, in the case of the United States, threatened to create a state in which polygyny was both legal and widely practiced (Strassberg 1997: 1504–5, n. 5). More recently, polygamy has been defended as an alternative sexual practice and family structure, like same-sex marriage, that is repressed by sexual prejudice and is deserving of legal protection and recognition in a liberal state (Chambers 1997: 81–83; May, this volume). Similar arguments are currently the basis for the strongest legal challenge to the criminalization of polygamy in modern times, a reference to the British Columbia Supreme Court on the constitutionality of the Canadian polygamy law under the Canadian Charter of Rights and Freedoms (BCCLA 2011: 3–4). I have argued, however, that polygamy poses social and ethical concerns in a liberal state that both distinguish it from same-sex and opposite-sex monogamous relationships and justify its continued criminalization (Strassberg 1997: 1615–18; Strassberg 2003b: 363–412).

It may well be that some of the feminist and gay rights support for polygamy is more reasonably explained as support for polyamory (Stacey 2009: 192). *Polyamory* is a recently invented term denoting a relationship form based on the belief that no one individual can meet all the needs of any other individual and that multiple loving relationships are necessary to allow individuals to realize their full sexual, emotional, intellectual and spiritual potential (Strassberg 2003a: 455). Since polyamory celebrates the individual, polyamorous relationships arise out of the voluntary and individual choice of partners based on romantic love and sexual attraction (*Ibid.*: 452). Informed by both the women's and gay rights movements, polyamory values both male and female sexual pleasure and can include multi-partner sexual and romantic relationships that are exclusively same-sex or opposite-sex or a mixture of both (*Ibid.*: 453). While polyamory is an umbrella term covering everything from individuals with multiple separate partners to open marriages, it is only the group marriage version of polyamory, called polyfidelity (*Ibid.*: 466), that could in any stretch of the imagination be potentially covered by laws criminalizing polygamy. For purposes of this chapter, therefore, references to polyamory in general should be understood as referring to polyfidelity in particular.

Some definitions of the criminal offense of polygamy, most notably that found in American jurisdictions following the Model Penal Code, arguably would not reach polyfidelity. Although there is no case law to this effect, it is likely that the Model Penal Code requirement that multiple cohabitation be an 'exercise of the purported right of plural marriage' would effectively exclude polyfidelity (Strassberg 2003b: 421). To begin with, the term 'plural marriage' is a specific reference to Mormon polygyny, as it is the term used by Mormons to describe marriages involving one husband and multiple wives (*Ibid.*: 424). In addition, the 'purported right' likely refers to the United States Supreme Court's 1878 rejection of the claim that plural marriage by Mormons was an exercise of religious freedom (Reynolds: 166). Polyfidelitious families certainly do not use the term plural marriage, and may not even use the term marriage at all, to describe their relationships (Strassberg 2003b: 425). In addition, they are more likely to view their conduct as an exercise of the right of intimate association, rather than a right to marry (*Ibid.*: 423). As a result, it would be difficult to argue that the Model Penal Code polygamy law gives clear notice, as criminal statutes must, that polyfidelity is covered conduct. However, polyfidelity involving some legally married partners could be criminalized in the United States under state bigamy laws that forbid cohabitation while concurrently married to another (Strassberg 2003b: 418–19).

There are other definitions of criminal polygamy, such as that found in Canadian law, that have a much greater likelihood of criminalizing polyfidelity. The current Canadian polygamy statute now in effect was purged of its original references to plural marriage and now simply prohibits entering into 'any kind of conjugal union with more than one person at the same time' (AGC: 9–10). In its filing in the Canadian constitutional polygamy case, the Attorney General of British Columbia has argued that the polygamy law will and should cover polyamorous relationships only to the extent that they fall within the language of the statute and have become 'marriages or marriage-like through the influence of a binding authority or otherwise' (AGBC: 122). Under this interpretation of the statute, most polyfidelitious relationships would be excluded due to an absence of either any kind of commitment ceremony or external authority understood as capable of 'binding' the parties to each other. However, as a requirement of a binding authority does not actually appear on the face of the statute, this interpretation by the Attorney General may well be an attempt to 'rewrite the provision [to exclude polyamory] in order that it pass constitutional muster' (Bailey 2010/11: 13–14).

In this chapter I will argue that despite the liberal discomfort it creates, criminalizing polygyny, with particular reference to Mormon fundamentalist polygyny, through polygamy laws, continues to be a justifiable social policy.

Although the reasons for criminalizing Mormon fundamentalist polygyny do not apply to polyfidelity as an alternative form of marriage and family, polyfidelity does raise some social and ethical concerns of its own. These concerns do not, however, rise to the level of requiring that polyamory be criminalized. Thus, to the extent that contemporary polygamy laws do apply to polyamory, they should be rewritten. Understanding the differences between polygyny and polyamory may help with this admittedly difficult task.

Polygyny

Contemporary polygyny seems to have two faces, one that is somewhat attractive to feminists and gay theorists, and another that is quite frightening. These two sides of polygyny are illustrated by two articles that appeared in the online version of the New York Times within two weeks of each other in January of 2010. The first article described a Muslim Malaysian family with four wives, each of whom is a highly educated and successful woman: a medical doctor, a lawyer, a college professor and a teacher (Gooch 2010). The article suggested that the doctor, lawyer and college professor, who were mostly financially independent, had chosen to become the second, third and fourth wives of their wealthy, industrialist husband because they had put off marriage to further their careers and were unable to find monogamous husbands by the time they wanted to marry. Their polygamous marriage provided them with an opportunity to be in a sexual relationship and have children in a socially conservative society that limited these activities to heterosexual marriage. During the week, the doctor, lawyer and professor had their own homes near their workplaces while their young children were cared for by the first wife at the family home. On weekends, they all converged on the family home, where they cooked together, shared clothes and enjoyed their sisterhood. From a feminist perspective, what is attractive about this polygynous family is that, although polygyny ultimately allowed these women to take on gender-typical roles as wives and mothers, at least they did so voluntarily and in a way that also allowed them to balance gender-atypical roles as professionals. It also may be an illustration of Simon May's argument that polygamy is not inherently vicious (May, in this volume).

In contrast, the second article described a police raid on a Jewish polygynous family in Israel, headed by a religious leader who views himself as the saviour of the universe (Kershner 2010). A raid by the Israeli police on his apartments in Tel Aviv turned up seventeen wives and forty children. While the women had joined the family willingly at first, they had subsequently been abused and terrorized into what became a state of enslavement. Here polygyny magnifies the worst anti-feminist aspects of heterosexual marriage, allowing a single abusive man to dominate and abuse more than one woman.

These two faces of international polygamy are also present in the predominant context for polygamy in the United States, fundamentalist Mormon polygamy. Professor Janet Bennion, an anthropologist who has done extensive field research living with Mormon polygamous families, observed polygamous wives who as mature adults voluntarily left mainstream, monogamous Mormon communities to enter into fundamentalist Mormon polygynous marriages. She describes them as flourishing in a way they were unable to do so in the absence of polygyny (Bennion 1998: 9, 65, 96). On the other hand, women who have escaped abusive polygynous marriages in fundamentalist communities have described conditions that more closely resemble the Israeli family (Strassberg 2003b: 395–402). Positive outcomes in polygyny seem to arise when mature women control and use the institution to meet their need for a family in a larger social and religious context that requires heterosexual marriage. In such cases, the polygynous family so created may be considerably less patriarchal in its day-to-day operation. However, when men and religious belief really control polygyny, it is a very different institution. This, I believe, is most typically the situation in fundamentalist Mormon polygyny, in large part because of the particular religious beliefs that make polygyny a religious practice for such fundamentalists.

Fundamentalist Mormons believe, as did the original historical Mormons, that God himself was once a mortal man who had achieved godhood (Strassberg 1997: 1579). This means that men can also ascend to godhood by creating the right foundation during earthly life. In addition to the initial requirement that a man be righteous, which means faithful and loyal adherence to Mormon Church doctrines and institutions, the primary earthly foundation for godhood is the accumulation of power over large numbers of people, for whom you will subsequently be a god in the Kingdom of Heaven (*Ibid.*). Such power can only be accumulated through the institution of celestial marriage, by which a woman is sealed to a man for all eternity, and by the birth in such a marriage of blood progeny, who are also subordinated to their patriarch for all eternity (*Ibid.*). Since only men can achieve godhood, salvation and eternal life for fundamentalist women requires that they enter into a polygynous union with a righteous man, bear him as many children as possible, and support the further expansion of his progeny by the addition of more wives (*Ibid.*: 1579–80). Rejection of polygyny by women is believed to result in damnation (Strassberg 2003b; 381–2). In addition, to ensure that they marry a righteous man, women must accept marriages that are approved by Church elders and often arranged by them as well (Strassberg 2003b: 366–37, 391).

Polygyny thus serves two religious purposes. First, it reinforces the hierarchy of men over women by, as the founder of the Mormon religion said, freeing men 'from the unnatural sexual influence women hold over men' in monogamous marriage (Foster 1981: 176). Second, it is a crucial instrument in making godhood possible by vastly expanding the progeny of men aspiring to god status. Consequently, it is the religious significance of procreation and patriarchy that must be understood as the driving force behind fundamentalist polygynous marriages. Contrary to the title of the Home Box Office cable television show, 'Big Love', fundamentalist Mormon marriages are not meant to be defined by love, although love may arise.

The role of coercion in how women come to be polygynous wives is the most troubling aspect of polygamy and the primary basis of its continued criminalization. However, coercion is not the case for all fundamentalist Mormon polygynous wives. Some join polygynous communities and polygynous marriages as mature adult converts to fundamentalism and are usually divorcees or widows with children, or never-married 'thirty-somethings' (*Ibid.*: 390–91). They typically come from the mainstream Mormon community which, although it has repudiated polygyny, maintains beliefs about godhood, celestial marriage and eternal power through blood progeny that make divorced women, widows with children, and older, never-married women disfavoured marriage partners (*Ibid.*). Such women are often both financially vulnerable and socially disconnected from mainstream Church culture due to their unmarried state and find that polygynous marriage addresses their needs for survival, sex, family, community and salvation (*Ibid.*). These relationships are no more coercive than many monogamous heterosexual relationships motivated by religious prohibitions on extra-marital sex and child-bearing and most closely resemble the Malaysian polygynous marriage profiled in the New York Times.

However, given fundamentalist beliefs about the purpose of polygyny to exponentially grow men's kingdoms through procreation, older women from outside of the fundamentalist community are only a small proportion of polygynous wives. The majority of such wives enter polygynous marriages from within the isolated polygynous community they grew up in (*Ibid.*: 393). Many, if not most, enter into arranged marriages as teenagers between the ages of twelve and eighteen (*Ibid.*: 366, 386; Bramham 2011). Most of these marriages are with middle-aged to older men who already have multiple wives and families (Strassberg 2003b: 366). This is because older men form the 'righteous' religious hierarchy and they give these teenage wives to themselves and each other (*Ibid.*: 391; Bramham 2011). Many of the younger men who might be natural objects of affection and attraction for these teenage and young adult women are ejected from the fundamentalist community, often as minor teenagers themselves, for the simple reason that polygyny cannot accommodate equal numbers of men and women, and the young men who threaten to undermine polygyny must be removed from the competition for women (Harris 2005: 1–2).

Anecdotal evidence suggests that a number of teenage wives are coerced into polygynous marriages by physical violence and threats of spiritual damnation (Strassberg 2003b: 366–68). These are girls who are raised to obey religious authority in isolated and closed communities, are taught to expect polygynous marriage, and are pulled out of school before high school because they will not need further education. If they don't actively resist marriage it may only be because they believe that resistance will be met with extreme punishment and that they have no real chance of escape from their community (*Ibid.*).

There are, at the same time, teenage girls in these communities who don't seem coerced into these marriages. They embrace their faith and consent to the marriage arranged for them (*Ibid.*: 373–74). However, as I have argued in greater detail elsewhere, religiously-motivated consent by teenage girls to polygynous marriage should be seen as uninformed, just as we see a teenager's religiously motivated refusal to accept life-saving medical procedures as insufficiently informed to amount to legal consent (*Ibid.*: 381–89). Although teenage girls do not risk certain or even likely death by consenting to become polygynous wives, they are consenting to sexual relations which will be designed to get them pregnant both as soon as possible and as many times as possible during the next 20–30 years. For young teenagers, any pregnancy is physically risky, and multiple early pregnancies will have debilitating effects over the long term. Beyond the health risks, however, are the life-changing effects of accumulating a large brood of children that she will largely raise on her own, or with the help of her similarly burdened sister-wives.

Indeed, just at the point a polygynous wife might become disenchanted with polygyny, she will find it extremely difficult to leave her marriage. Sarah Song has referred to this as the problem of 'exit' (2007: 160–62). Exit is difficult for wives married as teenagers due to their lack of education and exposure to the outside world, their financial dependence on the church and other polygynous wives, and their fear of losing their children and their eternal salvation (*Ibid.*: 400–04). This serves to make teenage consent to polygynous marriage both deeply life-changing and irreversible. Thus, these marriages should be viewed as coerced.

Many of these same exit difficulties are present for those adult polygynous women who can be presumed to enter into such marriages voluntarily. Their voluntary entrance into polygyny does not ensure voluntary exit (*Ibid.*). These coercive realities make me ambivalent at best about the decriminalization of polygynous marriages involving only mature adult women. Furthermore, any attempt to decriminalize polygyny involving only mature adult women must come to grips with the fact that fundamentalist Mormon polygyny, even at its best, is not an individual-focused alternative lifestyle designed to meet the needs of otherwise unmarriageable older Mormon women (*Ibid.*: 410; May in this volume). Rather, Mormon fundamentalist polygyny is largely and most successfully a community-based practice (*Ibid.*: 393), where the communities are inevitably theocracies that have been created by and around a male prophet (*Ibid.*: 405–06). Polygyny is an essential element of the political success of these theocracies because it allows for the control and concentration of sexual, reproductive and economic resources in the hands of the prophet and his favoured delegates. Given the specific religious significance of fundamentalist Mormon polygyny, decriminalizing mature polygynous marriages would not stop the coercive polygynous marriages of teenage girls. Teenage wives are the mainstay of Mormon fundamentalist polygyny for both practical and religious reasons. Consequently, the entire institution is inevitably tainted by the sexual coercion and reproductive exploitation of young women, not to mention the sexual exclusion and emotional cruelty displayed towards the young men summarily ejected from their families and communities[1].

This does not mean that I support the criminal prosecution of polygynous wives in general, which is simply a re-victimization, although some criminal penalty could be appropriate where polygynous wives become active coercive agents in the marriages of their own young daughters. Maintaining a crime of polygyny on the books is in large part a symbolic rejection of both the specific coercion of teenage and adult polygynous wives and the theocratic communities created by and around polygyny. As I have argued in more detail elsewhere, a more effective strategy against those aspects of polygyny that are most problematic may be to reassert government control and oversight over the economic and social institutions of polygynous communities while simultaneously working to empower both teenage girls and dissatisfied adult women in these communities (*Ibid.*: 430). However, I remain skeptical that such efforts can truly produce a kinder, gentler form of fundamentalist polygyny (May, in this volume). I suspect that the religious ideology driving Mormon fundamentalist polygyny is simply inconsistent with our desire to reform the institution.

Polyamory

There are a number of crucial distinctions between polygyny and polyamory that justify exclusion of polyamory from criminalization. To begin with, polyamory is not the developed social institution that polygyny is. Even the relatively new institution of Mormon fundamentalist polygyny, which was founded as a return to the patriarchal polygyny described in the Bible (Strassberg 1997: 1582), has been practised for more than 150 years (Strassberg 2003b: 353 n.3). Although there may have been antecedents to polyamory as far back as such nineteenth-century social experiments as the Oneida community (Foster 1997: 257–260), the roots of polyamory are more accurately traced back to the free love movement of the 1960s, the concurrent development of the women's and gay rights movements, and the practical experiences of certain utopian communities that existed through the 1970s and 1980s (Strassberg 2003a: 439–42). The term 'polyamory' itself only first appeared in print in 1990 (*Ibid.*: 439, n. 4). Around that time, a movement was borne that has spent the last two decades largely focused on itself: exploring its own theoretical underpinnings, creating a national community through print and internet media, and giving advice on the practical challenges of polyamorous life (*Ibid.* 442–43). Whether out of a fear of drawing too much attention to itself, or a lack of energy available for external focus caused by the internal demands of polyamorous relationships, polyamory has not developed the political/activist character of the women's/gay rights movements (*Ibid.*: 447).

Because there is no stable social institution of polyfidelity that can be easily studied and characterized (*Ibid.*), determining the impact of polyfidelity upon the adult individuals who choose to enter such relationships, upon the children who may be raised by polyfidelitious families, and upon society as a whole is, therefore, a matter of some speculation. Nonetheless, to the extent that polyfidelity has effectively been criminalized by the polygamy laws in such countries as Canada, or by bigamy laws in the United States, it is necessary to try to do so. In what follows, I shall use the movement's own writings and anecdotal descriptions to compare polyfidelity to polygamy.

Ideologically, polyamory begins with a focus on the individual and the conditions necessary for individuals to flourish. Its values are 'individual choice, voluntary cooperation, a healthy family life and positive romantic love' (Nearing 1992: 59) along with 'sexual equality, a non-possession orientation towards relationships, and a widening circle of spousal intimacy and true love' (*Ibid.*). Polyfidelity ensures that each individual has equal value within a multi-partner relationship by requiring that each person must be in a loving, although not necessarily sexual relationship, with each other 'marriage' partner (*Ibid.*: 10). Adding new partners to the 'marriage' thus requires the knowledge and full consent of each other member (*Ibid.*: 69, 26–7). Many couples interested in polyfidelity spend years looking for just one additional partner whom both partners love, and who wants to be 'married' to both of them (Northrop 1997: 40–42). Adding a fourth or fifth 'marriage' partner is even harder. Maintaining this complex web of relationships in the face of the inevitable jealousy than can arise requires a commitment to communication, emotional honesty, negotiation and trust as well as lots of family meetings. Egalitarian decision-making processes like consensus or majority democracy are used (Nearing 1992: 36–7). Thus, while fundamentalist Mormon polygyny is defined by obedience, patriarchy, and hierarchy, polyamory is defined by autonomy, egalitarianism, and democracy.

Another important distinction between polyfidelity and fundamentalist Mormon polygyny is that polyfidelity is not practiced by members of a pre-existing community who share religious beliefs, cultural bonds or difficult economic circumstances, nor is it imposed upon anyone (Strassberg 2003b: 413). Rather, it is a choice that individuals from anywhere in society may come to if they find themselves attracted to and in love with more than one person. This may arise as a combination of temperament and happenstance. As a result, polyfidelity neither arises out of, nor does it seek to create, a homogeneous and self-perpetuating community engaged in such group 'marriages' (*Ibid.*).

A direct focus on the particular concerns used to justify criminalizing fundamentalist Mormon polygyny also shows that polyfidelity does not cause the same individual or social harms. The primary reason for continuing to criminalize polygyny is to protect the teenage girls who are a significant source of plural wives. Polyfidelity, on the other hand, seeks to maximize the sexual and romantic connections between partners. As a result, these 'marriages' are not particularly interested in reproduction, let alone maximizing the number of children borne to the family (Strassberg 2003a: 492–94). Consequently, polyfidelity has no reproductive-based need to target teenage or young adult women.

In addition, a polyfidelitous 'marriage' seeking to expand is looking for an individual who is comfortable with sharing sexual and emotional intimacy with more than one person. Teenagers and young adults are quite unlikely to already be dissatisfied with monogamy and seeking multiple-party relationships for themselves. Furthermore, teenagers and young adults are not likely to be emotionally mature enough to deal with the jealousy that comes with sharing partners, or sufficiently self-aware and skilled at communication to live in a group (Strassberg 2003b: 426). Thus, the teenage girls of polyfidelitious families are presumably not going to be married off to other polyfidelitious families, nor are the teenage boys of polyfidelitous families going to be banished from their families and communities. Polyfidelity's emphasis on individual choice requires allowing any children the family might have to make their own life and relationship choices. In addition, unlike most polygynous families, polyfidelitous families do not live in isolated communities that exert almost total community control over the lives and minds of their children, from education to media exposure (*Ibid.*, 428). As a result, polyfidelitous families are not likely to have the power to coercively marry off their young teenage girls or brainwash them into wishing to enter into such marriages.

Although, unlike polygyny, entry into polyfidelity is limited to adults and is non-coercive, there is a potential 'dark side' (Slomiak 1997: 22) to such relationships. To begin with, it is a core principle of polyamory in general that jealousy is an unnecessary emotion that we have been socialized to feel, but can 'unlearn' (Strassberg 2003a: 456–60). Since jealousy makes it impossible for sexual and romantic partners to tolerate the existence of others (*Ibid.* 456–57), polyamory devotes considerable energy to helping its practitioners unlearn jealousy (West 1996: 110–59). However, if polyamorists are wrong, and jealousy is inevitable, then polyamory 'itself is coercive because it necessarily provokes jealousy and then demands of its practitioners that they accept what they cannot accept and pretend not to feel what they cannot help but feel' (Strassberg 2003a: 506). The invisible self-coercion demanded by polyamory may, in turn, generate a need to coerce other existing or potential partners.

Larger polyfidelitous families may be especially at risk for coercive internal dynamics. Although group decision-making in polyfidelity is ostensibly democratic, the reality of group dynamics is that individual differences between group members can produce power differentials that turn group decision-making from autonomous deliberation to coercive manipulation (*Ibid.*: 496–97). In larger polyfidelitious families, such power differentials can arise if some members of the family are sexually connected to more family members than others (*Ibid.*: 496). This occurs when, in a particular family, the family members are not sexually fully mutual, i.e. all the family members are not in sexual relationships with all other family members. Thus, in a triad, if one person has a sexual relationship with the two other triad members, but the two other members do not have a sexual relationship with each other, one person is the 'sexual hinge' (*Ibid.*, n. 312). In larger polyfidelitious families, especially those that are purely heterosexual, there are likely to be one or two individuals who are sexual hinges. In addition, even in the context of fully mutual sexual relationships within the family, each relationship is unique, and the level of connection will vary both from relationship to relationship and, within relationships, over time. Those family members who are in the most relationships or in the most intense relationships will likely have more power in the group (*Ibid.*). Other factors contributing to power differentials in polyfidelity can include links between particular members created by longer-term relationships, legal marriage, biological and/or legal parenthood and asset ownership. Family members not linked to others in such ways can be more vulnerable than those who have such links. Finally, personal charisma, verbal fluency and personal aggressiveness can create and/or exacerbate otherwise existing power differentials (*Ibid.*). Thus, with all that goes into the relationships that constitute polyfidelity, a procedural commitment to deliberative and democratic decision-making may be subverted by emotional dominance and vulnerability (*Ibid.*: 497).

The Kerista community, a twenty-five member San Francisco community credited with coining the word polyfidelity, suffered from just such coercive and manipulative group decision-making (Slomiak 1997: 20–26). This community began as two group marriages that ultimately merged into one marriage over a twenty-year period (*Ibid.*: 18–20). Although ideologically Kerista was committed to 'equality, democratic decision-making, and personal freedom' (*Ibid.*: 20), in reality, there was a social hierarchy that used highly effective techniques of emotional manipulation and intimidation to force conformity with the desires of powerful family members (*Ibid.*: 22–26). Pressure of this kind extended even to decisions such as the addition of new members to the marriage, which meant that ultimately some family members were coerced into sexual relationships with others to maintain the ideology of equality (*Ibid.*: 23).

Of particular interest in the Kerista community was the use of a threat of banishment to weld control over family members (*Ibid.*: 24). Because this community was an economic as well as family community, members stood to lose everything if banished: love, friends, home, and livelihood (*Ibid.*).

This threat of banishment successfully kept dissatisfied community members from challenging the family power brokers for many years (*Ibid.*). The example of Kerista, therefore, suggests that individuals in polyfidelity can have 'exit problems' similar to those of polygynous wives.

It is a paradox of polyfidelity that a commitment to individual autonomy ultimately places individuals in group 'marriages' capable of exercising much greater control over the individual than any single individual could possibly have exerted (Strassberg 2003a: 500–504). Larger polyfidelitous families have the capacity to take on the coercive and autonomy-depriving characteristics of a cult, as Kerista did. Whether this actually occurs may depend, at least in part, on two inter-related factors; the size of the family and the ideology driving it. Kerista ultimately involved a 25-person marriage, but started out as two associated group marriages sharing a vision to create a utopian community (Slomiak 1997: 19–20). Like Kerista, there are many polyfidelitious families with visions of utopian community at their core (Strassberg 2003a: 498). Such a focus on community is likely to drive attempts to expand the marriage to a size where the coercive potential becomes much greater (*Ibid.*: 498, n. 323). It may well be the case that many polyfidelitious groups larger than four adults have some kind of 'compelling communal dynamic' that helps both bring and hold them together (Nearing 1997: 22–23). In contrast, smaller polyfidelitious families may view themselves as merely larger nuclear families with no aspiration to grow bigger than the three or four romantically and sexually connected adults already involved (Northrop 1997: 40–42). This suggests that there may be an important difference between polyfidelity used as an alternative to the nuclear family and polyfidelity used as a basis for the organization of utopian communities. It is the latter that most significantly raises the spectre of coercive, autonomy destroying relationships. One way to ensure that this is less likely to occur would be to place a limit on the size of polyfidelitious families to perhaps no more than four adults.

Do the potential for coercion and difficulties of exit in polyfidelity justify the criminalization of polyfidelity? To begin with, allowing a mature adult to choose to engage in polyamorous relationships that may demand suppression of jealousy seems no worse than entering religious orders that demand suppression of sexuality. These may be impossible demands, and it may be an unwise exercise of an adult's personal autonomy to attempt such suppression, but this is no reason to prohibit the choice. In addition, although utopian/communal visions may even be commonplace in polyfidelity, there is no evidence to suggest that most polyfidelitious families do contain significantly more than four adult members. As such, they are not likely to have reached the tipping point at which individual autonomy is swallowed by the power of the group. Furthermore, it is not illegal for adults to join a cult. For a mature adult to choose to enter into a polyfidelitious family that has cult potential seems no worse than a mature adult entering a monogamous heterosexual marriage that has domestic abuse potential. Again, it is possibly unwise, but that alone is no reason to prohibit the choice.

If polyfidelity does not coerce teenagers into polyfidelitious relationships, and at worst allows adults to choose membership in a group that will demand unusual self-discipline and may become personally coercive, we may still ask what impact polyfidelity has upon children raised in such families. With no more than anecdotal data, these concerns are mostly speculation. On the positive side, polyfidelitious families may be the 'village' that Hillary Clinton said was needed to raise a child (Ravenhart 1997: 11), providing multiple adult parents to meet the varying needs of children. At the same time, we may ask whether there is any threat to children from living with multiple adults not biologically related to them in the 'sex positive' culture of polyamory (Strassberg 2003a: 452–53, 510–17). We know that family members and acquaintances are a major source of sexual abuse for children in general and that children living with only one parent have an elevated risk of such abuse (Finkelhor 1994). In polyfidelitous families with children, children will be living with one or more biologically unrelated adults. However, I do not believe that there is a significantly increased risk of sexual abuse for such children arising out of their family structure. In many polyfidelitous families, the adults will join the family prior to the birth of the child and will consider themselves co-equal parents of the child. Such parents would be very different than the boyfriends or after-acquired husband of a single mother. In addition, the 'sex positive' culture of polyamory could also serve to insulate children from such abuse, as

> polyfidelity provides multiple sexual outlets for adult family members. Furthermore, polyfidelity would seem unlikely to attract or tolerate latent pedophiles as family members because pedophiles do not have the adult relationship skills sufficient to survive the pressures and demands of polyfidelity. (Strassberg 2003b: 426)

Finally, a larger number of adult parents may minimize such children's exposure to daycare providers and babysitters, which are other potential sources of child sexual abuse.

A final reason for criminalizing polygyny is its central contribution to the creation of isolated theocratic communities that accumulate considerable economic resources, often at the expense of the women and children who help produce those resources (Strassberg 2003b: 409). Such communities substantially evade federal, state and local regulation in ways that hurt both vulnerable community members and the larger society as a whole. It is clear that polyfidelity poses no such threats. While some practitioners of polyfidelity may value communal living, they are not ideologically homogeneous and show little tendency to band together to create exclusive and truly independent polities (*Ibid.*: 428–29). Indeed, polyfidelity would wither without access to a large population of people not in such relationships from which to find willing and acceptable partners (*Ibid.*: 428).

In conclusion, I would note that the modern decriminalization of adultery, fornication and same-sex relationships has been based on the recognition of sex and love as crucial expressions of personal autonomy. I would argue that to the extent personal autonomy arguments are made the basis for decriminalizing polygyny, such arguments support decriminalization of polyamory much more than polygyny. Polyamorous relationships are based on love and sexual attraction. Mormon fundamentalist polygyny is about reproduction and patriarchy. Since these goals have been given a religious context, the strongest argument for decriminalization of polygyny is the freedom to practice one's religion. But such religious freedom cannot be supported when it destroys the autonomy of the very individuals in whose name claims of religious freedom are made.

Note

1 Simon May would characterize this impact on both young men and women as showing the viciousness of polygamy (May, in this volume). I would agree with him in general that it is only contingent viciousness, as polyamory does not produce the same harmful impact. I would argue that Mormon fundamentalist polygyny is inherently rather than contingently vicious. May's claim that polygyny and polyandry are not inherently vicious is based on an assumption that there is no coercion, no problem of exit, and no male domination (May, in this volume). However, he does conclude that the viciousness of the practice is 'parasitic on the underlying distribution of power between men and women' (*Ibid.*). Thus, we might agree as to the actual inherent viciousness of Mormon fundamentalist polygamy, which mandates a highly unequal distribution of power between men and women. I suspect that the reformed institution of polygamy he defends as not inherently vicious is actually polyamory rather than polygyny/polyandry, as the latter are gendered practices that cannot be reformed as he suggests without changing the cultural reality that makes them gendered.

References

Anapol, D. (1997), *Polyamory: The New Love Without Limits: Secrets of Sustainable Intimate Relationships*, San Rafael: IntiNet Resource Center.

Attorney General of British Columbia (AGBC), Closing Submissions, filed in The Supreme Court of British Columbia, Reference Concerning the Constitutionality of S. 293 of the Criminal Code of Canada, Vancouver Registry, S097767, http://stoppolygamyincanada.wordpress.com/court-documents/closing-statements-for-the-reference/ [accessed 17 March, 2011].

Attorney General of Canada (AGC), Closing Submissions, filed in The Supreme Court of British Columbia, Reference Concerning the Constitutionality of S. 293 of the Criminal Code of Canada, Vancouver Registry, S097767, http://stoppolygamyincanada.wordpress.com/court-documents/closing-statements-for-the-reference/ [accessed 17 March, 2011].

Bailey, M., (2009), "Should Polygamy Be Criminalized?", http://papers.ssrn.com/sol3/papers.cfm?abstract_id=1509459 [accessed 18 March, 2011].

Bennion, J. (1998), *Women of Principle: Female Networking in Contemporary Mormon Polygyny*, Oxford: Oxford University Press.

Bramham, D. (2011), 'Bountiful dads smuggled daughters, 12 into U.S. to "marry" accused pedophile', Vancouver Sun, February 25, 2011 http://www.vancouversun.com/life/Bountiful+dads+smuggled+daughters+into+marry+accused+pedophile/4343527/story.html [accessed 17 March, 2011].

British Columbia Civil Liberties Association (BCCLA), Opening Statement on Breach, filed in The Supreme Court of British Columbia, Reference Concerning the Constitutionality of S. 293 of the Criminal Code of Canada, Vancouver Registry, S097767, http://stoppolygamyincanada.wordpress.com/court-documents/british-columbia-civil-liberties-association-bccla-opening-statement/ [accessed 17 March, 2011].

Chambers, D. (1997), 'Polygamy and Same-Sex Marriage', *Hofstra Law Review*, 26: 53–83.

Finkelhor, D. (1994), 'Current Information on the Scope and Nature of Child Sexual Abuse', *Sexual Abuse of Children*, 4: 31–52.

Foster, L. (1981), *Religion and Sexuality: Three American Communal Experiments of the Nineteenth Century*, Oxford: Oxford University Press. Foster, L. (1997), *Free Love and Community: John Humphrey Noyes and the Oneida Perfectionists*, Chapel Hill: University of North Carolina Press.

Gooch, L. (2010), 'Malaysian Polygamy Club Draws Criticism', *International Herald Tribune*, January 6, http://www.nytimes.com/2010/01/06/world/asia/06malaysia.html?_r=1&emc=eta1

Harris, D. (2005), 'Hundreds of "'Lost Boys" Expelled by Polygamist Community', *ABC News*, June 15, 2005 http://abcnews.go.com/WNT/story?id=851753&page=1 [accessed 17 March, 2011].

Kershner, I. (2010), 'Israel Raids Polygamist Compound', *New York Times*, January 15, 2010, A4, http://www.nytimes.com/2010/01/15/world/middleeast/15harem.html?emc=tnt&tntemail0=y

Nearing, R. (1992), *Loving More: The Polyfidelity Primer*, Captain Cook, HI: PEP Publishing.

Nearing, R (1997), 'California Book of the Dead', *Loving More Magazine*, 9: 22–23.

Northrop, B. (1997), 'Threesome Makes It Last', *Best of Loving More*, 1: 40–42.

Ravenhart, R.W. and Ravenhart L.A. (1997), 'Help! I'm Going To Have A Baby', *Loving More Magazine*, 9: 10–11.

Reynolds v. United States, 98 U.S. 145 (1878).

Slomiak, M. (1997), 'Community: The Dark Side', *Best of Loving More*, 1: 18–26.

Song, S. (2007), *Justice, Gender, and the Politics of Multiculturalism*, Cambridge: Cambridge University Press.

Stacey, J. and Meadow, T. (2009), 'New Slants on the Slippery Slope: The Politics of Polygamy and Gay Family Rights in South Africa and the United States', *Politics & Society*, 37: 167–202.

Strassberg, M. (1997), 'Distinctions of Form or Substance: Monogamy, Polygamy and Same-Sex Marriage', *North Carolina Law Review*, 75: 1501–1624.

Strassberg, M. (2003), 'The Challenge of Post-Modern Polygamy: Considering Polyamory', *Capital University Law Review*, 31: 439–563.

Strassberg, M. (2003), 'The Crime of Polygamy', *Temple Political & Civil Rights Law Review*, 12: 353–431.

West, C. (1996), *Lesbian Polyfidelity*, San Francisco: Booklegger Publishing.

12

Sex and Relationships

Reflections on living outside the box

Dossie Easton

Introduction

For the past twenty years, I have worked as a licensed marriage and family therapist in San Francisco, seeing clients and relationships in private practice. I currently supervise two intern therapists who are preparing for licensure. I also teach many workshops and classes in the U.S., Canada, and Europe, both for participants in explorative sexualities and for professionals who wish to gain cultural competence in working positively with people whose lifestyles include BDSM and polyamory. I have worked formally in sex education and counselling since joining San Francisco Sex Information in 1973. Although I have read a lot of what has been published about sex and relationships I did not learn most of what I write about in libraries. I have been an active sex radical since 1961, consciously polyamorous since 1969, and proud co-author with Janet W. Hardy of *The Ethical Slut: Polyamory, Open Relationships and Other Adventures*.

I am profoundly grateful to my friends, lovers, colleagues, and clients for all that they have taught me over the past fifty years. I see myself as an experientialist: I believe what I experience. Whether or not I can prove it to anyone, what I feel is as palpably real to me as I assume everyone else's experiences are to them. So I base my understanding on my accumulated experience, and it is my firm belief that participant-observer is the best position from which to explore and understand sexualities which have rarely been observed with a friendly eye in our cultures. I am happy to note that friendly eyes are becoming more common, and it is a great blessing to me to now be able to live my life and do my work completely out of any closet.

Celebrating Diversity: We live in a society in which coupling and the nuclear family have achieved mythological status as the gold standard of love, sex, and relationship. We are instructed that people who really love each other will move in together and live as a couple. If, after five years or so, they are no longer happy living together and they separate, the relationship is deemed to have failed and they must not have truly loved each other. They are also told that they don't really love each other if they experience desire, fantasy, or actual sexual connection outside of the twosome.

Relationships that do not conform to the nuclear pattern are deemed dysfunctional: participants are pathologized as commitment-phobic, incapable of intimacy, suffering from disorders of attachment, and they get labelled as sex addicts and sluts. Our governments privilege the couple with legal and financial support, while our courts may punish people who widen their sexual horizons with punitive divorce settlements and loss of custody of their children. All this despite the fact that the 2000 census in the United States found that only 24.1 per cent of households consisted of nuclear families, compared with 40.7 per cent in 1970.

To better understand what is going on, we need to look at how we form our cultural and scientific beliefs and assumptions, in particular the common practice of trying to understand any phenomenon by reducing it down to one single first cause. Reductionist thinking works well for medical technology – when a group of symptoms can be traced back to a single cause, we can often treat the symptoms by cutting out or killing the cause.

In our quest for simple answers, we have acquired the habit of idealizing what is 'normal', by which is meant average. If 60 per cent of people are monogamous, does that mean that the other 40 per cent don't have meaningful relationships? If 60 per cent of people spend six hours a day watching television or surfing the internet, this might be 'normal', but probably not very healthy. If 60 per cent of the population is too scared or too shy to fully explore their sexual potential, maybe the rest of us could help them out.

We particularly tend to pathologize and sometimes criminalize sexual diversity. Alfred Kinsey wrote:

> The publicly pretended code of morals, our social organizations, our marriage customs, our sex laws, and our educational and religious systems are based upon an assumption that individuals are much alike sexually, and that it is an equally simple matter for them to confine their behaviour to the single pattern which the mores dictate ... Even the scientific discussions of sex show little understanding of the range of variation in human behaviour. More often the conclusions are limited by the personal experience of the author ... Abnormal may designate certain individuals ... (who) are not as usual in the population as a whole, but in that case, it is preferable to refer to such persons as rare. (Kinsey 1948:197–201)

I was four years old in 1948, growing up in a monocultural colourless town near Boston where how we claimed we lived was obviously the right way and all other ways were clearly inferior and inadequate. In 1962 I fled New England and moved to New York City to live in an immigrant neighbourhood where I got to know people from all over the world, who had fascinating and *different* ways of doing relationship, intimacy, communication, conflict, gender, and sex. I was entranced to be immediately transformed from a failure at being a soft-spoken, self-sacrificing, self-effacing candidate for wife and motherhood to being a powerful outspoken creative woman with chutzpah.

In this chapter, and in this volume, we intend to celebrate diversity in cultures, in families, in relationships, in kinship groups, in intentional communities, and in sex.

"*Normalcy*" is often enforced by legal or social opprobrium. Sex-negative forces attempt to limit sex by constraining access to birth control and disease prevention. This is particularly egregious in my own country, where schools are required to teach 'abstinence-only' sex education, which adds up to no education at all, and our teenagers face dreadful danger of disease and unwanted pregnancy when responsible and accurate information about sexual health is not available. Birth control clinics and access to abortion are constantly threatened, and there has been hysterical opposition to a vaccination programme that could protect young women from cervical cancer.

Most of us are taught that sex outside of whatever boundaries our culture espouses makes us bad people, 'dirty', unworthy of respect and fair game for anyone who decides to assault or rape us. We may be considered unfit parents, and in many countries around the world, could be jailed or even executed for sexual variance of any kind. In Northern Europe, the many countries that have eliminated oppressive laws criminalizing consensual sexual practices between adults seem to be doing just fine, and their citizens have not become maniacs or criminals. Such countries stand as a fine example that there are no societal dangers in permitting sexual diversity.

Modesty is enforced in most countries, particularly sexual modesty. What percentage of the world's population today has a master bedroom with a door that closes? If modesty were required to procreate, we would be extinct. Anthropology is rich with examples of how we lived before prudery took over. In one African culture studied by Beach and Ford, if you came across a couple of villagers enjoying sex in the tall grass, proper behaviour would be to hunker down with one heel firmly in your crotch and quietly rock yourself to orgasm, then leave, careful not to interrupt the cries of joy (Beach and Ford 1951).

Evolutionary science has a startling bias towards monogamy in studies of sexual behaviour. This is peculiar, seeing as few animals, including humans, are in fact monogamous[1]. I think we need to question the reductionism and sexism in our arguments about sexual norms; medical and psychological professionals routinely squash diversity by pathologizing anything in their field of ignorance. Evolutionary scientist Joan Roughgarden writes:

> Medicine seizes on the often tiny anatomical differences between people, and on differences in life experience, to differentiate them from an artificial template of normalcy and deny a wide range of people their human rights by defining them as diseased. (Roughgarden 2004)

On another front, too many religions seem to operate on the conviction that God hates sex, making sinners of us all. I have worked as a therapist with a client whose church elders called him frequently during his teenage years to make sure he wasn't masturbating, and another whose father showed her a knife when she was twelve years old and explained that he would have to kill her to protect his honour if she had sex before she was married. I often wonder if there is a political strategy in this. If everyone feels guilty, ashamed, and terrified that God does not accept them, does the population become easier to control? I prefer a gentler and more pleasure-positive spiritual awareness. My favourite quote on the subject comes from Sister Wendy Beckett, art critic and nun, who looks at the sexuality, sensuality, and nudity in much great art like this:

> Why (should) anybody not delight in the creative work of God? God made the body. (Will we) suggest that God made mistakes about certain parts of the body? ... He's done these shameful things and we must do our best to cover them up? This is not the faith. The faith is that God looked at his creation and thought that it was good, thought that it was beautiful, made in the image of God. (Beckett 1997)

We often ask 'What is sex for?' Not often do we reply that sex is good, a wonderful experience, in and of itself. Too often we try to harness sex to the support of societally approved goals. We can see in the present that basing relationships solely on passion and romance is not a very good strategy for creating long-term life partnerships, nor a predictor for skills at sharing a mortgage. And, on the other hand, why would we value virginity as the coin of exchange for a successful marriage?[2]

When our culture insists on affirming the nuclear family by defaming sex and desire in the name of stability we are being asked to become a lot less than we can be. We are told that our desire is dangerous and destructive. Limiting the dynamic flow of passionate energy to a crabbed, cramped pipette and damping the flame of desire down to a flicker until we manage to forget about it, in my experience, results in a lot of disappointed and frustrated people trapped in unrewarding relationships.

Our sex can be so much more than we have been taught is allowed. When we constrict sexuality, we in many ways strangle our creativity and our personal growth, which constitutes setting up roadblocks to societal and personal progress. When each of us stretches to become all that we have the capacity to be, we will be free to create the rainbow of relationships and sexualities, not to mention families and tribes that are truly our birthright. Because sex is wonderful and good for its own sake. Because it sets us dancing in delight, vibrating to amazing rhythms, travelling together in fantastic connections, and opening our hearts to love and spiritual connection. It is my experience and my firm belief that sexual freedom is spiritual freedom.

We were taught, at some time before we can remember, not to masturbate in the living room. Babes and toddlers explore all of their bodies, genitals just like their toes. We may have been taught that touching ourselves is dirty and disgusting, and many of us grew up in a sex-negative culture where we were taught that masturbation was wrong and unnatural.

Blinded in this blizzard of condemnation, how can we even imagine sex as something clean and good? Sex has the power to expand our awareness, to generate universal loving acceptance of each other and delight in each person's individuality, and to teach us to celebrate bringing our differences together to form new templates of what relationships can be.

Oxytocin: Our bodies evolved a rather remarkable hormone called oxytocin, which promotes bonding, increases trust, and are released in response to touch, massage, nursing, skin contact, and orgasm, whether alone or shared with another[3]. Oxytocin builds trust, a necessary way to identify our tribe from predators and dangerous animals, and our families from the neighbours. Oxytocin are the physiological expression of our capacity to bond with many people. We are arguably the world's most social animal, with a built in ability to build intimate connections into extended families, clans, tribes, cultures, and civilizations. Thus the expanded intimacy of sharing sex with a number of partners seems more likely to support than to destroy our societies.

What about romance? First, let me point out that, while romantic love is indeed an amazing journey, after the wonder and excitement of its beginning, this journey often proceeds into the dark and shadowy parts of our psyches. Struggle often ensues. Romantic love and the glory of *limerence*[4] is no predictor of a stable future relationship. Falling in love is wonderful, and I, for one, will never say no to that experience. I have, however, learned, as Khalil Gibran most beautifully put it: 'Even as (Love) is for your growth, so also is he for your pruning' (Gibran 1923). Sex and romance are wonderful for personal growth, but not so stable a rock on which to found our families.

We can observe that people in technologically advanced cultures tend to be more mobile in their relationships. The average person can expect to enjoy several important sexual relationships in a lifetime, and a number of lovely 'flings' might occur when one is not coupled. Our relationships may work very well for a few years, and then people may come to feel stuck or unhappy, and need to move on to the next part of their life. We could save ourselves a lot of grief if we accepted this as a fact and let go of finding something wrong with the relationship or, worse yet, some serious deficiency in that other person we used to love, that lets us feel justified about leaving. Only allowing the ending of a relationship because of catastrophic wrongness is a tribal custom we could well do without.

Perhaps it would be better to develop customs and rituals to protect and support us through times of endings and new beginnings. When all sexual relationships are not about making babies, when we enter into sexual connection to meet our needs for love and emotional growth, perhaps we don't have to get coupled to have a love life. We could create relationships that exist for their own sake, not in service to financial stability or reproductive goals or anything but delight and connection and exploration. We can use all this lovely bonding and trust to build relationships, extended families, and communities.

When we expand our freedom of choice we can generate enormous diversity in relationships, and thus enjoy abundant supplies of whatever each of us needs in our life, whether it be a fuck buddy, a meditation partner, a gentle lover or a rough and tumble affair. We can have intimate friends, many adults to help raise the kids, a sense of community, a culture that fits us and our sexuality, and maybe even new ways to nurture civilization.

Sexual Extended Families: Researcher and swinger James Ramey, in *Intimate Friendships* (1975), proposed that expanded sexual intimacy could become the foundation of modern extended families, bonded together through shared pleasures and intimacies, creating a tribe, a clan, that famous village we need to raise a child. Over the years I have belonged to a number of such families, some overlapping, some quite distinct, since I decided in 1969 to invest my security, not in my partnerships, but in my community. I have been rewarded with a shifting kaleidoscope of familial experience, unbelievable support while raising my child, and abundant supplies of free-flowing love.

The Ethics of Sluttery. Our notions about the rights and wrongs of family structures come from adaptations in relatively recent history to the situations we are living in. In the American melting pot, we are enriched by the rich diversity of ways people from all over the world build relationships and families. What would be the moral values of a sex-positive civilization of ethical sluts?

Ethics for me is about being kind to people, and treating my neighbours the way I'd like them to treat me. We can start from the notion that all sexual acts between consenting adults are just fine. I like to propose an expanded definition of consent for use in slut communities: consent is an active collaboration for the pleasure and wellbeing of all people involved in any interaction, including some who may not be present.

Slut ethics require respect for everyone, including all of your lover's other lovers. Everyone's boundaries need to be considered and honoured, especially the boundaries that are about feeling easy and comfortable and safe. Although we may ask a partner on occasion to stretch a bit to accommodate our needs – considering that we all grew up in a culture that never taught us how to stretch beyond our jealousy – we can negotiate agreements about how much stretching feels possible at this particular time. When we succeed in stretching today we acquire new skills that will support us in stretching further tomorrow, and so we generate a learning curve in the direction of more freedom. Nobody's needs or feelings should be discounted. When we cultivate the willingness to listen to each other we can really appreciate the emotions we are sharing in any interaction. Then we can become free to choose the boundaries of our relationships and of our families, and thus free to choose, even invent, the kinds of families we wish to build. We would be free to choose monogamy and if we did, it would actually be our choice.

One very important boundary we need to be serious about is taking the responsibility for our own emotions. We most commonly perceive our feelings as something that happens to us, rather than something that we do. We get in trouble when we are not willing to feel an emotion. We wind up projecting our fears and insecurities onto our lover or our lover's lover. When we feel bad we would love to be able to blame someone else, but all we accomplish when we do so is to disempower ourselves. When we find ways to feel our emotions and get the support we need to move through them and keep the flow going, then we can grow and evolve[5].

Let me give you an example from my own experience of how we might honour the entire family and still get needs met. I had a lover when my daughter was young who was married and also had kids. He and his wife occasionally declared sexual monogamy, usually for about three months, when there was a family difficulty to work through. This happened one November when his father had a heart attack. Taking a vacation from our sexual connection in no way shut me out of the family. I have very happy memories of Daniel and me roasting a bunch of ducks and a goose for Thanksgiving dinner while the kids played cheerily in the living room and Daniel's wife set out hors d'oeuvres.

Security is built on the foundations of honouring people's boundaries and being very conscious of what commitments we are making. In complex blended families commitments are agreements, not universal truths about the best way to make choices. I can count on my family if, for instance, I get seriously sick or need help, and I count on myself to help those close to me. This is my security.

Intimate relationships are not necessarily sexual. My longest life partner and co-parent was the gay man who raised my child with me for eight years. Our bond was profound, we fit together beautifully, and we might still be making home together if AIDS had not come along. Ethical sluts need to maintain really solid practices around safer sex and birth control – for me, that goes without saying, but it surely bears repeating.

A commitment to some form of predictability is part of most slut agreements. It is useful to talk about this and not just assume that you have the same picture of predictability that your partners do. How much advance notice of dates do you expect? Is it okay to flirt at a party, and which parties? (Perhaps not at church events or company picnics.) If we can't come home at the time we planned, how do we arrange phone calls and such? Who is out of bounds from your point of view: relatives, teachers, co-workers, your boss, your therapist? Important detail: when we are all at the same party, am I welcome to join any conversation you may be engaged in? Probably yes, but many people wind up hiding miserably in corners fearing that their partners don't want them around right now. Compare your pictures, then figure out how everyone can feel safe, free, and welcome.

Slut communities have developed some wonderful forms of matchmaking; it is so different from sneaking around when your partner will actually introduce you to that cute person you are feeling shy about. A lover of mine once started a great tradition. We were out at a club, and an attractive person had been eying me behind his back. When I told him about this as we were leaving, he gallantly helped me into my coat and then strode confidently over to the cutie in question, pen in hand, to say, 'My lady would like you to have her phone number'.

We work on being particularly thoughtful about our lover's partners. We can't assume they want to play with us, and it would be appalling to assume that someone should share sex with us just to be polite. When we are invited into some sex that we don't want, we find ways to be gentle and compassionate when we decline an invitation: 'No thanks, that doesn't fit for me right now, but thank you, I'm flattered'.

We remember to honour the gifts we bring to each other. We share our delights, we express our gratitude, we remember to honour the hospitality of partners and roommates and children and parents and everyone who is welcoming us into their family. To do this we practice getting bigger than our judgments. I may not be wildly enthusiastic about straight macho men or competitive beauty queens, but I am a grown-up, and I can usually find positive ways to deal with people in my intimate circles that I might not myself have chosen. These efforts have been rewarded with some surprisingly deep friendships with people I was not initially drawn to.

The ultimate slut ethic is to tell the truth as much as is humanly possible. If we tell the truth in a kindly manner with due regard for the feelings of the person we are telling it to, then all of our interactions will be based on truth and that makes life so much cleaner and easier. This can be difficult: we have all learned to keep our crushes, our fantasies, and our desires profoundly secret to protect our partners and conceal our shame. We may well fear that our partner will find some of our truths uncomfortable. But sharing our individual truth is how we learn that crushes are normal, fantasies are normal, desire is normal, our interest in sex is healthy and loving and normal. We need to get comfortable with our sexual truth. So practice. Tell the truth in a supportive and compassionate manner, and keep on telling it.

What about kids? Kids benefit from having a big extended family, multiple coparents, siblings, aunts, uncles, and many households available to them. The opportunity to experience multiple family cultures is hugely beneficial – kids in tribes learn that there are a lot of different ways to live together. Some families talk easily about conflict, others do not. Some family cultures are noisy and active, others more quiet and serene. Kids learn diversity and grow up with abundant resources and skills for dealing with family and relationship problems. We evolved to grow up in big extended families like our ancestral tribes; we can reclaim our ancestral skills at getting along.

It can be difficult when our children go to school and other kids tell them that their families are wrong. In schools our kids meet others who have been deliberately denied information about sex, for reproduction or for pleasure, and our kids may be confronted with scorn and humiliation, even violence, for being open-minded and knowledgeable about sex, same sex relationships, and the like. One six-year-old girl I knew came home from school all upset, because the other kids insisted that if her mother wasn't married and wasn't a virgin, then her mother was going to hell. The child came home terrified. Our kids have a right to be safe from religious oppression.

On the positive side, at a polyamory workshop I recently attended I ran into a man in his forties whom I had co-parented back when he was four. He was mighty proud that a member of his constellation of parents had written *The Ethical Slut*, and I was proud to see him exercising *his* family values.

Many Intimacies: There exists a huge diversity of ways in which to relate and connect that include sex. Everyone of us can enjoy and benefit from variety in relationships within our own lives. This is what being a slut means to me. I can form relationships with different people that feature different kinds of connection and commitment. I can relate to people who are different from me, and others who are similar, and I can learn from all of them.

To me, sexual connections are all relationships. Even if we meet in a club and go to one of our homes for a few hours of steamy sex and never meet again, we have still met and connected. We have related. The commitment in a one night stand is to share pleasure in the present moment and unburden ourselves of fretting about the future. Other relationships endure over time, ranging from many years of regular connection and family membership, through occasional dates spread over a remarkable period of time, to perhaps living together, all three or four or five of us.

Or not. I look to my nearly twenty-year relationship with my co-author Janet as an example. Since 1992, we have been lovers, best friends, co-teachers of many workshops, and co-authors of five books about sexual lifestyles. Our creative process is profoundly connected to our sexual relationship: we write and think and play and edit and work and play some more. We cook together too. We have never lived together.

We have profound differences in how we manage our physical environments and money, and we could never make agreements we could both live with about everyday life. Most of the time we have known each other we have been in primary relationships with other people – hers male, mine female. I think one of the things that make our connection work over time is that we don't expect to get married. We share play and sex and writing together and editing and love. Lots of love.

We can find nourishment in many different connections – we no longer have to blame our spouses for what they cannot provide, we simply look for it elsewhere. So we each become empowered to seek whatever we need at any particular time in our life. Do remember that needs and desires are not fixed traits: as we grow and change, so do our passions and ambitions.

Skilled sluts develop very sophisticated boundaries, which might differ from one person to the next, or expand with a given person over time. Boundaries in relationships are how we know where I end and you begin, and they tell us what we each own and are responsible for in any interaction. People with strong, clear, flexible boundaries are easy to relate to. They know how to take care of themselves, and offer the space for you to take care of yourself. Then we can care for each other in whatever ways fit the occasion.

Bad sex certainly exists. If we connect our genitals with no intention of making any personal connection, if we withhold ourselves and our feelings, if we treat our partners without respect, if we fail to honour their boundaries, if we disregard their consent, if we force sexual connection with outright assault or with bullying or emotional blackmail, we will continue to have very limited sex, and a lot of unpleasant experiences. I see sex as sacred – that means we should not profane it.

> *Clean Love:* Can you imagine love without jealousy, without possessiveness, love cleaned of all its clinginess and desperation? Let's try. We can take some thoughts from Buddhism: What would it be like to love without attachment? Or to open our hearts to someone with no expectation beyond another heart opening in return? Loving just for the joy of it, regardless of what we might get back? (Easton and Hardy 2009:131)

Imagine a Sex-Positive Culture. How shall we evolve the nuclear family beyond the boundaries of prudery? I think it is a challenge to open our hearts and minds, as well as bodies, to really connect with others. It requires openness in spirit as well as sex. Sex is by its nature an intimate connection; we need to be willing to get vulnerable with each other. We need to develop the skills to own our vulnerabilities so that we can become compassionate both with others and with ourselves. Then we become free to open our hearts, and journey together in erotically expanded awareness.

Good sex is a profoundly altered state of consciousness, a journey into our deeper selves and our spiritual possibilities. We live in a culture whose dominant religion insists that spirituality and sexuality are antithetical – in my experience, nothing could be further from the truth. Good sex is a journey into intimacy. Sharing vulnerability generates intimacy. I recommend investing serious time and energy into sex: when we slow down and savour every part of our bodies, our sensations, and our amazing capacities for pleasure, sex becomes much more than 'getting off'. Sex at its finest is about travelling in ecstasy.

Sex Is Infinite. A fully realized sexuality can be, for all our human intents or purposes, an infinite territory for expansion and exploration: of each other, of connection, and of ourselves. Sex is so much more than just satisfying a need or releasing some pressure. Orgasm is a rich field that can be mined for many treasures; our wonderful bodies are blissfully equipped with many pathways to joyous climax. Our nervous systems provide us with a wealth of sensitive nerves and erectile tissue, many paths into our sensuality, and nearly unlimited possibilities for happy stimulus and response.

Our entire bodies are sex organs – warm skins, pulsing veins, pounding hearts, muscles that rise to meet a warm hand, hips designed to rock and reach, powerful thighs, sensitive ears and lips and tongues – even our scalps are richly innervated. Our brains light up in very special ways, switching our attention from mundane thoughts and worries into another kind of awakening that can completely immerse us in ecstasy. There is no part of us that can't experience pleasure and that does not partake of Eros.

Even more remarkable, we have the capacity to raise erotic energy, as practised in Indian and Tibetan Tantra, Native American Quodoushka, and Chinese Taoist He Qi, as the driving force that opens us into transcendent states of consciousness. We are truly amazing creatures when we discover the full range of our erotic capabilities.

Personal Growth: When we pathologize desire we cause great damage to the individual. We cage the imagination, forbid exploration of the life force, and degrade self-loving masturbation. We make everyone of us guilty of something forbidden, and give each of us something shameful to hide, while we are told, and often tell ourselves, over and over, that we are not okay.

One path to healing this epidemic of distress is to insist on the freedom to become all that we can be, in sex, in love, and in life. When we allow ourselves diverse connections, these unique intimacies provide us with remarkable opportunities to know ourselves better. Each lover provides us with an entirely individual mirror in which we can see and experience parts of ourselves we may never have noticed before, and affirm these parts as desirable and lovable. We learn yet more as we provide these intimate mirrors to each of our lovers, as seeing them in our unique way allows them to see more of themselves. A diverse sex life can empower us to be all that we can be.

We don't need to try to turn these relationships into anything except themselves: each relationship we enter into will seek its own level like water, and flow into the form that fits it, when we allow it to. Sustainable relationships need not be based on exclusive sexual attention, or, for that matter, on territoriality, or ownership, or any of the ways in which we commoditize ourselves. We each get to decide how much sustainability we are looking for in all our relationships, or in any particular one. The results for me have been amazing adventures, floods of wisdom and creativity, and a life rich in support and love.

The real purpose of sex is that sex is valuable in and of itself, for its own sake. The connections we make with people are not the purpose of sex, these are the benefits we can create when we follow our desire. We now refer to these connections as 'friends with benefits', realizing that we can include sex in our friendships, and discarding the myth that sex without coupling is doomed to be cold, distant, and disconnected.

What if the real purpose of sex is ecstasy? What if ecstasy has its rightful place in our social and personal ecologies even if it never gets us more food or gets our sperm into the race? Neuroscientists Andrew Newberg and colleagues have this to say on the subject:

> We believe, in fact, that the neurological machinery of transcendence may have arisen from the neural circuitry that evolved for mating and sexual experience. The language of mysticism hints at this connection: Mystics of all times and cultures have used the same expressive terms to describe their ineffable experiences: *bliss, rapture, ecstasy,* and *exaltation.* They speak of losing themselves in a sublime sense of union, of melting into elation, and of the total satisfactions of desires.

> We believe that it is no coincidence that this is also the language of sexual pleasure. Nor is it surprising, because the very neurological structures and pathways involved in transcendent experience – including the arousal, quiescent, and limbic systems – evolved primarily to link sexual climax to the powerful sensations of orgasm.... An evolutionary perspective suggests that the neurobiology of mystical experience arose, at least in part, from the mechanism of the sexual response. (Newberg *et al.* 2001: 125–26)

What sex can be is enormous. Huge potential, massive awakenings that draw us into the present moment like nothing else, and open us to acceptance of ourselves and each other in profound ways. When we allow desire to be our teacher, and passion to fuel our journey, difference dissolves, and we participate in generating the constant stream of love that is the animating force of this universe that is our home. In this process we give birth to loving supportive connections that can bring us together into free-flowing families and tribes. Then perhaps we can envision building a future civilization firmly founded on love.

Notes

1 For further information, read the excellent books *The Myth of Monogamy* (Barash and Lipton 2001) and *Sex at Dawn* (Ryan and Jetha 2010).

2 For a view from a radically different culture, read Judith Stacey's chapter in *Unhitched*, in which she explicates how the Mosuo people of southwestern China have created family structures that entirely separate desire from domesticity.

3 Interview with Judith Lipton, co-author of *The Myth of Monogamy*, May 2011.

4 Limerence: was coined by psychologist Dorothy Tennov to describe the blindingly obsessive aspects of the state of mind we know as 'falling in love' (Tennov 1979).

5 For an in-depth discussion of how this can work please read *The Ethical Slut*, particularly the chapters on 'Roadmaps through Jealousy' and 'Embracing Conflict' (Easton and Hardy 2009: 108–160).

References

Barash, D.P. and Lipton, J.E. (2001), *The Myth of Monogamy: Fidelity and Infidelity in Animals and People*, New York: W.H. Freeman & Co.

Beach, F.A. and Ford, C.S. (1951), *Patterns of Sexual Behavior*, New York: Harper & Rowe.

Beckett, W. (1997), Conversation with Bill Moyers, New Television Workshop, WBGH, Boston.

Easton, D. and Hardy, J.W. (2000), *When Someone You Love Is Kinky*, Oakland: Greenery Press.

Easton, D. and Hardy, J.W. (2001), *The New Bottoming Book*, Oakland: Greenery Press.

Easton, D. and Hardy, J.W. (2003), *The New Topping Book*, Oakland: Greenery Press.

Easton, D. and Hardy, J.W. (2004), *Radical Ecstasy*, Oakland: Greenery Press.

Easton, D. and Hardy, J.W. (2009), *The Ethical Slut: a Practical Guide to Polyamory, Open Relationships & Other Adventures, Second Edition*, Berkeley: Celestial Arts.

Hrdy, S.B. (1999), *Mother Nature: Maternal Instincts and How They Shape the Human Species*, New York: Ballantine Books.

Kinsey, A.C., Pomeroy, W.B. and Martin, C.E. (1948), *Sexual Behavior in the Human Male*, Philadelphia and London: W.H. Saunders.

Morin, J. (1996), *The Erotic Mind*, New York: Harper Paperbacks.

Newberg, A., D'Aquill, E. and Rouse, V. (2001), *Why God Won't Go Away: Brain Science and the Biology of Belief*, New York: Ballantine Books.

Ramey, J. (1975), *Intimate Friendships*, New York: Prentice Hall Trade.

Roughgarden, J. (2004), *Evolution's Rainbow: Diversity, Gender and Sexuality in Nature and People*, Berkeley: University of California Press.

Ryan, C. and Jetha, C. (2010), *Sex at Dawn: the Prehistoric Origins of Modern Sexuality*, New York: Harper-Collins Publishers.

Stacey, J. (2011), *Unhitched: love, marriage, and family values from West Hollywood to Western China*, New York: New York University Press.

Tennov, D. (1979), *Love and Limerence*, Maryland: Scarborough House.

13

Human Cloning and the Family in the New Millennium

Kerry Lynn Macintosh

Imagine the following scenario: A woman lies on a table in a hospital, attempting to give birth to her first child. Her doctor urges her to push. She does, with all her might. Suddenly a baby boy slips out of the birth canal and into the waiting hands of her husband.

The birth of a first-born son is a common event, one that is celebrated the world over. But this newborn baby is anything but ordinary. He is a human clone.

How did this birth come about? The woman's husband had dysfunctional sperm. Efforts to conceive a child through sexual intercourse and in vitro fertilisation failed, so the couple decided to try human cloning. A doctor retrieved eggs from the woman and removed the nuclei. Then, he fused to each egg a somatic cell of the husband, such as a skin or muscle cell. A few of these reconstructed eggs developed into embryos. The doctor placed one embryo in the woman, who became pregnant and delivered a baby who shared the nuclear DNA of her husband.

This scenario is science fiction today but could become reality in the near future. Therefore, this chapter will explore the practical and ideological consequences when human cloning is used to have children.

Scientific research over the past fifteen years has greatly improved cloning technology. Further advances may make it possible for humans to reproduce through cloning in the near future

The first mammal to be cloned was a sheep named Dolly. Her creator, Ian Wilmut, started with mammary tissue harvested from a Finn Dorset sheep. He extracted cells from the tissue and coaxed them into a quiescent state. Each one of these cells carried within it the nuclear DNA of the tissue donor. Working with enucleated eggs of Scottish Blackface sheep (a different breed), Wilmut used electricity to merge one cell into each egg. In this manner he created twenty-nine embryos that bore the nuclear DNA of the original Finn

Dorset sheep. He transferred these embryos into thirteen surrogate sheep. One Scottish Blackface sheep became pregnant and delivered Dolly: a Finn Dorset lamb. In terms of lambs born per embryos transferred, this initial experiment achieved a birth rate of approximately 3 per cent (Wilmut *et al.* 1997: 811).

Since 1997, when Wilmut first introduced Dolly to an astonished world, scientists have improved the efficiency of animal cloning. For example, birth rates for cloned cattle can now reach as high as 20 per cent (Niemann *et al.* 2008: 153). For cloned mice, birth rates can run as high as 13 or 14 per cent, depending on the genotype of the donor mouse and the type of cell used for the cloning (Inoue *et al.* 2009: 567; Inoue *et al.* 2010: 498).

To be sure, some animal clones miscarry or die shortly after birth (National Academies 2002: 40). Placental abnormalities are believed to account for many of these losses (Cibelli *et al.* 2002). However, most animal clones that survive the neonatal period exhibit normal patterns of growth and development and appear to be healthy (Center for Veterinary Medicine 2008: 156–68, 176–81, 328–29; Cibelli *et al.* 2002; Inoue *et al.* 2002).

In short, though animal cloning is not yet perfected, recent data indicate that birth rates are increasing and healthy offspring are common. Researchers who experiment on animals may eventually improve the technology to the point where it becomes efficient and safe.

Meanwhile, other scientists are working to create embryonic stem cells from cloned human embryos. If they can learn how to create stem cell lines from the DNA of individuals with specific diseases, medical researchers can study the cells and test potential drugs on them in the laboratory. One day, scientists may even use cloned stem cells to create DNA-matched tissues or organs for patients who need them (President's Council on Bioethics 2002: 130–33). Towards such ends, researchers have already cloned human blastocysts, that is, human embryos several days old and containing hundreds of cells (French *et al.* 2008). This is a significant milestone, because in human reproduction, embryos ordinarily implant in the womb after reaching the blastocyst stage of development. Once medical researchers learn how to create healthy cloned blastocysts, and share that information with the world, it will be a relatively simple matter for a fertility doctor to read that information, create blastocysts, and transfer them to the womb of a patient.

Human cloning cannot create duplicate human beings. The most likely practical use of the technology is to help people have children

However, in order for human cloning to become commonplace, more than technical proficiency is required. There must be a market. The need for a market raises the question: why would anyone want to conceive a child through cloning technology?

People who assign too much power to genes sometimes imagine that cloning is a method of copying existing persons with desirable characteristics, such as great thinkers or star athletes. Others suppose the technology can be used to resurrect dictators or recreate lost loved ones (Macintosh 2005: 26–27). Nothing could be farther from the truth.

Consider the results of experiments in cloning animals. Animal clones are born as infants of their species, and not as full-grown adult copies. Indeed, clones frequently exhibit coat patterns, sizes, weights, and behaviours that differ from those of their DNA donors; moreover, if multiple animals are cloned simultaneously from the same DNA, the clones differ from each other (Archer *et al.* 2003; Center for Veterinary Medicine 2008: 495; Galli *et al.* 2003; Shin *et al.* 2002; Wells *et al.* 1999: 1003). The biological reasons for these variations are too complex to explore in detail in this brief chapter. However, one point deserves special mention: even when two animals have the same DNA, variations in the environmental factors that each animal experiences during gestation and after birth lead to differences in gene expression and phenotype (Macintosh 2005: 24–25).

Human clones, like animal clones, must be born as babies. And like animal clones, human clones are bound to differ from their DNA donors in gene expression and phenotype for biological reasons. However, humans are more intellectually complex than animals, so it is important to also consider the non-biological impacts that differing environments will have. A human clone born in the new millennium will be raised in a different family, era, and culture than his or her genetic progenitor, leading to differences in acquired traits such as personality, values and tastes (*Ibid.*: 25).

These realities render human cloning useless to dictators who wish to maintain a perpetual reign through their clones, or politicians who want to clone a master race. More poignant goals, such as the resurrection of a child who died too young, are also impossible to achieve. All cloning can do is create a new baby with a unique phenotype and personality.

Why, then, would anyone want to use human cloning? The value of the technology lies in this fact: cloning is a method of *asexual* reproduction. A person who cannot reproduce sexually can nevertheless transmit his or her DNA to the next generation via cloning.

For example, consider a man who lacks sperm, or a woman whose eggs are aged or otherwise dysfunctional. Such individuals are incapable of transmitting genes to the next generation through sexual intercourse or in vitro fertilisation. In order to have children to raise, they must resort to donor gametes or adoption. In the future, however, they may turn to cloning as a means of conceiving the genetic offspring they desire (Eibert 2002: 1101–02).

Gay or lesbian couples might also benefit from cloning. Though not infertile, these couples can produce offspring through sexual reproduction only in cooperation with egg or sperm donors from outside their marriages or partnerships. Cloning offers them the opportunity to conceive a child who bears the DNA of one partner, rather than one partner plus one outsider (Macintosh 2005: 37). In the case of a lesbian couple, one woman could provide eggs and a womb and the other the DNA for the cloning. In the case of a gay couple, one of the two men could contribute the DNA for the cloning[1].

Finally, cloning could take some of the pressure off of single women whose biological clocks are ticking. Today, they are becoming single mothers by choice, procreating with sperm donors to beat the clock and hoping to find a suitable marriage partner later on (see Graham in this volume). But this strategy has a drawback: some romantic partners will not be enthusiastic about marrying into a family that already has a child. Cloning would free single women to take their time in finding a partner and building a healthy relationship, secure in the knowledge that they can reproduce asexually if medically necessary (Silver 2002: 1041).

In sum, cloning is a more egalitarian method of reproduction. What you need to conceive genetic offspring is DNA. Everyone has that, even those who are infertile, gay or lesbian, or destined to marry later in life. Moreover, cloning allows such individuals to bypass some tricky issues associated with collaborative reproduction. If a child is not conceived with donated sperm or eggs, parents need not agonize over whether to disclose the fact of donation to their child. Nor need parents construct elaborate narratives that portray the donor as unimportant and themselves as 'real' parents in an effort to reinforce family bonds and safeguard themselves against rejection (see Gurnham in this volume).

Unfortunately, the fertile majority has been slow to recognise the potential benefits of human cloning. Indeed, just the reverse: human cloning is a science that has drawn tremendous legislative fire. Around the world, many nations have enacted laws to prohibit human cloning (Kunich 2003: 63–83). For example, the United Kingdom first criminalized reproductive cloning ten years ago, through enactment of the Human Reproductive Cloning Act 2001 (*Ibid.*: 67). Parliament has since eliminated the need for a specific act on cloning by amending the Human Fertilisation and Embryology Act (HFEA). The HFEA provides that no person is allowed to transfer an embryo to a woman unless the embryo is 'permitted'. To qualify as 'permitted', an embryo must be created through fertilisation of 'permitted' eggs by 'permitted' sperm – i.e. eggs and sperm that have been produced by or extracted from ovaries and testes and that have not been altered in nuclear or mitochondrial DNA (Human Fertilisation and Embryology Act 1990, as amended, sections 3(2), 3ZA). These provisions preclude human cloning for two reasons: cloning uses eggs that have been altered through the removal of their nuclear DNA; and cloning creates embryos by means other than fertilisation.

In the United States, the legal landscape is more complicated. Due to disagreements over the morality of stem cell research involving cloned embryos, the United States Congress has been unable to enact a federal law on human cloning. Instead, a growing number of American states have enacted laws that prohibit reproductive cloning and prescribe stiff prison sentences for violators (Macintosh 2005: 75–80, 85–88).

However, even the most draconian anti-cloning laws will not put a stop to human cloning. Individuals who live in countries with restrictive laws already travel across borders to access assisted reproductive technologies. Tomorrow those who wish to reproduce asexually will travel abroad to locations where cloning is legal and come home pregnant (Macintosh 2005: 118). Chances are that their use of cloning will not be detected, as many children resemble one parent or the other.

Claims that cloning will create dysfunctional families are speculative and based on scientific fallacies

Despite the futility of attempting to control the human drive to reproduce, critics have insisted that human cloning must be banned. Their objections to the technology are multitudinous and range from the secular (for example, cloning is bad because it might lead to eugenic programs) to religious (for example, humans should not play God). I have debunked these objections at length elsewhere (Macintosh 2005). Here I will concentrate on concerns that are relevant to the family.

Critics claim that prospective parents will select DNA with an eye towards creating a child with desirable traits. For example, if the person who donated DNA for the cloning procedure was a brilliant physicist, the parents will hold unreasonable expectations that their child will also become a brilliant physicist. Failure to respect the child's individuality and right to forge his own path will generate familial conflict (National Bioethics Advisory Commission 1997: 69–70; President's Council on Bioethics 2002: 103).

Critics also claim there will be conflict and confusion when a child is cloned from a prospective parent. For example, suppose a husband and wife agree to clone a daughter from the DNA of the wife. Later on, if there is marital discord, the husband may project his resentment of the wife onto the daughter and treat her poorly. Conversely, if the husband and wife have a positive relationship, the husband may fall in love with the daughter who is the mirror image of his wife (President's Council on Bioethics 2002: 111).

Claims such as these implicitly assume that parents will perceive cloning as a copying process. I have two points in response. First, experiments have established the individuality and uniqueness of animal clones. Human clones will likewise be individual and unique. They will have their own looks, intellects, talents, personalities, and dreams. Parents will have no scientific basis for holding unreasonable expectations or projecting feelings for others onto a cloned child.

Second, even if many parents are ignorant of the scientific realities of human cloning, it is not necessary to prohibit the technology, for a less restrictive solution is readily available. The government could require education and counselling for prospective parents to ensure they are prepared to embrace the individuality and uniqueness of their child.

Children conceived through cloning will be psychologically healthy and the families to which they belong will function well

Once speculative harms are set aside, it becomes possible to draw a predictive analogy. For decades, infertile men and women, gays and lesbians, and single women have conceived children with the aid of assisted reproductive technologies such as in vitro fertilisation, intracytoplasmic sperm injection, donor insemination, and egg donation. These individuals will use human cloning for the same purpose (having children) and for the same reason (inability to procreate through sexual intercourse within a partnership). Given these similar parental characteristics and motivations, the experiences of families formed through assisted reproduction offer a reasonable forecast of what families formed through human cloning can expect.

Compared with those who are spontaneously conceived, children conceived through in vitro fertilisation, donor insemination, and egg donation do not show an increased risk of psychological problems (Shelton *et al.* 2009: 386, 390). Rather, children conceived with the aid of assisted reproductive technologies are well-adjusted (Barnes *et al.* 2004: 1486; Golombok *et al.* 2002: 837; Murray, MacCallum and Golombok 2006: 617) and remain so as adolescents and young adults (Wagenaar *et al.* 2009: 1912; Wilson *et al.* 2011: 1217). Their parents are also psychologically healthy and enjoy good relationships with them (Barnes *et al.* 2004: 1485–86; Golombok *et al.* 2002: 837–38; Murray *et al.* 2006: 616–17).

These positive outcomes are not surprising. Assisted reproductive technologies involve expense, effort, and even some physical pain. No one uses these technologies unless he or she is extraordinarily committed to the twin goals of conceiving and parenting a child. Indeed, some research indicates that families formed through assisted reproduction function *better* than families formed through sexual intercourse or adoption (Barnes *et al.* 2004: 1485–86; Golombok *et al.* 2002: 838).

To be sure, a child conceived through cloning will share nuclear DNA with only one of his parents. The same is true of children conceived with the aid of donor sperm or eggs, who have a genetic link to one of their parents and not the other. Yet, children and families created through donor gametes appear to function as well as children and families created through standard in vitro fertilisation, indicating that a genetic link to both parents is not required in order for children and families to flourish (Golombok *et al.* 2002: 837; Murray *et al.* 2006: 616; Shelton *et al.* 2009: 390).

Challenges to the happiness of children conceived through cloning are more likely to come from outside the family. Peers, teachers, employers, and others who are ignorant of basic scientific principles may assume the children are copies until they get to know them as individuals. But the risk that the members of a minority group might suffer from prejudice is not an ethical basis for banning their existence (Pence 1997: 46). Indeed, anti-cloning legislation can only make a bad situation worse, since it stigmatizes cloned children as unworthy of existence (Macintosh 2005: 121).

The legal relation of human clones to their parents can be clarified through appropriate legislation

Critics also raise practical concerns about families created through human cloning. They worry that the social relationships and legal status of persons within the family unit will be unclear (National Bioethics Advisory Commission 1997: 70; President's Council on Bioethics 2002: 110; Harris 2004: 77–83). To illustrate the point, consider once again the hypothetical scenario from the start of this chapter. There, a couple created a cloned embryo from the eggs of the woman and DNA of the man. The woman gestated the embryo and gave birth to a baby boy. Is the man the father of the child, or is he the brother of the child? And is the woman the mother of the child?

This conundrum exists because cloning makes asexual reproduction possible without eliminating the prevailing paradigm of sexual reproduction. If one sticks with the sexual reproduction paradigm, it appears that the persons who last reproduced were the *parents* of the man, meaning that the child is his twin brother. But if one adopts an asexual reproduction paradigm, the man passed his genes to the next generation and is the child's genetic father.

How, then, should one choose between these two competing paradigms? I submit that a functional approach is most practical. In the scenario, the man is infertile. He and his wife turned to cloning because sexual reproduction was not possible for him. Their intention is to raise the boy as their son. Therefore, the boy will experience them as parents, and they will experience him as a son. The asexual reproduction paradigm better describes the situation, and the law should acknowledge the child as the son of the couple. This solution has an added benefit: it is consistent with the biological motherhood of the woman, who gestated the child.

By contrast, a sexual reproduction paradigm does not fit the facts. Siblings ordinarily grow up together in the same household with the parents who made the decision to conceive them. The hypothetical scenario is different: the man, who has already reached maturity, is the one deciding to conceive the child. His wife gestated the child, and he and she will be the ones to raise the child. Functionally, the child is a son, and it makes no sense to treat him as a younger brother of the man.

Assuming the asexual reproduction paradigm best describes the social circumstances of the hypothetical family, the next question is whether the law of parentage is adequate. At first glance, one might think not. After all, existing statutes were written to deal with the parentage of children conceived through sexual reproduction. Upon closer inspection, however, it appears that some statutes and common law principles may attribute parentage correctly in cases of asexual reproduction (at least in the United States and United Kingdom).

In the United States, eighteen states substantially adopted the Uniform Parentage Act (UPA) in its original 1973 form (West Group 2001: 377). The National Conference of Commissioners on Uniform State Laws issued a revised text of the UPA in 2000 and amended it in 2002. Nine states (including six that had previously adopted the 1973 version) have substantially adopted the revised UPA (Thomson Reuters 2010: 4). All in all, twenty-one states have some version of the UPA.

In its 2002 incarnation, the UPA added provisions addressing the parentage of children born through assisted reproduction. These provisions probably would not apply to children conceived through cloning, since cloning is not included within the definition of assisted reproduction (*Ibid*, UPA section 102(4) at 12). However, the UPA also includes general provisions that may be broad enough to establish parentage for many heterosexual couples who clone.

Consider the hypothetical scenario. Under the original and revised UPA, when a child is born to a woman, she is the mother of that child (West Group 2001: UPA section 3(1) at 391; Thomson Reuters 2010: UPA section 201(a)(1) at 21). Therefore, since the woman in the scenario gave birth to the baby boy, she is considered the mother of that child. Further, under the UPA, her husband is presumed to be the father of the child. (West Group 2001: UPA section 4(a)(1)at 393; Thomson Reuters 2010: UPA section 204(a)(1) at 23). Unless that presumption is rebutted, a father-child relationship will be established (Thomson Reuters 2010: UPA section 201(b)(1) at 21).

The outcome is similar even if the facts are altered to make the woman the infertile one. If she conceives a daughter using her own DNA, so long as she gives birth to the daughter, she is the mother and her husband is still presumed to be the father of the daughter. Thus, when a man and woman who are married to each other utilize human cloning to overcome infertility the UPA assigns parentage to them (Price 2010: 145–46).

In the United Kingdom, cloned embryos are not 'permitted' embryos that may legally be transferred to a woman. Therefore, the parentage rules for children of assisted reproduction contained in the Human Fertilisation and

Embryology Act (HFEA) do not apply. Nevertheless, common law principles may still accommodate human cloning to some extent. For example, suppose the man and woman from the hypothetical scenario travelled abroad to obtain cloning services and returned home to the U.K., where their son was born. Under the common law, it appears that the woman is the mother of the boy because she gave birth to the child. The man is presumed to be the father because he is married to the mother (Cretney *et al.* 2002: 523–24). If the child is the clone of the woman, rather than the man, the presumptions as to legal parentage of the child are the same (*Ibid.*).

Granted, some courts may balk at applying existing statutes or common law principles to a technology as novel and controversial as human cloning. Moreover, existing law may not protect all families formed through cloning. For example, the UPA fails to address the parentage of gay and lesbian couples who have children through assisted reproductive technologies, let alone through cloning (Byrn 2007: 171). However, the very fact that lawmakers in the United States and United Kingdom have begun to address the parentage of children born through assisted reproduction shows that laws can be amended to deal with new technologies and families. Should the parentage of children born through cloning require further clarification, legislators have the power to act.

Human cloning undermines social and religious dogmas that are based on the naturalness of sexual reproduction

If cloning does not pose a serious threat to the family, and if parentage laws are readily amended, why has society reacted so negatively to the prospect that infertile, gay or lesbian, or single individuals might use cloning to have children?

Until the advent of cloning, sexual reproduction was the norm for mammalian species, including human beings. Throughout human history, men had sexual intercourse with women and children were born as a result. This history makes sexual reproduction appear to be the natural means of procreating for our species.

Many social and religious beliefs have been based on this biological foundation. For example, secular opponents of gay marriage appeal to the biology of sexual reproduction to justify their position. They argue that marriage is for heterosexuals because only one man and one woman can join their bodies through sex and procreate together (Girgis *et al.* 2011: 253–57).

Similar reasoning is evident in Roman Catholic teachings on assisted reproduction and cloning. In 2008, the Congregation for the Doctrine of the Faith released an instruction addressing bioethical issues. According to the Congregation, procreation must occur in the context of marriage, where a man and woman give of themselves (through sexual intercourse) to create new life in cooperation with God (Congregation for the Doctrine for the Faith 2008: paragraph 6). The Congregation asserts that this principle is rooted in the laws of nature (*Ibid.*). The Congregation rejects as unethical reproductive technologies that substitute for sexual intercourse between husband and wife. Thus, it disapproves of in vitro fertilisation, intracytoplasmic sperm injection, and the use of sperm or eggs donated by third parties outside the marriage (*Ibid.* paragraphs 12, 14, 16, 17).

The Congregation reserves special condemnation for human cloning. Some of its objections echo the fallacies discussed earlier in this chapter. For example, the Congregation claims that cloning forces a specific genetic identity on a person, thereby condemning him to 'biological slavery' (*Ibid.* paragraph 29). There is no scientific basis for this claim. As animal experiments in cloning have demonstrated, genes are not destiny. This is fortunate; otherwise, we all would be biological slaves from the moment we were conceived.

However, the Congregation's opposition to human cloning has deeper roots. As it notes, cloning is not only unconnected to sexual intercourse between marriage partners, but also has no link to sexuality (*Ibid.* paragraph 28). In other words, the problem with cloning is that it is a form of *asexual* reproduction; as such, it runs counter to natural law as perceived by the Roman Catholic Church.

Thus, human cloning inspires opposition in part because it contravenes social and religious dogmas. Those who might procreate through cloning are incipient rule-breakers. Anti-cloning laws are necessary to deter and punish such violations.

But there is a deeper reason for opposition to human cloning. Through the forbidden fruit of cloning, humanity has acquired new knowledge: mammalian reproduction can be asexual rather than sexual. This knowledge is threatening to the existing order because it challenges dogmas premised on the naturalness of sexual reproduction at their core. Traditionalists may hope that legal bans will suppress not only cloning but also this dangerous knowledge. However, efforts to hide scientific facts rarely succeed. Legal or not, cloning invites us to reexamine social and religious dogmas. It is a force that may contribute to greater acceptance of diverse families of all kinds.

Human cloning will not harm nuclear families but will challenge the nuclear family ideal

As discussed in this book, a nuclear family consists of one man and woman, typically married, who conceive children through sexual intercourse. In discussing human cloning, it is important to consider the technology's impact on nuclear families as such, before considering its impact on the nuclear family as paradigm or sanctioned ideal.

To begin, many families created through human cloning will come quite close to the paradigmatic nuclear family in both their structure and intention. For example, consider the hypothetical scenario that appears at the beginning of this chapter. There, the family consists of one man, married to one woman, with a cloned son. The child bears the DNA of only one parent, rather than the standard two. However, by using cloning, the man and woman avoided the need to incorporate the DNA of a sperm donor into their family. Cloning allowed them to approximate the nuclear family despite the man's medical disability.

Other families created through human cloning will deviate more strongly from the nuclear family ideal. Gay and lesbian couples may find that cloning is an attractive means of conceiving genetic offspring while excluding the DNA of gamete donors. Unlike the standard nuclear family, these families will be headed by two men or two women. Similarly, single women may sometimes procreate through cloning even though they never do find a romantic partner who is willing and able to play the social role of father.

Still, relatively few people will have the resources and motivation to utilize human cloning for reproductive purposes. Sexual intercourse between men and women, which is fun and free, will continue to be a far more popular option, resulting in the procreation of countless children within nuclear families. For billions of people around the world, the nuclear family will continue to serve in the new millennium as the foundation for interpersonal relationships, child-rearing, and economic survival. Thus, human cloning does not threaten nuclear families as such.

Rather, what human cloning has done is challenge the nuclear family *as ideal*. By revealing that humans may be able to procreate asexually, cloning has undermined the argument that the nuclear family is and should be privileged for biological reasons.

Those who oppose human cloning can rattle their swords and threaten prosecution of anyone who dares to conceive a child in an unsanctioned manner. Ultimately, however, anti-cloning laws will prove impotent for two reasons. First, for all its power and majesty, even the law cannot turn back the hands of time and return us to a biologically simpler era in which sexual reproduction was the only option. Second, prospective parents will find ways of circumventing anti-cloning laws, such as travelling offshore to conceive their children. The more happy and healthy children are born through cloning, the more obvious it will become that the nuclear family ideal can no longer dominate the concept of family in the new millennium.

Note

1 In order to conceive a child through cloning, a gay couple would still need the assistance of an egg donor and gestational surrogate. The egg donor would pass a tiny amount of DNA to the child via the mitochondria in her egg. However, neither the donor nor the surrogate would pass nuclear DNA to the child.

References

Archer, G.S., Friend, T.H., Piedrahita, J., Nevill, C.H. and Walker, S. (2003), 'Behavioral Variation among Cloned Pigs', *Applied Animal Behaviour Science*, 82: 151–61.

Barnes, J., Sutcliffe, A.H., Kristoffersen, I., Loft, A., Wennerholm, U., Tarlatzis, B.C., Kantaris, X., Nekkebroek, J., Madsen, S.V. and Bonduelle, M. (2004), 'The Influence of Assisted Reproduction on Family Functioning and Children's Socio-emotional Development: Results from a European Study', *Human Reproduction*, 19: 1480–87.

Byrn, M.P. (2007), 'From Right to Wrong: A Critique of the 2000 Uniform Parentage Act', *U.C.L.A. Women's L.J.* 163–227.

Center for Veterinary Medicine, U.S. Food and Drug Administration, Department of Health and Human Services (2008), *Animal Cloning: A Risk Assessment* http://www.fda.gov/AnimalVeterinary/SafetyHealth/AnimalCloning/ucm055489.htm [accessed October 2011].

Cibelli, J.B., Campbell, K.H., Seidel, G.W., West, M.D., Lanza, R.P. (2002), 'The Health Profile of Cloned Animals', *Nature Biotechnology*, 20: 13–14.

Congregation for the Doctrine of the Faith (2008), 'Instruction *Dignitas Personae*: Bioethical Questions and the Dignity of the Person', *Origins*, 38: 437–49.

Cretney, S.M., Masson, J.M. and Bailey-Harris, R. (2002), *Principles of Family Law, Seventh Edition*, London: Sweet & Maxwell.

Eibert, M.D. (2002), 'Human Cloning: Myths, Medical Benefits and Constitutional Rights', *Hastings L.J.*, 35: 1097–1116.

French, A.J., Adams, C.A., Anderson, L.S., Kitchen, J.R., Hughes, M.R., Wood, S.H. (2008), 'Development of Human Cloned Blastocysts Following Somatic Cell Nuclear Transfer with Adult Fibroblasts', *Stem Cells*, 26: 485–93.

Galli, C., Lagutina, I., Crotti, G., Colleoni, S., Turini, P., Ponderato, N., Duchi, R. and Lazzari, G. (2003), 'Pregnancy: A Cloned Horse Born to Its Dam Twin', *Nature*, 424: 635.

Girgis, S., George, R.P. and Anderson, R.T. (2011), 'What Is Marriage?', *Harvard Journal of Law and Public Policy*, 34: 245–87.

Golombok, S., Brewaeys, A., Giavazzi, M.T., Guerra, D., MacCallum, F. and Rust, J. (2002), 'The European Study of Assisted Reproduction Families: The Transition to Adolescence', *Human Reproduction*, 17: 830–40.

Harris J. (2004), *On Cloning*, London and New York: Routledge.

Human Fertilisation and Embryology Act 1990, as amended in 2008.

Inoue, K., Kohda, T, Lee, J., Ogonuki, N., Mochida, K., Noguchi, Y., Tanemura, K., Kaneko-Ishino, T., Ishino, F. and Ogura, A. (2002), 'Faithful Expression of Imprinted Genes in Cloned Mice', *Science*, 295: 297.

Inoue, K., Ogonuki, N., Mekada, K., Yoshiki, A., Sado, T. and Ogura, A. (2009), 'Sex-Reversed Somatic Cell Cloning in the Mouse', *J. Reprod. & Development*, 55: 566–69.

Inoue, K., Kohda, T., Sugimoto, M., Sado, T., Ogonuki, N., Matoba, S., Shiura, H., Ikeda, R., Mochida, K., Fujii, T., Sawai, K, Otte, A.P., Tian, X.C., Yang, X., Ishino, F., Abe, K. and Ogura, A. (2010), 'Impeding Xist Expression from the Active X Chromosome Improves Mouse Somatic Cell Nuclear Transfer', *Science*, 330: 496–99.

Kunich, J.C. (2003), *The Naked Clone: How Cloning Bans Threaten Our Personal Rights*, Westport, Connecticut: Praeger Publishers.

Macintosh, K.L. (2005), *Illegal Beings: Human Clones and the Law,* Cambridge: Cambridge University Press.

Murray, C., MacCallum, F. and Golombok, S. (2006), 'Egg Donation Parents and Their Children: Follow-up at Age 12 Years', *Fertility and Sterility*, 85: 610–18.

The National Academies (2002), *Scientific and Medical Aspects of Human Cloning*, Washington, D.C.: National Academy Press.

National Bioethics Advisory Commission (1997), *Cloning Human Beings, Report and Recommendations of the National Bioethics Advisory Commission*, Rockville, Maryland: The National Bioethics Advisory Commission.

Niemann, H., Tian, X.C., King, W.A. and Lee, R.S.F (2008), 'Epigenetic Reprogramming in Embryonic and Foetal Development upon Somatic Cell Nuclear Transfer Cloning', *Reproduction*, 135: 151–63.

Pence, G.E. (1998), *Who's Afraid of Human Cloning?*, Lanham, Maryland: Rowman & Littlefield Publishers, Inc.

The President's Council on Bioethics (2002), *Human Cloning and Human Dignity*, Washington, D.C.: The President's Council on Bioethics.

Price, W.N. II (2010), 'Am I My Son? Human Clones and the Modern Family', *Columbia Science and Technology Law Review*, 11: 119–51.

Shelton, K.H., Boivin, J., Hay, D., van den Bree, M.B.M., Rice, F.J., Harold, G.T. and Thapar, A. (2009), 'Examining Differences in Psychological Adjustment Problems Among Children Conceived by Assisted Reproductive Technologies', *International Journal of Behavioral Development*, 33: 385–92.

Shin, T., Kraemer, D., Pryor, J., Liu, L., Rugila, J., Howe, L., Buck, S., Murphy, K., Lyons, L. and Westhusin, M. (2002), 'A Cat Cloned by Nuclear Transplantation', *Nature*, 415: 859.

Silver, L. (2002), 'Public Policy Crafted in Response to Public Ignorance is Bad Public Policy', *Hastings Law Journal*, 53: 1037–47.

Thomson Reuters (2010), *Uniform Laws Annotated, Volume 9B: Matrimonial, Family & Health Laws, 2010 Cumulative Annual Pocket Part*, New York: Thomson Reuters.

Wagenaar, K., Wagenaar, K., van Weissenbruch, M.M., Knol, D.L., Cohen-Kettenis, P.T., Delemarre-van de Waal, H.A. and Huisman, J. (2009), 'Behavior and Socioemotional Functioning in 9-18-year-old Children Born After In Vitro Fertilization', *Fertility and Sterility*, 92: 1907–14.

Wells, D.N., Misica, P.M. and Tervit, H.R. (1999), 'Production of Cloned Calves Following Nuclear Transfer with Cultured Adult Mural Granulosa Cells', *Biology of Reproduction*, 60: 996–1005.

West Group (2001), *Uniform Laws Annotated, Volume 9B: Matrimonial, Family & Health Laws*, Eagan, Minnesota: West Group.

Wilmut, I., Schnieke, E., Mcwhir, A., Kind, J and Campbell, K.H.S. (1997), 'Viable Offspring Derived from Fetal and Adult Mammalian Cells', *Nature*, 385: 810–13.

Wilson, C.L., Fisher, J.R., Hammarberg, K., Amor, D.J. and Halliday, J.L. (2011), 'Looking Downstream: A Review of the Literature on Physical and Psychosocial Health Outcomes in Adolescents and Young Adults Who Were Conceived by ART', *Human Reproduction*, 26: 1209–19.

14

Moral and Legal Constraints on Human Reproductive Cloning

Melinda Roberts

Goals of this paper

Does moral law limit the families we may permissibly choose to construct? Should human law do the same? Or do both morality and the law instead permit the family to proliferate, whether by rhyme or reason or not, in whatever direction potential procreators might happen to have in mind? Is, in other words, the rule that governs procreative choice just the very simple 'anything goes'?

One argument in favour of the 'anything goes' rule has seemed particularly compelling. According to that argument, which borrows its logic from what is called the *nonidentity problem* (Parfit 1987: 363), the choice that brings a person into existence cannot *harm* that person provided that person's existence itself is worth having. In this paper, I find fault with that argument as it arises in the context of human reproductive cloning. But both the argument itself and the objection I shall suggest apply to many other reproductive technologies as well – and indeed to procreative choice generally, whether technologized or not.

The logic of the nonidentity problem may seem highly exculpatory from a legal point of view and – arguably – from a moral point of view as well. But any close inspection will reveal that things are not quite so simple. In this paper, I explore the difficult issues raised by nonidentity logic. I argue that that logic fails in any case in which we can trace an *alternate, and better, route* into existence for a particular child available to agents just prior to choice. In such cases, the argument that concludes 'no harm done' loses all force. On the basis of the harm that we can then easily discern, we find ourselves nicely positioned to argue both that the child has suffered a moral wrong and that the state is entirely justified in regulating the choices we make for the purpose of rescuing offspring from that particular harm going forward.

The analysis I propose may seem at odds with a certain idea that has a great deal of force among moral philosophers and is at least taken seriously within the law as well. That is the basic *consequentialist* idea that agents cannot have done anything wrong if they have maximized wellbeing for people. I will argue, however, that we can avoid any tension by simply giving to that necessary condition on wrongdoing a *person-affecting*, or *person-based*, construction instead of a more traditional *aggregative* construction.

Human reproductive cloning is the focus of the next part of my paper. My conclusion is not that all applications of human reproductive cloning are morally and legally problematic. It is rather that some are and some aren't – with everything turning on whether or not the special logic of the nonidentity problem in fact *succeeds* in showing 'no harm done'.

Finally, I consider a particularly trenchant objection against my claim that human cloning, in at least some cases, impermissibly harms the very offspring it helps to produce. According to that objection, if it is permissible to impose what is arguably the *deeper* harm on a given person – the harm of never existing at all – then it should be permissible as well to impose the *shallower* harm on that same person – the harm of existing as a genetic multiple. I conclude with a response to that puzzle.

Does the logic of the nonidentity problem undo claims of harm whenever the existence is worth having?

Does 'anything go' when it comes to procreative choice? We understand, of course, that that's not the rule when the issue is how we are to conduct ourselves in respect of the children we already have. While we think parents surely must be accorded some discretion regarding how they deal with their own children, we understand that that discretion is far from absolute. Some parents on at least some occasions treat their children in ways that no plausible moral theory can deem permissible. And any credible legal system will give the community license on some occasions to protect children against some of the serious harms their parents would otherwise be likely to inflict.

But the *construction* of the family – the *procreative* choices, that is, that determine the size and constituency of a particular family going forward – may be thought to be different. Choices to bring a child into existence may seem to be governed – categorically, across the board – by the special, and highly exculpatory, logic of the nonidentity problem[1]. The idea is this. Whether a given choice damages the very child it causes to exist is surely, at least from the child's own point of view, moot. After all, the child's interests ordinarily weigh *in favour of* existence – or at least not *against* existence[2]. Stripping the agents of their right to procreate will only bring it about that the child *will never exist at all*. Perhaps an alternate, seemingly better (that is, less damaging) choice would have produced a *distinct* child, one *nonidentical* to the original, in place of the original. And perhaps that child would have been better off than the original. But that *alternate* choice (at least very probably) would have done nothing to improve things for the *original* child. We are thus left with no basis on which to conclude that the original child has been harmed by the choice agents in fact made. No better-for-the-child alternate choice *entails* 'no harm done' to that child.

We see the same logic at play in far more ordinary cases. Thus, even the well-executed surgical procedure may leave you with a limp. But if you would otherwise have necessarily been left paralyzed for life, we don't think the surgeon who has performed the procedure has *harmed* you. Similarly, the well-executed reproductive technology may leave the child it brings into existence *disadvantaged* in some way. It may cause the child, not just to exist, but also to bear a certain burden. But if that same child could never otherwise have existed at all, then the use of that technology cannot plausibly be said to have *harmed* the child[3].

The logic of the nonidentity problem has been widely understood to support the use of many innovative reproductive technologies – including, for example, intracytoplasmic sperm injection (ICSI), in vitro fertilisation (IVF), aggressive drug therapies (high doses of, for example, clomiphene) and human reproductive cloning – against their critics[4]. Unable to identify any clear victim, critics have instead fashioned speculative arguments against whatever technology it is that offends them. But such arguments should always be greeted with suspicion. If we truly are blocked from establishing harm-to-offspring, it is difficult to see how we are not blocked as well from establishing any serious objection against any of those technologies.

Nonidentity logic may seem unassailable. In fact, however, it cannot be relied on to defend each and every procreative choice. Rather, it supports the 'no harm done' result when it is limited to the case in which agents *could have done no more for the child than they have*. But it fails miserably in any case in which what agents have done is simply part of the causal sequence of acts and events that leads to the existence of a particular child and an *alternate, less burdensome route into existence* for that same child was available to the agents just prior to choice. In both scenarios, it is perfectly correct to say that the act under scrutiny 'brings the child into existence'. But under the former, perfectly reasonable principle, the burden that comes with the act is one that agents (practically, that is, physically) *cannot avoid* if the child is to exist at all; the burden is (we can say) *critical* to the child's coming into existence at all (or at least to the *probability* of the child's coming into existence being higher than it is under any alternative choice). And under the latter, fallacious principle, the burden that comes with the act could have been avoided had agents opted for some other stepping stone into existence on behalf of the particular child rather than the one that creates the burden. When the latter principle rather than the former has been deployed for the purpose of showing 'no harm done', critics of any particular technology have far more than mere speculation to draw on. For in those cases we can easily sidestep the inference to 'no harm done'.

Moreover, we can, in such cases, establish that harm has been done not in some exotic (and arguably morally and legally irrelevant) sense of the term 'harm' but rather in an *ordinary* and *intuitive* – that is, *comparative* – sense. In my view, then, we can – and I believe should – concede (contra Benatar 2006) that in many cases existence is, from the child's own point of view, a good thing. We should concede, that is, that in many cases existence is better, and certainly not worse, than never having existed at all. And we can – and again I think should – concede (contra Harman 2009, and Steinbock 2009) that no harm is done to the child *unless* agents have made that child worse off when they could have made that same child better off. We can – and should – accept, that is, an intuitive, ordinary, comparative account (as opposed to an 'objective list' account, or a 'minimal decent threshold' account) of *harm*, or *loss*. We can – and should – instead say that a person is harmed by a given act performed in a given possible scenario (or 'future' or 'world') *only if* that act makes that person *worse off* than that person is in some alternate scenario – *only if*, that is, the agents could have performed some *alternate* act that would have made things *better for that same person*.

But we can concede all these points but still insist that the act that brings the child into an existence worth having may well *harm* the child. What is important is whether the act – and any injuries or adverse effects it might produce – was *critical* to that child's coming into existence. Could the agents have acted otherwise and still brought that very same child into a better existence?

We would certainly say that the surgery that leaves you with a limp *harms* you had it so happened that an alternate and better procedure – say, an Ace bandage rather than a bone graft – was available to your surgeon. And so should we say that the procreative choice that leaves the child damaged *harms* that child if an alternative, better means of bringing that same child into existence is available.

What applications of nonidentity logic, then, often overlook is that a particular procreative choice is not always the *only* path into existence for a given child. If multiple paths into existence are available, and if some of those paths are better for that child than others, and if agents could have chosen a path that was better for the child and instead have chosen a path that was worse, then what they have done *harms* the child. And if that harm cannot be justified – if, for example, there is no showing that the only way to avoid harming the one child is to impose a more serious harm on still another person or that same harm on *many* other children – then agents have not only *harmed* but have also *wronged* the child. And they have wronged the child both morally – they have done less for the child when they could have done more at no cost to anyone else – and legally – tort law remedies should be understood to be available and laws regulating the agents' conduct recognized as valid constitutional measures necessary to protect children from the harm that they would otherwise incur[5].

But this is very general. We can't just *say* that other, better routes into existence are sometimes available to agents in the context of – for example – human reproductive cloning. We must instead *prove* that point. I will turn to that argument later in this paper. But first a discussion of certain underlying connections between morality and the law is in order.

Morality and the law

It seems that any plausible moral theory will share with any credible legal system one important goal – that of promoting the 'general welfare' or, alternately, the 'public welfare' or the 'common welfare'. These are expressions O.W. Holmes used in describing the goals and function of law (Holmes 1881). Relatedly, he exhorts judges to read the law 'recogniz[ing] their duty of weighing considerations of social advantage' (Holmes 1897: 467).

Restated in purely moral terms, the idea here could be read this way: an act is morally permissible *if and only if* nothing agents could have done in place of that act would have created still more wellbeing for people – would have, that is, done still more to promote the common good. The resulting moral principle is inherently *consequentialist* and inherently *maximizing*. But as far as I can see there is no reason to think that it is also *aggregative*. We thus have the option of instead endorsing a *person-affecting*, or *person-based*, form of maximizing consequentialism.

Reference to the *common* good need not, in other words, be construed as a reference to the *aggregate* good. It can instead be taken as a reference to the good that is done for each person *as an individual* – more for one person, perhaps, than for another, but with the goal being not the maximization of the *aggregate*, or *summation*, of individual wellbeing levels but rather *for each person* the maximization of wellbeing *for that person* (with the necessary caveats in place to address cases in which agents cannot create more wellbeing for one person without creating less for another).

Similarly, when Holmes invokes the common good in his discussions of how the law is to be read, there is no indication that the good he is referring to is measured by summing up the wellbeing levels of all the individuals who belong to a given population. Far more plausibly, the common good consists not in *aggregate* wellbeing but rather in the varying amounts of the good enjoyed by varying numbers of people[6]. At least in many cases, the fact that we can *count* means we need not *aggregate* (Roberts 2002: 326–333, 347–348). We needn't say that one choice produces more wellbeing *in the aggregate* than another. We can instead in many cases simply note that one choice produces more wellbeing for *at least some people* and less for none – or assigns *fewer people* to a lower wellbeing level, or etc. – than another does. Tricky, perhaps, to detail, person-based principles in the end yield a far more plausible picture of what morality requires.

These two ways of understanding the common good – the aggregative reading and the person-based reading – will yield very different results when applied to procreative choice. That that is so can be seen in the context of human reproductive cloning. The argument against human reproductive cloning is in many cases going to be effectively blocked if our starting point is aggregative consequentialism. Specifically, if the technology of cloning is applied in a way that adds to the population and if adding to the population maximizes wellbeing in the aggregate, then aggregative consequentialism is going to favour cloning. And that is so, even in the case in which *not* adding to the population and not cloning happens to be the choice that maximizes wellbeing *for each and every person who does or ever will exist.*

Suppose, as the following table suggests, that agents have the options of cloning a single, consenting adult source to produce between one and four new people – children – genetically identical to that source. And suppose that they also have the option of not cloning at all.

Table 14.1 Human Reproductive Cloning

	a1 = produce via cloning from an adult clone source p1 as a singleton	a2 = produce via same procedure p1 and p2 as two genetically identical individuals	a3 = produce via same procedure p1, p2 and p3 as three genetically identical individuals	a4 = produce via same procedure p1, p2, p3 and p4 as four genetically identical individuals	a5 = avoid cloning altogether and produce no additional individuals at all
p1	+10	+9	+8	+7	*
p2	*	+9	+8	+7	*
p3	*	*	+8	+7	*
p4	*	*	*	+7	*

The asterisk (*) signifies that the indicated person never exists under the indicated choice; numbers indicate relative overall, lifetime wellbeing levels.

As long as p1–p4 are additional people and agents had no way of producing genetically distinct additional people at higher wellbeing levels, aggregative consequentialism is going to imply that a4 is obligatory and that a1, a2, a3 and a5 are wrong.

In contrast, person-based consequentialism – depending, of course, on its details – can easily find a4 wrong. As I understand it, a main tenet of a person-based approach is the so-called *person-affecting*, or *person-based*, intuition. According to that intuition, an act can be 'bad' only *if* it is 'bad for' some person or another. In other words: an act performed in a given scenario, or possible future or world w, is wrong *only if* it *harms* – that is, makes things, relative to some alternate world w', *worse for* – a person who does or will exist at w (Parfit 1987: 363). Still another basic tenet will surely be the following. If a person is harmed *without any justification at all* at a world w at which that person does or will exist, then the act that harms that person is *wrong*. So, if the harm is justified, then the harm won't ground a finding of wrongdoing. But if it isn't, it will.

Applying these basic tenets to Table 14.1, and understanding that harm is imposed in any case in which agents could have created more wellbeing for a person and have instead created less, we can infer that a1 is perfectly permissible. In contrast, a4 harms a person who does or will exist at a world where that act is performed – namely, p1. And that harm itself remains unjustified: agents can avoid that harm to p1 by performing a1 instead, where a1 (i) makes things better for p1 than a4 does but (ii) doesn't impose any harm – at least, doesn't impose any *morally significant* harm – anyone at all.[7] a4, we can thus conclude, is wrong.

Nonidentity logic and human reproductive cloning

My analysis, when coupled with the facts displayed in Table 14.1, shows that a4 *harms* and indeed *wrongs* p1. But why should we think that 'the facts' displayed by Table 14.1 have anything to do with 'real life'? Why should we think Table 14.1 represents the alternatives that would be available to agents in any actual cloning scenario?

To establish the relevance of the table for 'real life', we must argue two points. First, we must argue that there are grounds for thinking that p1 is indeed worse off as one of – say – four genetically identical individuals than p1 is as a genetic singleton. And, second, we must show that agents had the ability to make p1 better off – that an option like a1 would be genuinely available to agents in normal cloning scenarios and that a4 and its effects are not themselves *critical* to p1's coming into existence. We must, in other words, show that the special logic of the nonidentity problem in fact fails.

Macintosh (in this volume) describes a number of grounds for prohibiting human reproductive cloning and then points out just how weak those grounds in fact are. Consider, for example, the claim that the families cloning may help to create may be dysfunctional in certain ways or the claim that parentage of any cloned offspring will be difficult to establish for legal purposes. Macintosh's argument that these claims are speculative seems exactly right. There is no reason to think that the family created via cloning is at any particular risk of becoming dysfunctional. And many societies are by now adept at addressing issues of parental rights in the context of adoption, including in the case where the adopted child is genetically related to one of the two parents but not the other. Distinctions will need to be drawn. But surely we will be able to use that expertise to address issues that will arise in the case where the child is not just genetically related to, but rather shares the full genome of, one parent but not the other.

Macintosh also properly dispenses with the various arguments against cloning that derive from religious dogma. Faith may help an agent decide whether to produce a child by way of cloning. But the faith that some people have should not play any role in deciding how *everyone* in society should conduct their lives.

At the same time, the international groundswell of legislation prohibiting human reproductive cloning shows that the prospect of human cloning is highly controversial – more troubling to many than is, say, the right of early abortion. Why are all of these people so worried? Do the objections against cloning truly fail across the board?

We begin with the point that a person's being brought into existence as one of four genetically identical multiples rather than as a genetic singleton really does constitute a burden or a disadvantage – something it would 'ideally' have been better for a given person to have lived without, something that *harms* that person. We begin with the point that a4 can indeed be expected to be *worse for* p1 than a1 is. Here we – just for the moment – put aside whether the special logic of procreative choice in the end forces us to say that what *looks* to be harm is really *not* harm at all.

We can, I believe, easily articulate a basis for the claim that existing as one of four rather than just one of one is indeed worrisome. Neither you nor I would want to look out into the world and discover that our genetic identity – our genome – had been shared without our consent for the reproductive purposes of other people. Whether we have a moral or constitutional *right* of genetic control is not anything we need to decide in order to be very confident that we *want to exercise* a certain level of genetic control – and that taking that control out of our hands imposes a genuine harm, or loss, against us. Thus, I don't want my gametes shared (courtesy of, for example, the technician in charge of the cryopreservation of my ova) without my consent. Still less do I want my entire genome shared without my consent.

But we can't reasonably take that position – and insist that we do indeed have an interest in exercising a certain level of genetic control and that stripping us of that control *harms* us – and also take the position that the offspring we produce, whether for our personal childrearing purposes or in order to help our patients or our clients or still others achieve their own childrearing ends, have no parallel interest. We can't reasonably take the position that *our* wellbeing has legal and moral significance, and that we can be harmed by a certain sort of choice, but that *their* wellbeing does not have the same sort of moral significance and that they can't be harmed by a very similar sort of choice.

Similarly, I can't reasonably take the position that I have an interest in keeping – say – my left kidney and at the same time take the position that you have no parallel interest in keeping yours. If your taking my kidney constitutes a harm to me – represents, that is, a case in which you as moral agent have created less wellbeing for me when you could have created more – then so does my taking your kidney constitute a harm to you. Now, on occasion such harms may permissibly be imposed. But we cannot expect that latter debate to reach any correct conclusion unless we begin the debate with the recognition of *all* the harms that our many alternative choices may impose – including the harm that is imposed on you when I take your kidney.

The same analysis holds in the case of human reproductive cloning. The thought here is not at all that our genes make us who we are or determine our 'destiny' – or that the process of human reproductive cloning will produce people who are the *exact duplicates* of each other. Much goes into who we are beyond our genes. Nor does our left kidney make us who we are. But we still don't want to lose it without our consent.

Now, it might be argued that losing our left kidney *makes a difference* to us in a way that losing our genetic uniqueness – that is, being made to share our genome with others – cannot. But innovations in genetic technology give rise to worries – or at least fantasies – that quickly reveal just how naïve this argument in fact is. Do we think it makes a *difference to us* if, after we have produced our own child, our frozen embryos are handed off to other infertile couples so that they may produce their own child without our consent? Yes. We want to be the ones to make the call; we want to exercise that level of genetic control.

It might be objected that the fact that we *want* to retain genetic control does not on its own prove either harm or risk of harm. Perhaps our desire instead does no more than reveal a certain squeamishness on our part when it comes to our bodily parts – or a fetishism about our genetic identity. Perhaps our desire is itself arbitrary or irrational. We thus need to be able to give at least a rough account of *why* the duplication of our own genome in another constitutes a loss. We need to be able to say just how the case is one in which agents could have created more wellbeing for a person and have instead created less.

I believe that our genetic identity, while it does not determine who we are or our destiny in life, is part of what we offer the world. If our genomes can be obtained from many different sources, then the value of what we have to offer the world is diminished. My children's hearts and minds may not be as wonderful as I think they are. But if you want what you perceive to be the riches that can be mined from the genomic stream that makes up my little clan, you shall have to convince one or the other of them to have a child with you. If you can obtain those riches elsewhere, my children will not have as much to offer you. And it makes things *better for them* that they have a lot to offer; it's an *advantage to them* that in your eyes they have something you cannot get elsewhere. That their value is increased in your eyes is of value to them. You should not be permitted to cheat them out of their due by taking their genomes without their consent from the saliva they leave behind when they go to the dentist.

* * *

But now, of course, we must address the second point. We must show just why the special logic of procreative choice fails in the context of human reproductive cloning. Yes, existing as a genetic multiple as opposed to a genetic singleton *looks* to be a disadvantage. If, however, the act under scrutiny and the disadvantage it seems to inflict are *critical* to the coming into existence of the apparent victim, then we shall have no choice but to infer 'no harm done'.

It is useful to return to Table 14.1 at this point. To reach the result that a4 does not harm p1, it is not enough to establish that a4 brings p1 into existence. One would need to establish as well that there exists *no alternate means* of bringing p1 into existence that *makes things better* for p1 – that p1 cannot be *both* brought into existence *and* accorded a desirable level of genetic control.

But surely there *is* an alternate and better route into existence for p1. Surely, that is, there is a way of bringing p1 into existence *and* according to p1 the same level of genetic control we want for ourselves.

The choice of a1 is, in other words, an alternative that we can anticipate would actually be available to agents in any 'real life' case. Perhaps the particular *mechanics* of the cloning procedure mean that all four genetically identical embryos must be created if p1 is ever to exist at all[8]. But that does not mean that all four genetically identical embryos need to be allowed to develop into four genetically identical ('full-fledged') persons. After all, the agents could allow the one embryo to develop into p1 while destroying any remaining embryos[9]. p1 would then exist, not as one of *many*, but as one of *one*[10].

We must, accordingly, recognize that the logic of the nonidentity problem simply does not fit at least some cases involving human reproductive cloning. Because alternative, better routes into existence are clearly available to agents prior to choice, we cannot infer 'no harm done' on the basis of that logic.

My conclusion here is *not* that *every* cloning choice harms the person it brings into existence. On some occasions, the sound application of nonidentity logic will indeed allow us to construct a compelling argument for the 'no harm done' result. Consider, for example, the choice of a1. Let's suppose that a1 brings p1 into existence by way of cloning DNA derived from an adult clone source and that p1, accordingly, is genetically identical to that adult clone source. In this case, it seems that p1 has no other, better route into existence. Being brought into existence without the desirable level of genetic control, in this case, is indeed *critical* to p1's coming into existence to begin with. And we should conclude 'no harm done'.

Macintosh's opening scenario involves similar facts. There, a woman gives birth to a son, the genetic clone of the woman's infertile husband. It's true that the son has been deprived of a certain level of genetic control. Because the man and the child are genetically identical, the man would remain perfectly able to clone *both* himself *and the child* again and again. But it's also true that that particular child would not have been any better off had his mother achieved her pregnancy through donor sperm. For then that *particular* child would never have existed at all. Nor would that child have been better off had his mother arranged for the cryopreservation of the embryo and then waited until her spouse died before having that embryo transferred to her uterus. For then the child would have been deprived of the parenting that the man himself was (presumably) willing to provide. Thus, while the child certainly *lacks* a certain level of genetic control, it is not at all clear that he has been on balance *harmed* in a morally or legally relevant sense.

More generally, the determination of harm in a given case involves an assessment of *all* the alternatives available to the agents just prior to choice. If *any* alternative exists that make things better for the child than does the procreative choice under scrutiny – if *any* alternative both avoids the disadvantage and still manages to bring that very same child into existence – then the child is *harmed*. But if on the other hand the choice reflects the *best agents can do for that particular child*, then, we should agree, 'no harm done'.

If it is permissible not to bring a child into existence at all, how can it be wrong to bring a child into existence as a genetic multiple?

The foregoing discussion establishes, I believe, that human reproductive cloning in some cases can be expected to harm the very offspring it brings into existence, depending on the facts of the particular case. I believe that that harm can easily serve as a basis for a finding of moral *and* legal wrongdoing.

But there is an argument – a puzzle, really – that would seem to undermine my conclusion. As we have seen, if the agents' choice not to perform a4 is replaced by a1, then what they do will make things *better* for p1 than a4 does. But, of course, their choice not to perform a4 could instead be replaced by a5. Rather than make things *better* for p1 than a4 does, agents could, in other words, make things *worse*. After all, it is surely better for p1 to exist under a4 than it is for p1 never to exist at all under a5. Or so I will concede for purposes here.

But with this recognition the problem arises. If the *lesser* harm that a4 imposes on p1 counts against a4, then surely the *greater* harm of never existing at all counts still more heavily against a5. Yet we do *not* think that a5 is wrong. We think, rather, that it is perfectly permissible not to bring p1 into existence at all. But if it really is permissible for agents to impose the *greater* harm on p1, then how can it not also be permissible for them to impose the *lesser* harm on p1 – to perform, that is, a4 in place of a5 or a1[11]?

It might seem discouraging that this particular puzzle – this objection – isn't the least bit susceptible to a seemingly obvious solution. Thus, one *wants* to say that it is just obvious – a matter of common sense – that *existing* and *future* people matter morally in a way that *merely possible* people do not. One could then concede that leaving a child out of existence altogether can harm that child but insist that that harm itself is devoid of moral significance.

The principle would be this: the child's *modal* status determines the child's *moral* status, and the *child's* moral status determines the moral status of the *harm*[12]. Because the merely possible do not, in other words, matter morally, the harms they incur cannot *count against* the choices that impose those harms.

But the seemingly commonsensical notion that people can be divided between those who matter morally and those who don't – that *modal* status determines *moral* status – cannot be made to work. A number of cases compel us to recognize that the merely possible *do* matter morally – and in just the way that we ourselves matter morally.

One case that makes this point clearly is *Addition Plus*[13]. Suppose that we can make *existing* people better off only by bringing into existence still other people whom we *avoidably* treat very badly. And suppose that we in fact choose not to bring those other people into existence at all. Our choice seems clearly permissible. The difficulty is that that result seems unavailable to us if we think that modal status determines moral status. After all, if the *merely possible* do not matter morally and if that, in turn, means that the harms they incur have no moral significance whatsoever, then the choice to harm *existing* people – by failing to provide them with, for example, slaves or organ donors – will presumably turn out to be *wrong*. For that choice makes existing people worse off when we could have made those same people better off at no cost *to anyone* who *matters morally*.

This shows that the merely possible do, after all, matter morally. At least in some cases, the harms they incur can indeed make the otherwise wrong choice to impose still other harms on existing people perfectly permissible (Roberts 2010; Roberts 2011).

Fortunately, however, we can defend the result that it is perfectly permissible to leave a child out of existence altogether and yet still wrong to bring that child into existence as a genetic multiple on other grounds. The new strategy is this. We concede, as before, that leaving a child out of an existence worth having harms that child, and that that harm is deeper than the harm of existing as a genetic multiple. We can also recognize that the merely possible have the same moral status as existing and future people. But we now insist that to say a given person has moral status is just to say, not that the harms that person may incur matter in a categorical or across-the-board way, but rather that they matter *variably*. More specifically, we can say that a harm to a person matters morally if and only if it is imposed on that person at a world where that person does or will exist[14]. And we can then analyse the problem case as follows. Yes, it indeed harms p1 to leave p1 out of an existence worth having, and that harm is indeed deeper than the harm of bringing p1 into existence as a genetic multiple. But that deeper harm, we can now assert, has no moral significance at all. It *does not* count against a5 or in any roundabout way in favour of any alternate choice. It cannot, in other words, make the otherwise permissible a5 wrong. In contrast, the harm of existing as a genetic multiple, though shallower, has full moral significance. It *counts against* a4 and in a roundabout way in favour of the alternate choice a1 that avoid it.

Our puzzle is then solved. We have explained just how it can be perfectly permissible to leave a given child out of existence altogether but still wrong to bring that same child into existence as a genetic multiple. a5 may well, in other words, be perfectly permissible, even as a4 is clearly wrong. In the world of contemporary moral theory, this strategy for solving our puzzle and others like it is highly controversial[15]. I hope, though, that the law at least – or at least Holmes! – would find it plausible.

Notes

1 See Parfit 1987: 363. David Heyd calls the special rules he believes applicable to procreative choice 'genethics' (Heyd 1992, 2009). John Robertson has also appealed to this special logic (see Robertson 2004a: 344, and generally Robertson 1994) but does recognize that it is limited in some ways (Robertson 2004b: 15). See also Macintosh, this collection.

2 The only exception would seem to be the case of the genuinely *wrongful life* – the case, that is, where the child would inevitably and unavoidably be so diseased that his or her life would be *less* than worth living. But that is hardly the ordinary case.

3 At least it seems not do so in any 'morally relevant sense' (Parfit 1987: 374) – in any sense, that is, that *counts against* the particular application of the technology itself or make that otherwise *permissible* application into a moral *wrong*. One might, of course, challenge my analogy. One might argue that it makes no sense to say that the scenario in which one exists and suffers in a certain way is better than or at least no worse than the scenario in which one never exists at all. On this view, there would be a disanalogy between arguing 'no harm done' in the surgical case and arguing 'no harm done' in the reproductive case. It is not clear, however, that the highly technical argument against the cogency of comparisons involving scenarios in which the subject never exists can in fact successfully be made. For a summary of the current debate on that issue, see Roberts 2011. In any case, if it so happens that such comparisons are not cogent, it is simply going to make it more difficult to establish that the particular technology harms its apparent victim. We still, in other words, would seem forced to conclude, in both the surgical case and the reproductive case, 'no harm done'.

4 One risk associated with many reproductive technologies involves multiple pregnancy, which can occur in any case in which the number of embryos transferred to the uterus is not strictly limited or (in the case of drug therapies) fetal reduction is not applied (Robertson 2004b: 10; 2007). The risk associated with ICSI is of a different sort. There, the concern has been that ICSI itself is associated with certain birth defects which in nature occur very rarely (Robertson 2004b: 9–10). Human reproductive cloning, even in the case in which agents take steps to avoid multiple pregnancy, is associated with still another sort of risk. That risk is a main subject of this paper.

5   Of course, as just noted, the imposition of harm can be morally, and indeed legally, justified by the fact that the choice to do anything else would have led to a more serious harm being imposed on another person or the same harm being imposed on many other persons. But that just means that the logic that governs at least some of the new reproductive technologies is perfectly routine and not special at all. That is, for purposes of resolving the particular issue, we should do what we usually do when a conflict scenario arises: we should balance the parties' interests and particularly balance the harm we think will be imposed on the particular child by one choice against the harm we think will be imposed on others by another choice. We can predict, however, that it will often be the child's interests that prevail. The cheaper technology – which is itself often the technology that will produce more offspring per procedure – may benefit the child's *parents*, or their *fertility specialist*, in some way. Human reproductive cloning may – for example – insure that one's children are genetically related to oneself. But if doing things in that way is what is worse *for the child*, then my suspicion is that things ought not be done in that way. I will not, however, fully develop that argument here.

6   I believe this point holds whether we are talking about Holmes *or* John Stuart Mill.

7   For an account that explains why the harm to p1 that a4 imposes can't be justified by the fact that a1 arguably *does* impose an arguably still *deeper* harm than a4 does on each of p2, p3 and p4 when it leaves those people out of existence altogether – that explains, that is, just why the harm that a4 arguably imposes on p2, p3 and p4 s devoid of moral significance – see the concluding part of this paper.

8   This is so whether the cloning procedure uses genetic materials derived from an adult (and presumably consenting) clone source, as in Table 14.1, or instead involves the cloning of a human embryo, itself created using in vitro fertilisation.

9   Perhaps the agents would not have been interested in the production of p1 as a singleton. Perhaps they want four – or a hundred, or a thousand – genetically identical individuals or none at all. No matter. Regardless of what they *want*, if the alternative of producing p1 as a singleton is available to the agents just prior to choice, then the agents *harm* p1 when they produce p1 as one of (perhaps many) genetically identical individuals.

10 I presented earlier versions of this argument in Roberts 1996, 1998 and 1999. As in the case of human reproductive cloning, the logic of the nonidentity problem also fails in the case of multiple fetal pregnancy. Not *all* of the people developing from the fetuses involved in a multiple fetal pregnancy can exist and not suffer the impairments that are by now clearly associated with pregnancies involving three or more fetuses developing within the same uterus. But *some* of them could. That better-for-some outcome could be achieved in either of two ways: reducing the number of ova fertilized and transferred to begin with or selectively reducing the number of fetuses once the pregnancy is established. Harm is thus easily established (Roberts 2007).

11 A similar but not identical puzzle is suggested by McMahan 2006.

12 While there is some controversy as to whether such comparisons can cogently be made, it is far from conclusive that they can't. Accordingly, it would be a mistake to try to ground the view that bringing a person into existence as one of (perhaps) many genetically identical individuals is wrong while leaving that same person out of existence altogether may be perfectly permissible on the controversial, and

highly technical, position that the claim that it is worse for a person never to exist at all is not fully cogent (Roberts 2011).

13   Roberts 2011; Roberts 2010.

14   I have elsewhere called this principle *Variabilism* (Roberts 2011; Roberts 2010).

15   Specifically, contemporary moral philosophers are divided regarding what we should say about 'the Asymmetry', according to which it would be wrong to bring the miserable child into existence even as it is perfectly permissible to leave the happy child out of existence. See generally Roberts 2011; Roberts 2010.

References

Benatar, D. (2006), *Better Never to Have Been: The Harm of Coming into Existence*, Oxford: Clarendon Press.

Harman, E. (2004), 'Can we Harm and Benefit in Creating?', *Philosophical Perspectives*, 18: 89–113.

Harman, E. (2009), 'Harming as Causing Harm', in M.A. Roberts and D.T. Wasserman (eds), *Harming Future Persons: Ethics, Genetics and the Nonidentity Problem*, Dordrecht: Springer, 137–154.

Heyd, D. (1992), *Genethics: Moral Issues in the Creation of People*, Berkeley: University of California Press.

Heyd, D. (2009), 'The Intractability of the Nonidentity Problem', in M.A. Roberts and D.T. Wasserman (eds), *Harming Future Persons: Ethics, Genetics and the Nonidentity Problem*, Dordrecht: Springer, 3–25.

Holmes, O.W. (1881), *The Common Law*, Boston: Little Brown and Co.

Holmes, O.W. (1897), 'The Path of the Law', *Harvard Law Review*, 10: 457.

McMahan, J. (2006), 'Paradoxes of Abortion and Prenatal Injury', *Ethics*, 116: 625–55.

Roberts, M.A. (1996), 'Human Cloning: A Case of No Harm Done?', *Journal. of Medicine and Philosophy*, 21: 537–54.

Roberts, M.A. (1998), *Child Versus Childmaker: Future Persons and Present Duties in Ethics and the Law*, Lanham, M.D.: Rowman & Littlefield.

Roberts, M.A. (1999), 'Cloning and Harming: Children, Future Persons and the "Best Interest" Test', *Notre Dame Jo. of Law, Ethics & Public Policy*, 13: 37–61.

Roberts, M.A. (2007), 'Supernumerary Pregnancy, Collective Harm and Two Forms of the Nonidentity Problem', 34 *Journal of Law, Medicine & Ethics*, 277–292.

Roberts, M.A. (2010), *Abortion and the Moral Significance of Merely Possible Persons: Finding Middle Ground in Hard Cases*, Dordrecht: Springer.

Roberts, M.A. (2011), 'The Asymmetry: A Solution', *Theoria*, 77: 333–367.

Robertson, J.A. (1994), *Children of Choice: Freedom and the New Reproductive Technologies*, Princeton, NJ: Princeton University Press.

Robertson, J.A. (2004a), 'Gay and Lesbian Access to Assisted Reproductive Technology', *Case Western Reserve Law Review*, 55: 323–372.

Robertson, J.A. (2004b), 'Procreative Liberty and Harm to Offspring in Assisted Reproduction', *American Journal of Law and Medicine*, 30(7): 7–40.

Steinbock, B. (2009), 'Wrongful Life and Procreative Decisions', in M.A. Roberts and D.T. Wasserman (eds), *Harming Future Persons: Ethics, Genetics and the Nonidentity Problem*, Dordrecht: Springer, 155–178.

Name Index

Subject Index

Lightning Source UK Ltd.
Milton Keynes UK
UKOW04f0706080614

233039UK00005B/71/P